GREAT
SOUTH
LAND

Rob Mundle

ABC
Books

The ABC 'Wave' device is a trademark of the Australian Broadcasting Corporation and is used under licence by HarperCollins*Publishers* Australia.

First published in Australia in 2015
by HarperCollins*Publishers* Australia Pty Limited
ABN 36 009 913 517
harpercollins.com.au

HarperCollins*Publishers*
Level 13, 201 Elizabeth Street, Sydney NSW 2000, Australia
Unit D1, Apollo Drive, Rosedale, Auckland 0632, New Zealand
A 53, Sector 57, Noida, UP, India
1 London Bridge Street, London, SE1 9GF, United Kingdom
2 Bloor Street East, 20th floor, Toronto, Ontario M4W 1A8, Canada
195 Broadway, New York NY 10007, USA

National Library of Australia Cataloguing-in-Publication data:

Mundle, Rob, author.
   Great South land : how Dutch sailors discovered New Holland
   and left Australia to an English pirate ...
   / Rob Mundle.
   ISBN: 978 0 7333 3237 1 (hardback)
   ISBN: 978 1 4607 0560 5 (ebook)
   Subjects: Explorers – Netherlands.
   Explorers – Great Britain.
   Australia – Discovery and exploration – Dutch.
   Australia –Discovery and exploration – British.
994.01

Cover design by Hazel Lam, HarperCollins Design Studio
Cover image by Lisa Wiltse / Fairfax Syndication
Typeset in Bembo Std by Kirby Jones
Maps by Map Illustrations www.mapillustrations.com.au
Printed and bound in Australia by Griffin Press
The papers used by HarperCollins in the manufacture of this book are a natural, recyclable product made from wood grown in sustainable plantation forests. The fibre source and manufacturing processes meet recognised international environmental standards, and carry certification.

To the brave seafarers and explorers who sailed their ships beyond the horizon and into the unknown, searching for new lands on history-making voyages

Contents

Contents

GREAT SOUTH LAND

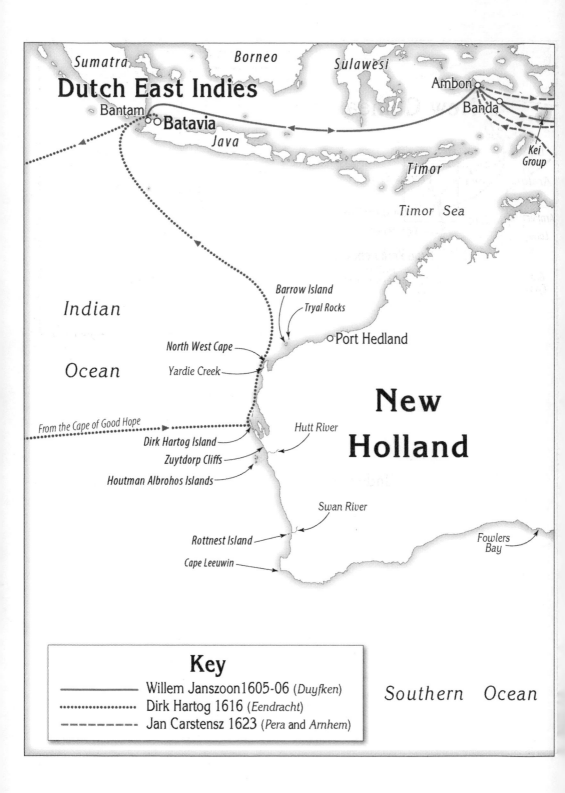

Sumatra

Borneo

Sulawesi

Dutch East Indies

Ambon

Bantam

Banda

Batavia

Java

Kei
Group

Timor

Timor Sea

Indian

Barrow Island

Tryal Rocks

North West Cape

Port Hedland

Ocean

Yardie Creek

New

From the Cape of Good Hope

Hutt River

Holland

Dirk Hartog Island

Zuytdorp Cliffs

Houtman Albrohos Islands

Swan River

Rottnest Island

Fowlers
Bay

Cape Leeuwin

Key

———————— Willem Janszoon 1605-06 (*Duyfken*)

••••••••••••••• Dirk Hartog 1616 (*Eendracht*)

— — — — — Jan Carstensz 1623 (*Pera* and *Arnhem*)

Southern Ocean

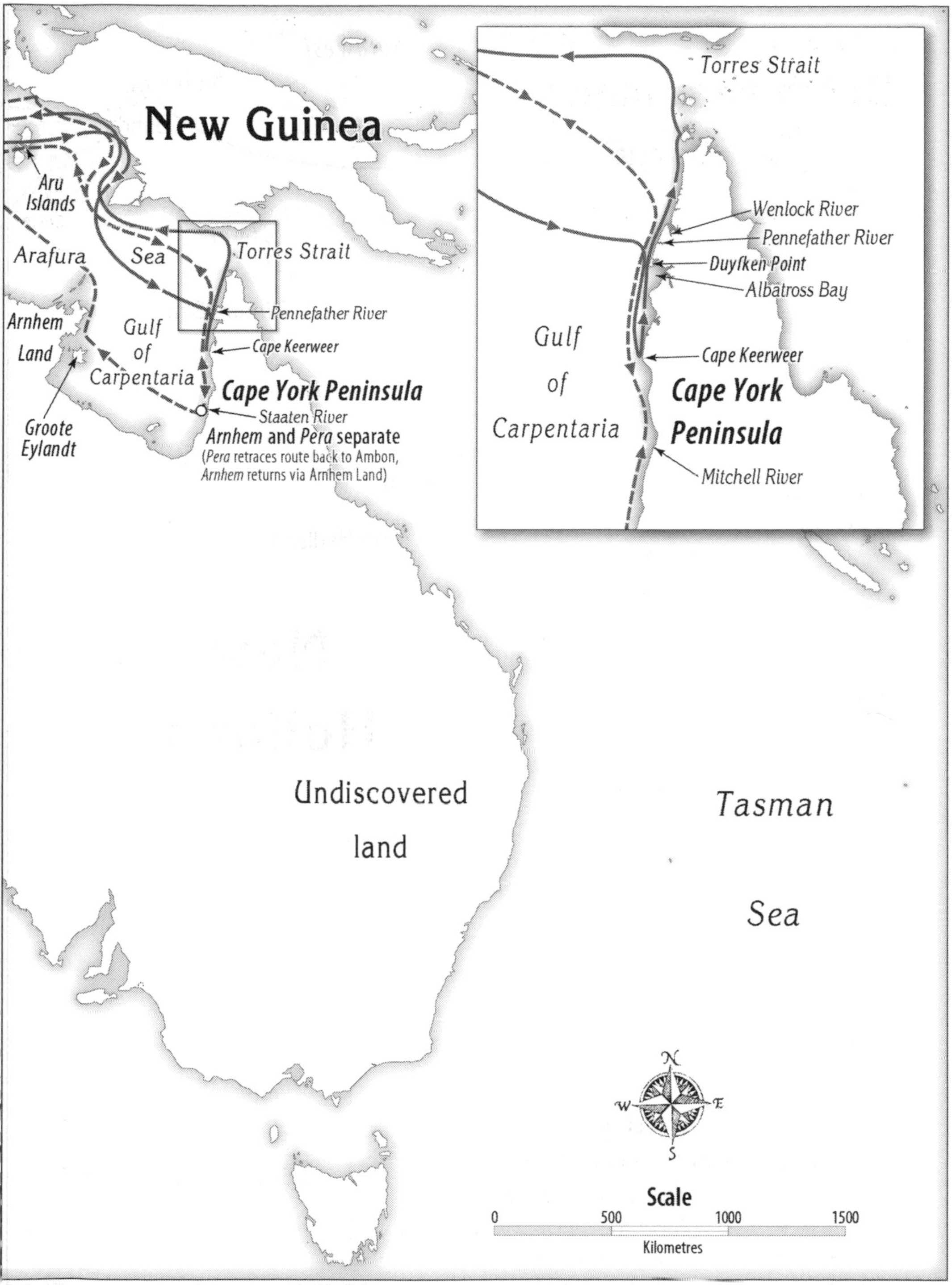

New Guinea
Aru Islands
Arafura Sea
Torres Strait
Pennefather River
Arnhem Land
Gulf of Carpentaria
Cape Keerweer
Cape York Peninsula
Groote Eylandt
Staaten River
Arnhem and Pera separate
(Pera retraces route back to Ambon, Arnhem returns via Arnhem Land)
Torres Strait
Wenlock River
Pennefather River
Duyfken Point
Albatross Bay
Gulf of Carpentaria
Cape Keerweer
Cape York Peninsula
Mitchell River
Undiscovered land
Tasman Sea
N
W
E
S
Scale
0
500
1000
1500
Kilometres

Sumatra

Borneo

Dutch East Indies

Sulawesi

Macassar

Ambon
Banda

New
Guinea

To Mauritius

Batavia   Java

Timor

Arafura Sea

Torres
Strait

Timor Sea

Cape
York
Peninsula

Gulf
of
Carpentaria

Indian

Dampier
Archipelago
(Rosemary Island)

King Sound,
(Dampier, 1688)

Ocean

Roebuck Bay

North West Cape

New

From the Cape of Good Hope

Shark Bay

Holland

Houtman Albrohos Islands

Southern   Ocean

Scale

0   500   1000   1500

Kilometres

From Mauritius

Key

———————— Abel Tasman 1642 (*Heemskerck* and *Zeehaen*)

•••••••••••••• Abel Tasman 1644 (*Limmen*, *Zeemeeuw* and *Braek*)

– – – – – – – William Dampier 1699 (*Roebuck*)

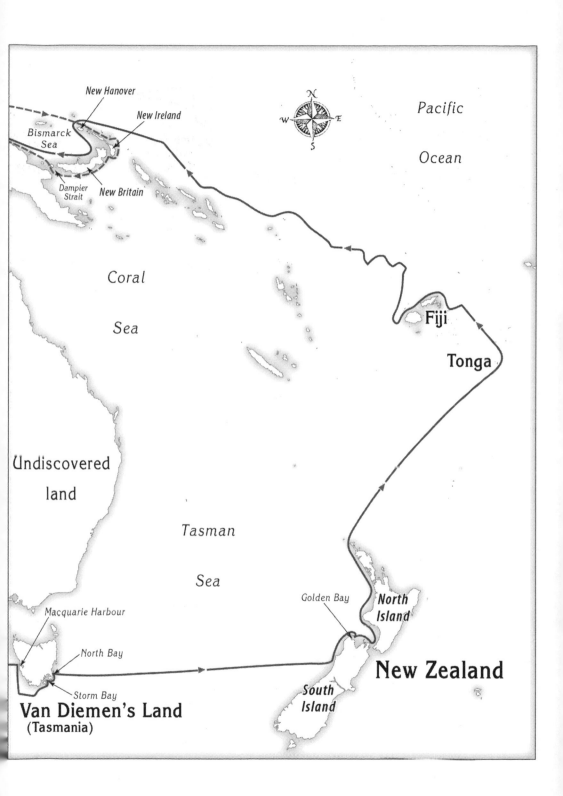

January 1688

On 15 January 1688 – almost 100 years to the day before Captain Arthur Phillip arrived in Botany Bay as commander of the First Fleet – another English ship, the sixteen-gun *Cygnet*, was running downwind on a gentle breeze while closing on the coast of the same continent. *Cygnet*, however, was passing the island of Timor, 2000 nautical miles to the north-west of where Phillip would anchor HMS *Sirius* and go ashore to establish the first British colony in the Great South Land.

To get to this point, *Cygnet*, under the captaincy of Charles Swan and with William Dampier as navigator, had crossed the Pacific from the coast of Mexico to the East Indies with a 140-man crew, comprising a bunch of unruly seafarers, young and old ... and pirates all. If they had one thing in common it was that every one of them had taken to the high seas so they could reap the rewards that came through pillaging and plundering enemy ships and ports anywhere they desired.

The decision had already been made that from this point, to avoid attack from enemy ships, they would sail a looping course that would eventually take them to the north-west and on to India, claiming what prizes they could along the way. However, the elements caused a change to that plan soon after *Cygnet* cleared the south-western end of Timor and entered the Timor Sea. Dampier would later note:

> Being now clear of all the islands we stood off south, intending to touch at New Holland, a part of Terra Australis Incognita, to see what that country would afford us. Indeed as the winds were, we could not now keep our intended course (which was first westerly and then northerly) without going to New Holland unless we had gone back again among the islands: but this was not a good time of the year to be among any islands to the south of the Equator, unless in a good harbour.

As *Cygnet* sailed away from Timor, there was a strong westerly wind blasting across the Timor Sea, so strong that the water's surface resembled a stippled, undulating canvas of deep blues and churning whitecaps. Each time one of the larger waves smashed into the ship's topsides on the windward side, a geyser-like plume of spray would explode skywards, then, once caught by the wind, shoot horizontally across the deck, peppering the face of any sailor not quick or nimble enough to avoid it.

As strong as the wind was, though, the conditions made for superb sailing. With only two courses and the mizzen set, and occasionally a reefed main-topsail, *Cygnet* was reaching across the wind at around 5 knots, her proud bow wave making her look as though she had a bone between her teeth.

Even so, there was a large element of caution being exercised: charts probably based on the discoveries of Dutch explorer Abel Tasman, when he was in the region decades earlier, revealed the existence of a shoal between *Cygnet*'s position and the coast:

> About 10 o'clock at night we tacked and stood to the northward for fear of running on a shoal which is laid down in our charts in latitude 13 degrees 50 minutes or thereabouts … In the morning as soon as it was day we saw the shoal right ahead … a small spit of sand, just appearing above the water's edge, with several rocks about it, eight or ten foot high above water.

Dutch cartography, and prudent seamanship, had saved the day.

The coast of New Holland hove into view 'in the latitude of 16 degrees 50 minutes [south]' on 4 January 1688. There was no suitable anchorage apparent, so they cruised along the shoreline for about 15 leagues until they spotted 'a pretty deep bay with abundance of islands in it, and a very good place to anchor in or to haul ashore'.

This was what is now known as King Sound, a large and magnificently scenic waterway in the Kimberley region of Western Australia. *Cygnet* came to anchor 'two mile from the shore in 29 fathom, good hard sand and clean ground'.

All aboard the ship soon noticed the amazing difference between low and high tide: among the largest in the world. Taking this into consideration, they set about looking for a suitable site where the ship could be put aground and careened so her hull could be cleaned below the waterline. A nearby sandy cove proved ideal:

> When we had been here about a week we hauled our
> ship into a small sandy cove at a spring tide as far as she
> would float; and at low-water she was left dry and the
> sand dry without us near half a mile; for the sea rises
> and falls here about five fathom … All the neap tides we
> lay wholly aground, for the sea did not come near us by
> about a hundred yards.

The careening gave the men time to cure their cabin fever; they went ashore and set up a camp site. During the day, those not working on cleaning the hull were otherwise employed – checking the rig, mending sails or gathering food. It is also apparent that Dampier spent much time investigating the region and observing the native animals and flora. His description of the indigenous population was – like those of Dutch explorers before him – largely unfavourable:

The inhabitants of this country are the miserablest
people in the world … They have no sort of clothes but
a piece of the rind of a tree, tied like a girdle about their
waists, and a handful of long grass, or three or four
small green boughs full of leaves thrust under their
girdle to cover their nakedness … I did not perceive
that they did worship anything … They did at first
endeavour with their weapons to frighten us … Some
of them had wooden swords, others had a sort of lances.
The sword is a piece of wood shaped somewhat like a
cutlass. The lance is a long straight pole sharp at one
end, and hardened afterwards by heat. I saw no iron nor
any other sort of metal; therefore it is probable they use
stone-hatchets, as some Indians in America do … These
people speak somewhat through the throat; but we
could not understand one word that they said.

The visitors did try to make direct contact with the inhabitants
of a nearby small island, but when they landed close to a group
of forty men, women and children (who must have thought
they were looking at aliens), the locals made threatening
gestures with their 'lances and swords'. It took a single musket
shot into the air to send the entire group scampering away
into the distance. Dampier wrote: '[They made] a doleful
noise as if we had been coming to devour them'.

But it was Dampier's theory regarding the continent on
which they had landed that was particularly insightful:

New Holland is a very large tract of land. It is not yet
determined whether it is an island or a main continent;
but I am certain that it joins neither to Asia, Africa, nor
America.

This was the observation of a man who, by the time his
seafaring adventures were complete many years later, could
stand proudly among the heroes of English maritime
exploration. It is safe to say that much of his work influenced
the 1770 expedition of James Cook, which would decisively
prove that Dampier's hypothesis was indeed correct.

Yet while Cook is now recognised as a legend in the
annals of Australian history – the grand seafarer who found,
explored and mapped the entire length of the continent's east
coast – this English pirate-cum-explorer surely deserves to
stand beside him. He is recognised as the first man to
circumnavigate the world three times, and the first English
explorer to visit the coast of Australia on two occasions:
eleven years after the 1688 voyage, he would lead an extended
exploration into the waters of what he would name Shark's
Bay, east of Dirk Hartog Island, before continuing north
from there.

He would also publish four remarkable volumes detailing
his journeys and discoveries, the likes of which had until then
been unknown. These works, which told of another world,
inspired ordinary folk to dream of travelling to places that
even the most active minds could not imagine.

It could also be postulated that, had harrowing winter weather not prevented Dampier's expedition from sailing around Cape Horn on his expedition in 1699, he would have sailed to the west and, consequently, be recognised today as the man who discovered the eastern coast of Australia. At this time there was still conjecture as to the existence or otherwise of the Great South Land. While the west coast of New Holland was known to exist, he was commissioned by the Admiralty to go in search of what he referred to as Terra Australis, which remained an enigma – it was thought by many to be separate from New Holland. Dampier agreed to the Admiralty's directive but he also asked to be given a free hand for this voyage of discovery. Regardless of whether or not he would succeed, the one extraordinary fact in the history of the world as we know it is that, over countless centuries of maritime exploration, this huge tract of land – the Great South Land – while being the longtime motherland of its Indigenous population, was never claimed by any country, not even the homelands of the earliest documented discoverers.

It was only when the English settled there – not for any strategic reason, but because they needed a distant repository for convicts held in their grossly overcrowded prisons – that settlement of this little known land became important. Equally extraordinary is the fact that, despite the slowness of English expansion across the land after they had arrived, no other nation took the opportunity to capture any part of it. Because of this, the country stands today as the largest single nation on Earth that is completely surrounded by sea.

The existence or otherwise of the Great South Land had been a contentious and prolific debate for thousands of years. But it was not until early in the seventeenth century, after a sea route to Asia via the Cape of Good Hope was established, that solid evidence of a great landmass in the southern hemisphere began to emerge, piece by piece.

However, it would not be maritime explorers who would confirm the existence of the previously unknown land. Instead, it was all because of spices, and the rivalry between the Portuguese, Dutch and English, who were literally fighting for control of the hugely lucrative spice trade out of Asia. It was a contest in which the Dutch would finally triumph – and which would lead to a completely unexpected revelation: the last great find for the map of the world – a large tract of habitable land which, within two centuries, would be recognised as 'Australia'.

CHAPTER ONE

The Spice Trade – Camels and Caravels

1415 to 1605

For centuries it had been little more than a sheltered Asian village lying between two rivers in a large bay on the northern coast of Java; a picturesque location from where local fishermen could put to sea in small boats and pursue a catch, or sail to nearby islands to trade. But in less than a decade in the early seventeenth century, there came a dramatic change of lifestyle for the local populace: this remote outpost was transformed into a bustling, European-style seaport. Large ships – all square-riggers and flying the Dutch flag – continually sailed into the bay and anchored offshore, adjacent to the port that had been hastily built to meet commercial demands.

After the cargoes these ships brought from Europe were unloaded from small boats that had ferried them ashore, an ant-like procession of labourers carried heavy casks from the godowns – waterfront warehouses – to the same boats. They were then transported out to the ships. Those casks contained what had become modern-day gold in Europe: spices!

The East Indies had long been the primary source for the majority of these spices, however the presence of so many large ships in the port signalled that the method of transporting them to Europe had changed dramatically.

Captured from the Sultan of Bantam in 1619, this port, then known as Batavia, soon became the most powerful manifestation of the Dutch presence in the East Indies. Previously known as Jacatra (today Jakarta), it was renamed after the original Roman name for the Netherlands. Its location on the island of Java gave the Dutch control over the strategically important Sunda Strait, which separates Java from Sumatra and allows access to other parts of the region. A huge fort, Batavia Castle, was built there as a residence for the Governor-General of the Dutch East Indies, the pre-eminent Dutch official of the region. The castle's walls surrounded a large city that became the centre of operations for the world's very first multinational corporation. The likes of Batavia were unprecedented in this part of the world: it has been described as having straight and broad avenues, with extensive tree-lined canals. There were also two rivers: one ran through the town, while the other encircled its walls.

The substantial wealth of the VOC – the Vereenigde Oost-Indische Compagnie, or United East India Company – was built around the European spice trade. As a virtual monopoly, the company was able to wield all the powers of a nation. Its expansion and resulting dominance of maritime trade, particularly in the East Indies, drove it to success that was almost beyond imagination.

The number of ships in the VOC fleet was greater than that of some of the largest European navies. By 1669 – when it was considered to be the richest privately funded company in the world – it had a fleet of 150 merchant ships and 40 warships, 50,000 employees and its own army comprising 10,000 soldiers.

During the life span of the VOC, from 1602 to 1796, a total of 4785 ships sailed under its flag. Over that period, the company employed nearly one million people in its Asian trade operations. By comparison, the VOC's nearest competitor, the English East India Company, had fewer than 2700 ships in its fleet, and carried only 20 per cent of the VOC's volume of cargo.

Incredibly, the company was able to return an annual dividend of 18 per cent for almost 200 years, due to the policy followed by its directors in Amsterdam of reinvesting much of their substantial annual profits back into the business.

But the VOC would also become the catalyst for the discovery of Terra Australis Incognita – the Unknown South Land – after tens of thousands of years of anonymity. It was the corporation's determination to find new markets and sources in the region, as well as maintaining its stranglehold on the European trade by delivering cargoes of spices as quickly as possible, that led to these historic discoveries.

*

The considerable benefits spices brought to food and lifestyle had made them an important part of everyday life in southern Asia and the Middle East before the Christian era. They had been traded in Europe since medieval times.

Initially, pepper was the preferred spice in Europe, for three reasons: it enhanced the flavour of food, it was used as a preservative and, for some, it disguised the revolting taste of months-old meat. The latter point was no better explained than by a famous sixteenth-century German writer and satirist, Johann Fischart, in his work *Gargantua*: 'Over a stinking meat one … likes to put … pepper.'

Beside pepper, the most sought-after spice was the clove because of its numerous applications: flavouring food, as a preservative, as a mild anaesthetic, for use in perfumes, for embalming the dead, and to disguise bad breath. Other spices of importance included nutmeg, ginger, turmeric, cinnamon and cardamom. Some came from India, and others from the Spice Islands fringing the Molucca Sea (now part of Indonesia).

Between the eighth and fifteenth centuries, these spices had often been transported to Europe, at least part of the way, by caravans of camels. Some were conveyed by boat up the Red Sea before being carried by caravan over the dusty desert to Alexandria in Egypt. These spices were then shipped across the Mediterranean to Venice, from where they were distributed throughout Europe.

Both routes involved long, painstakingly slow and very costly procedures. Regional taxes or payment demands by pirates saw a dozen or more rapacious individuals claiming a levy on each shipment. Consequently, the market price for spices in Europe became inordinately expensive. Still, the demand was there and profits were high.

Around 1419, the Portuguese, under the determined leadership of Prince Henry the Navigator, began a systematic push south along the west coast of Africa, in a bid to find a new route to Asia and gain a share in those vast riches.

Apart from the dangers faced by the seafarers aboard the ships searching for a solution, there was a significant concern from within their ranks: many went to sea in fear and trepidation because maritime legend had them believing that once they approached Cape Bojidor in Morocco, they would be sailing towards the edge of the world, a place where oceanic monsters lurked. But by 1434 these explorers had managed to progress beyond the cape and the theory was disproved.

Around this time, explorers were also able to make great gains as a consequence of the design and construction of the first caravels – ships capable of sailing faster and more efficiently than any other vessels. Maritime exploration was also becoming safer, and the plotting of positions more accurate due to advances in methods of navigation using the stars.

By the mid-fifteenth century, a greater sense of urgency was brought to bear on the search for a sea route, when the Ottomans overthrew the Byzantine Empire and established a realm which encircled much of the Mediterranean and Red Seas as well as the Persian Gulf. This victory gave the Ottomans a stranglehold over access to existing spice routes to Europe and, consequently, the opportunity to impose even greater taxes on the spices transiting their domain.

The beginning of the end of the well-trodden trade paths through Asia came in 1497 with the voyage of a great Portuguese sailor and determined explorer, Dom Vasco da Gama. He was acting under orders from King John II of Portugal, 'The Perfect Prince', who is recognised for revitalising his country's economy in the late fifteenth century through foreign trade.

John II had already spent a decade searching for an alternative spice route. In 1487, he had sent two spies overland to East Africa and India, their commission being to report back with whatever information they could compile regarding the existing spice trade, its costs and transport arrangements.

A year later, in 1488, King John's quest had received a fortuitous boost when Captain Bartolomeu Diaz returned home with news that he had successfully rounded the southern tip of Africa, which he had named 'Cape of Storms' (Cabo das Tormentas). He had then sailed an additional 450 nautical miles to the east-north-east along the southern coast of Africa, reaching Rio do Infante (now the Great Fish River, in South

Africa) before returning home. John II was so optimistic about what rounding the cape meant to his plan that he renamed it the Cape of Good Hope (Cabo da Boa Esperança). Diaz's success put paid to another longstanding belief: the theory that the Indian Ocean was land-locked, which had stood for around 1400 years.

Diaz's news was enough to convince John II – armed with the intelligence from his spies – that his much sought-after sea route from Portugal to Asia was likely there for the finding, and that cargo ships would soon be transporting hundreds of tons of spices to Lisbon more quickly and far more economically than the existing operation. Portugal would then control the spice trade into Europe, set the price and reap the benefits of immense profits. Not surprisingly, then, he accelerated plans for da Gama to lead a four-ship expedition that would try to discover a viable sea route between Portugal and Asia.

John II had already rejected requests from Italian Christopher Columbus to fund a plan to sail to the Spice Islands, China and India on a westerly course across the Atlantic. Columbus estimated that the Spice Islands could be reached after sailing west for only 2400 nautical miles; John II was sure it would be faster to sail there via the Cape of Good Hope, should that prove possible.

Columbus finally found the necessary support for his voyage from the Spanish monarchy and set sail in 1492. After a nine-week passage across the Atlantic, he discovered islands he was convinced were part of the Spice Islands. His mistaken belief that he had crossed into the Indian Ocean prompted him to name the islands – which were actually in the Bahamas – the Indies.

The reason for his mistake was simple: because his calculations had the circumference of the Earth considerably smaller than it really was, he had estimated that a degree equalled 45 nautical miles instead of 60. Applying this formula, he believed that he had sailed considerably further west than he had actually travelled.

Five years later, Italian-born English explorer John Cabot suffered a similar fate after sailing west across the Atlantic. He claimed his landfall in the name of England, thinking he had found the east coast of Asia. Instead, it was Canada, probably Newfoundland. Regardless, the discoveries by Columbus and Cabot would later prove to be significant – far more than they could have ever imagined. They had revealed parts of the world previously unknown to Europeans.

Meanwhile, the Portuguese pressed on with their plans to reach the Spice Islands by sailing in the other direction. On 8 July 1497, da Gama and his four ships, carrying 170 crew, sailed out of Lisbon's harbour, heading south. His flagship was the 84-foot, three-masted carrack *São Gabriel*, and her sister ship, *São Rafael*, was captained by da Gama's brother Paulo. King Manuel I, who had now come to the throne, was as enthusiastic about the mission as his predecessor John II had been.

Ten months later, after rounding the Cape of Good Hope and entering the Indian Ocean, Vasco da Gama etched his name into maritime history by being the first European to sail directly from Europe to India. It was an epic voyage of more than 12,000 nautical miles, some of it through previously unknown waters and often under the most challenging of conditions. Excepting ice and snow, the men experienced the full gamut of nature's moods – from Atlantic storms to frustrating calms in the sweltering equatorial zone. Making their test even more arduous was the fact that their ungainly ships, the design of which was considerably different from a caravel, struggled to sail to windward.

Da Gama's fleet arrived in Calicut (now Kozhikode), 220 nautical miles north of India's southern tip, on 20 May 1498. Three months later on 29 August, with his four ships laden with spices, da Gama set out for home, eager to declare to his king that the hoped-for trade route to India did indeed exist.

Unfortunately, while the mission had been successful to date, the passage back to Lisbon was beset by drama and widespread illness, particularly scurvy. On the outward journey, da Gama's flotilla had traversed the Indian Ocean in just twenty-three days, but because of a punishing monsoon season, the voyage from Calicut to Malindi on the east coast of Africa took 132 days. An alarming number of crew died during this time – so many, in fact, that there were insufficient able-bodied men to sail all four ships over the remaining 6200 nautical miles home. Consequently, da Gama decided to scuttle *São Rafael* and transfer the healthy crew to the other vessels.

When da Gama finally reached Lisbon a year after departing Calicut, a hero's welcome awaited him. He was fêted by royalty and given a celebratory parade through the town. Little wonder: Manuel I recognised that the majority of the riches associated with the spice trade were now destined to flow to Portugal, as da Gama's efforts had exceeded all expectations. The cargo of spices the remaining three ships carried back to Lisbon was worth six times more than the cost of the expedition. More importantly, the monopoly Venetian merchants held over the distribution of spices in Europe had been broken: a fact put beyond doubt when da Gama's second venture to India in 1502 with a fleet of ten ships returned a fiftyfold profit.

Later, Portuguese explorer Ferdinand Magellan would go even further and make the largest mark of all in the pages of maritime achievement. In 1519 he set out on a three-year voyage that would see him discover a route round the base of South America and become the first to circumnavigate the world. There was a secondary aspect to this achievement, one that again reinforced the value of the commercial trade that stood to be developed through contact with Asian ports. Apart from delivering a rich cargo of spices, he brought home exotic fabrics which fetched prices in England up to three thousand percent above their cost price.

Yet the immediate challenge for the Portuguese was to protect their own interests, and this could only be done by defending the sea lane discovered by da Gama against all rivals. A succession of fortified ports was established to deter foreign usurpers, especially along the east coast of Africa. It was a bold, often brutal operation orchestrated by Afonso de Albuquerque, who was appointed the Portuguese viceroy of India in 1508. On many occasions, any among the local population opposing the establishment of these defensive garrisons were ruthlessly slaughtered.

Portugal's control of the trade would last for almost the entire sixteenth century, in defiance of Europe's other major maritime powers. The Dutch didn't care, because their ships were being employed to carry the spices from Lisbon to ports throughout Europe. But the English, in particular, were getting restless: they wanted a share of the business. They knew, however, that their ships would never be able to ply the well-protected Portuguese route around the Cape of Good Hope, so they started looking for a possible alternative: to the north-west over the top of the New World, now North America, or a north-east passage that would cross the unexplored icy waters to the north of Russia, either of which would hopefully lead to the Spice Islands.

In 1580, while these possibilities were being contemplated, a sudden and dramatic change came over the European scene: the Spanish overran Portugal in what was essentially a battle to control succession to the Portuguese throne, which the Spanish saw as being under threat from a pretender, Dom António, Prior of Crato.

The Spanish victory had little immediate impact on Portugal's domination of the spice trade, but it did mean that Spain's ongoing enemy in the Eighty Years War, the Dutch, were promptly relieved of the profitable opportunity to distribute spices across Europe by sea. Their response was to no longer recognise Portugal's monopoly and instead go about creating their own commercial enterprise. However, the Dutch, like the English, believed there was no way they could achieve success by going head-to-head with the Portuguese along the same route, so they too decided to search for a passage in the north.

Dutch navigator and cartographer Willem Barentsz was the first of many directed to undertake this challenge.

His first mission, in 1594, out of Texel in the Netherlands, was to the north-east where it was hoped a passage would be discovered along the coast of Siberia. It almost ended in disaster when a polar bear they had captured and hauled aboard their boat went beserk and had to be shot. On reaching Novaya Zemlya, 2000 nautical miles from their starting point, they were forced to turn back after their course was blocked by massive icebergs.

Undeterred, Barentsz was named pilot for a six-ship expedition which set sail the following year. This expedition too was confronted by a savage polar bear which attacked and killed two sailors. This time, Barentz reached the Kara Sea off the coast of Siberia where, despite it being summer, the sea was still frozen. He had no option but to again turn back.

On his third mission, yet again to the north-east, his expedition became ice-bound for almost a year on Novaya Zemlya Island. The only opportunity for the sixteen men and the cabin boy to escape certain death was to take two of their small boats and try to sail to safety. This they did, but Barentsz and five others had died by the time the boats reached Kola Peninsula where they were rescued by a Russian merchant vessel. Subsequently his efforts were recognised when the Barents Sea north of Russia and Norway was named in his honour.

The quest to find passages to and from the Atlantic across the top of North America or Europe continued for centuries after Barentsz's first endeavours. In 1778, Captain Cook famously sailed into the Arctic Circle from the Pacific Ocean in the hope that he could find a way to the Atlantic and thus eliminate the need to navigate the storm-ravaged waters off Cape Horn. However, this mission failed when he was confronted by an impenetrable wall of ice some twelve feet high that stretched from horizon to horizon.

Others followed, but it was a full century after Captain Cook's failed attempt on what was known as the 'north-west passage' that Finnish-born Adolf Erik Nordenskiöld achieved the first breakthrough when he pioneered a way across the northern coast of Eurasia from the Atlantic and proved the existence of a north-east passage. Incredibly, it wasn't until 1903 that Norway's remarkable Arctic and Antarctic explorer, Roald Amundsen, accompanied by six men aboard a small,

45-ton fishing boat named *Gjøa* survived two winters in the Arctic Circle before proving the existence of the north-west passage from the Atlantic to the Pacific Ocean. This achievement proved invaluable for Amundsen personally as the Netsilik Inuit people he met along the way impressed upon him how wearing clothing made from animal skins, instead of heavy, woollen jackets, repelled the cold and wet far more efficiently. He later used this knowledge to great benefit on his expeditions across the wastelands of Antarctica and the Arctic Circle.

The Dutch and the English, having failed to find an 'over the top' route to the Spice Islands, both decided the only option was to challenge the Portuguese and Spanish head-on by sailing the known course to Asia via the Cape of Good Hope. In their favour was the fact that in 1588 the Spanish Armada had been all but destroyed when it sought to invade Elizabethan England, so the Spanish Navy's potency was greatly reduced. This resounding victory for the English had been achieved with the assistance of their then ally, the Dutch.

Ironically, the English and Dutch would soon become intense rivals in the spice trade, a fact that would ultimately lead to the discovery of New Holland by the Dutch and, eventually, confirmation that this was the Great South Land. It was the knowledge of the existence of so much of this landmass that sparked the interest of William Dampier, the man who went so close to proving the Great South Land and New Holland were one and the same.

England's first commercial move into the spice trade came on the very last day of 1600, when a Royal Charter declared the formation of the Governor and Company of Merchants of London Trading into the East Indies, which would later become known as the East India Company (EIC). A year later, Sir James Lancaster led the company's first expedition into the East Indies, establishing a factory in Bantam in 1603, the same year as the Dutch. This inevitably led to strong rivalry and eventually conflict between the two sides. Such was the commercial value of the spice trade, many other nations followed the lead of the English and the Dutch in eventually forming their own East India companies: the Danish (1616), Portuguese (1628), French (1664), Swedish (1731) and Austrians (1776).

The United East India Company (VOC) was established two years after the English formed their East India Company. However, the Dutch were more efficient and effective in their pursuit of the business. Theirs was a conglomerate of mercantile enterprises that would soon be unmatched in the commercial world. The VOC was the first business ever to issue stock and was given the authority by the Government of the Netherlands to strike its own currency and maintain its own navy and army. It also had the right to establish colonies and build the forts necessary to defend them.

This was the period recognised in history as the Dutch Golden Age, a time when they led the world in commerce, science, art and military activity. This Golden Age had come after the seven northern provinces of the Low Countries – Gelderland, Holland, Zeeland, Utrecht, Friesland, Overijssel and Groningen – combined to form the Republic of the United Netherlands in 1579.

Moves by the VOC to break the Spanish–Portuguese stranglehold on the trade were immediate. On 18 December 1603, the first VOC fleet sailed out of home waters bound for the Spice Islands, but their orders went well beyond those of a trading mission. They were directed to attack every Portuguese stronghold they came across in East Africa and Goa, in what would later be recognised as the Dutch–Portuguese War.

This exercise was not as successful as hoped when it came to victories over the Portuguese, but the one Portuguese bastion to fall was probably the most valuable: the spice island of Amboyna (Ambon). This success in 1605 gave the VOC the geographical foothold it needed to control the bulk of the spice trade and subsequently establish its own empire in the region, laying claim to the remainder of the Spice Islands (Moluccas).

The English would benefit directly from Dutch domination in the region by being allowed access, alongside the Dutch, to commercial trade with India. The French were also provided entrée to the Spice Islands and India, but did not operate on the same level as the Dutch or English.

The Dutch acted quickly to display their strength in the region, and over the next fifteen years built hundreds of bases, from minimalist ventures to massive centres of commerce.

Initially, two or three fleets of VOC ships sailed from the Netherlands to the region each year. Most returned home with cargoes of spices, but colourful silk and cotton fabrics from India were also in high demand. Before long, the Dutch market went beyond just Europe: they were trading Indian silk with the Japanese, and porcelain, tea and silk with the Chinese. As almost every cargo returned profits hundreds of times greater than its original cost, the VOC was soon reaping a harvest of cash unimaginable only a few years earlier.

But unheard-of profits from its existing colonies were not enough. To maintain its edge over competitors, the VOC realised it must also seek out unknown coasts, ports and peoples that might present new market opportunities.

In 1605, the Governor of Ambon, Frederik de Houtman, was sent a directive from the VOC headquarters in Amsterdam stating: 'There must be more charting, mapping and exploring of the lands further east of the Spice Islands and a renewed search for a passage through to the Pacific Ocean.' More specifically, the directive was that he concentrate his search on 'the great land of New Guinea and other East and Southlands'.

On hearing of the order, the Admiral of the Dutch Fleet, Steven van der Haghen, had no doubt as to the man for the job. He unequivocally recommended Captain Willem Janszoon, *Duyfken*'s captain.

Janszoon himself was quick to realise that this would be no simple undertaking. Still, he had no hesitation in saying yes. Preparations for the voyage commenced immediately and, much to the captain's delight, he was able to select his own small crew. Among the men he chose was his good friend Jan Rosengeyn, a very able mariner with thousands upon thousands of sea miles to his credit.

The fact that this passage of exploration was destined to sail into cyclone season indicates the VOC felt a sense of urgency: the company wanted to ensure they laid claim as quickly as they could to the largest possible amount of territory in this now very lucrative region. They certainly did not want any of the Iberians asserting their authority over currently undiscovered lands that held potential for vast profits – lands that for centuries had been mooted to exist.

The theory that there was a continent somewhere in the region dated all the way back to ancient times. It was believed that the weight of the European landmass had to be balanced by a similarly large landmass on the opposite side of the world. Some surmised that if there *was* land on the opposite side of the known realm, it would not be habitable due to 'the fury of the sun, which burns the intermediate zone'. At the same time, there were legends which related to an undiscovered continent that was a land of riches, a suggestion that could well have influenced the Dutch interest in exploring beyond the Spice Islands.

It was 18 November 1605 when *Duyfken* was guided away from the Javanese port of Bantam for the start of this bold expedition. As she glided towards the open sea, there was considerable speculation among those in Bantam as to the true reason for the voyage.

One theory that surfaced was that Janszoon was heading in search of the fabled King Solomon's gold mines, which were rumoured to lie to the east, and had already given their name to the Solomon Islands. This belief was confirmed in a journal written by Englishman Captain John Saris, an employee of the English East India Company and Governor of Bantam. He wrote:

> The eighteenth, here departed a small pinnace of the
> Flemmings, for the discovery of the land called Nova
> Guinea, which, as it is said, affordeth great store of Gold ...

There is little doubt that this information would have reached English ears half a world away, all eager to know what their trading rivals were out to achieve.

Duyfken's new course, of no determinable distance, would take her crew into a part of the world never previously traversed. The duration of their voyage could be months or more than a year, and the dangers they might face, from stormy weather, hazards to navigation and people they might encounter, could not be gauged.

Regardless of these dangers, the VOC was obviously determined to stay ahead of the English and others with interests in the spice trade. Because of this, should Janszoon return to Bantam with confirmation that the fables about the mythical land of riches were indeed fact, the VOC would secretly and swiftly move to exploit any commercial opportunity.

CHAPTER TWO

A Step into a New World

Early 1606

It was high summer in the southern hemisphere's low latitudes – the cyclone season – and the weather was steamy.

This was not the ideal time of year for a small vessel to be crossing an immense expanse of tropical ocean, especially in an age when storm forecasting was a matter of no more than instinct and a weather eye. But Willem Janszoon had no alternative: he was following orders from his VOC superiors. He and his crew were constantly scanning the horizon – as was the lookout, perched on a small platform on the mainmast about eight metres above the deck.

Duyfken (*Little Dove*) lived up to her name: she measured about 65 feet in overall length and 19 feet at maximum beam, and had a displacement of 45 tons. Small as she was, there was no questioning her seaworthiness. She had already sailed more than 18,000 nautical miles from her home port in the Netherlands, and on many voyages among the Spice Islands, before the journey that had brought her to this position in the Arafura Sea, north of what would one day be Arnhem Land.

Her crew was likewise small in number, consisting of no more than twenty, some of them believed to be one-time *watergeuzen*, literally 'sea beggars', former pirates or privateers, then in the employ of the VOC. Theirs was a tough life, as the tiny ship offered very little in the way of creature comforts. There were no cabins per se, so they slept where they chose – on deck or in the cargo hold, located in the waist of the ship. It's unlikely that these men had hammocks, as this form of sleeping apparatus was barely known in Europe at the time. Making their predicament even worse, surely close to intolerable, was that this was the time of year when they had to cope with day after day of torrential rain – an average of twenty-one days per month – and nearly 100 per cent humidity.

Despite her small size and the fact that she was being used for exploration, *Duyfken* was well armed and fast. She was classified as a *jaght* (the origin of the English word 'yacht'): a fast vessel capable of pursuing pirate or enemy vessels and engaging them effectively in battle. Even so, her hull was designed for high volume, a feature that ensured that, when she was in her commercial role, the maximum amount of cargo could be put aboard and delivered back to Europe.

In profile, she featured a heavily curved, crescent-like sheerline, and a sterncastle that extended forward from a high, teardrop-shaped stern to a point more than one-third of her overall length. There was also a small forecastle. Her rig comprised three masts and six sails; the foremast was raked slightly towards the bow, while the mainmast and mizzen were vertical. The bowsprit, which was mounted at deck level above a bow that was shaped like the back end of a bull, pointed high into the heavens and carried a rectangular spritsail, while the fore and mainmasts were each rigged with two square sails. The mizzenmast had a triangular lateen sail which, along with the spritsail, was usually set to help neutralise the pressure on the rudder and thus make the life of the helmsman easier.

There were no steering wheels in those early days of long-haul sailing. Instead, ships were controlled using a whipstaff, a vertical pivoted lever that poked through the deck and was attached to the tiller below. To direct the ship, the helmsman on deck would push the lever athwartships – to one side or the other – and as he did, the tiller attached to the rudder head moved in the opposite direction and turned the rudder. It was crude but effective steering.

Duyfken's ability to be fast under sail was not crucial to the success of this mission, but it helped, as did the fact that she had a shallow draft – less than 10 feet: a feature that decreased the chance of running aground in these never-before-seen waters.

This was Janszoon's first experience as an explorer. Details of his early life are vague, but it is known that he was born around 1570 in Amsterdam. His surname is sometimes abbreviated to Jansz. ('Janszoon' means Son of Jansz (John).)

His desire to go to sea for a life of challenge and excitement developed at a young age, so he studied mathematics, and navigation in particular. Life's big adventure started for him at age sixteen, when he became a cadet sailor.

There would have been many memorable moments as he ventured offshore on his first few passages – surely none more so than two years after he became a mariner when, while sailing in the English Channel, he and his shipmates on deck watched in near disbelief as the Spanish Armada was comprehensively destroyed by a squadron of English naval ships.

Second in command of the English fleet in that battle was the legendary Sir Francis Drake, a man who was in the process of making an indelible mark on maritime history. The young Willem Janszoon would ultimately do likewise.

In 1598, at the age of twenty-eight, Janszoon sailed on his first voyage to the Spice Islands. It was an intoxicating experience, one that involved foreign intrigue, previously inconceivable destinations, the excitement of trading and the potential for sea battles to protect Dutch commercial interests in the region. The culmination of these remarkable events became the catalyst for his moment in history.

Five years after that initial voyage east, in 1603, Janszoon's impressive abilities as a seafarer and fighter were recognised when he was first appointed captain of a ship: *Duyfken*. In this capacity he made his third passage to the Dutch East Indies, this time as part of a flotilla of twelve ships.

By now, the European spice trade had become so valuable that Spanish, Portuguese and Dutch ships were regularly locked in conflict, defending their commercial interests, or trying to gain others. *Duyfken* was often involved in battles, the most notable of which was in 1605, when the Dutch took Ambon from the Portuguese.

Janszoon continued to command *Duyfken* on passages through the Spice Islands until 1605. His ship was lying at anchor in the port of Bantam, Java, when he was advised that his next voyage would not see him returning home. Instead, it would be something out of the ordinary, a voyage of exploration.

*

As she sailed east, *Duyfken* wove her way through many islands, large and small, including Ambon, which Janszoon had helped to wrest from the Portuguese. *Duyfken* then headed for the Banda Islands, and while there, it is almost certain that Janszoon gathered valuable information relating to the region to the south-east, which he had been instructed to explore. It is likely that men from these islands had fished the coast of Australia, 600 nautical miles away, for hundreds of years, and therefore were able to advise the captain on what he might expect to find.

(Matthew Flinders would see clear evidence of the distance fishermen from islands to the north had travelled to Australian shores during his circumnavigation in 1802-03. It was when his ship *Investigator* was near Cape Wilberforce, on the western coast of the Gulf of Carpentaria, that he sighted six large vessels, each weighing about 25 tons, hauled up on the shore. Their origin was certainly not local, as the Indigenous people only used small canoes. His observations led him to conclude that these vessels, manned by Macassan fishermen, originated from the island of Sulawesi.)

Duyfken sailed on to the Kai and Aru Islands, in the south-eastern reaches of the Moluccas, before Janszoon set a course for the coast of what was referred to as New Guinea (today Papua). The ship made her way towards the south-westernmost point of that coast, about 2000 nautical miles east of her departure point in Bantam. Whenever possible, Janszoon went ashore to obtain fresh food and water. This was especially important when *Duyfken* was on the coast of New Guinea as it was their last anticipated landfall before she headed into the Arafura Sea.

On the first stage of this part of the voyage, Janszoon sailed about 250 nautical miles south before turning east-south-east. No doubt all on board were eagerly anticipating what might lie ahead. Was it possible they were sailing into a seemingly endless stretch of ocean, or would they actually discover new lands, and potential new sources of profit?

Duyfken's progress across the Arafura Sea and into what is now known as the Gulf of Carpentaria must have been slow. At least she was sailing downwind most of the time, but her hull was no doubt fouled by weed and crustaceans, so her average speed would rarely have been above 4 knots, at best 6.

Considerable caution would have been applied around the clock. At night, Janszoon would probably have elected to heave to, or proceed very slowly under reduced sail, perhaps on a reciprocal course that would guarantee their safety. Then, when the first glimmer of daylight could be seen in the eastern sky, all hands would have been roused so full sail could be set and the desired course resumed. Fortunately for the captain and his men, the first half of February 1606 brought the benefit of a waxing moon, something that made night-time navigation a little easier.

The actual date is debatable, but it was either late February or early March when, for the first time since leaving New Guinea weeks earlier, there was cause for excitement. The man aloft could see the faint outline of land ahead!

There's little doubt this Dutchman would not have realised the personal significance of this moment: he was the first European recognised to have sighted the coast of what would, one day, be known as Australia.

Janszoon would have scurried hand over hand up the rope ratlines to the lookout's platform on the mainmast so he too could get the best possible view. Initially, the land ahead could be seen as a low, dark outline on the horizon, but as it continued to expand, speculation must have grown accordingly. Was this part of an island, or a much larger tract of land, or part of New Guinea? Most importantly for all on board, whatever they had discovered, it did not exist on the map of the known world.

Prudent navigation continued to be applied as *Duyfken* closed on the coast. The depth of water was checked constantly, while every available man looked for navigational hazards – reefs or shallow water.

Anticipation gained momentum as the landmass lengthened every hour. Although it remained low in profile, it was obviously a sizeable coastline. With time came the finer definition: long ribbons of sand, and a backdrop of rich green vegetation with gently rolling hills in the distance. The most prominent feature of the coastline, and possibly the first land sighted, was a headland that Matthew Flinders would later name Duyfken Point in honour of the Janszoon expedition. It is located just south of the mining town of Weipa, today the largest community on the entire coast of the Gulf of Carpentaria.

Janszoon apparently elected to change course by a few degrees to the north and search for a suitable anchorage close to the shoreline. He spotted what seemed an ideal location when *Duyfken* was off what is now known as Pennefather River, a waterway that he named Rivier met het Bosch – River with the Bush. It lies 110 nautical miles down the east coast of the gulf from the tip of Cape York, and 25 nautical miles north of Weipa.

Once the anchor was set and the sails furled, the ship's small boat was lowered over the side so Janszoon could be rowed ashore. A few minutes later, when the boat's bow nudged the edge of the sandy beach, Janszoon unknowingly became the first confirmed European to set foot on the world's largest island and smallest continent, Australia.

He and his men would have been well satisfied by their discovery, though the evidence suggests they believed it was part of New Guinea, less than 400 nautical miles to the north. On the chart Janszoon or an associate created of their voyage, the coast where they landed and subsequently explored is designated 'Nova Guinea'. What is believed to be an accurate copy of this map, made in about 1670, still survives. It forms part of the extensive Atlas Blaeu–van der Hem, which contains many of the greatest treasures of Dutch map-making, and which in the eighteenth century ended up in the Austrian National Library in Vienna, where it was rediscovered in the 1920s.

Chances are that Janszoon was already realising there was little likelihood of finding ports whose inhabitants could become trading partners of the VOC in this part of the world as the vegetation, despite being green, was of a poor quality, and there was no sign of any inhabitants. However, his plan was to continue his exploration over some distance as he had to pursue the other part of his directive from headquarters: to search for a passage east into the Pacific.

The lack of surviving journals and logs from this historic voyage exposes it to much speculation, but at the same time, logic can fill in some gaps. Janszoon must have been confident that his only option was to sail south as he knew the coast of New Guinea was to the north, so when he returned to *Duyfken*, set the sails and weighed anchor, that was his chosen course.

Again, great caution would have been paramount as the small ship cruised along the shoreline: there was no knowing what dangers might be lurking off *Duyfken*'s bow. The crew would have reduced the sail area considerably as the wind strength increased, simply to ensure that progress was slow.

Duyfken would have crossed the 30 nautical mile wide expanse of what Janszoon named Vliege Baij (Fly Bay) because of the proliferation of flies. It was later renamed Albatross Bay in honour of a ship that transported people and supplies there.

Janszoon reached the place where the Archer River flows into the gulf, then continued sailing south, until he decided to terminate *Duyfken*'s journey at a point he named Cape Keerweer, which translates to Cape Turnaround.

Why did he suddenly turn back? The answer has been revealed in documents from another voyage undertaken nearly forty years later. In 1644, when Abel Tasman was directed to explore this region on his second voyage of discovery, he was advised that Janszoon had found 'that vast regions were for the greater part uncultivated ... so that no information was obtained touching the exact situation of the country and regarding the commodities obtainable and in demand there; our men having, by want of provisions and other necessities, been compelled to return and give up the discovery they had begun'.

But the document also suggests another reason why the voyage came to such a sudden end: parts of the area were 'inhabited by savage, cruel, black barbarians who slew some of our sailors'. Without question, the main reason why Janszoon abandoned his mission and returned home was because nearly half his crew were slaughtered.

The incident occurred when *Duyfken* was 100 nautical miles south of the Pennefather River. It is thought that Janszoon, along with the majority of his crew, went ashore, possibly to investigate what food and water supplies might be found. They were confronted by a number of Aboriginal men, who attacked them with spears, killing eight of them. This situation was as tragic as it was historic: not only was it the first time that Aboriginal people had been confronted by white men but it was also the first time there was a confrontation between the two sides and loss of life.

Some researchers are adamant that confirmation of this attack exists in the folklore of the Wik-Mungkan people, who still live in this region. A book written by members of this community contains an account of Janszoon's landing that, despite appearing to be somewhat embellished, is said to have been handed down through the generations.

In such circumstances, the survivors of the attack could do nothing but retreat to the ship. Seafaring logic would have confirmed for Janszoon that, with almost half his crew killed, it would have been near impossible to continue his exploration effectively and safely: he had barely enough men left to sail her, even in benign conditions. And the conditions could well be far from benign: this was the cyclone season, when heavy rain and strong winds are a normal part of life.

His decision was to turn back and head towards the Aru Islands, off the coast of New Guinea.

Yet, shorthanded as he was, Janszoon refused to abandon his exploration of this uncharted coast. With *Duyfken* forced to return north, he took the opportunity to proceed along the coast until he had to change course to the north-west and head for the Aru Islands. The ship again made her way across Fly Bay then passed Pennefather River before reaching another estuary flowing into the ocean, now named the Wenlock River.

It was here that tragedy is believed to have struck once more. This is how the incident is described on one Perth-based website which has tracked the VOC history:

It was at this river that Janszoon made the decision to accompany a longboat crew who rowed up the estuary in search of a desperately needed food source. As Janszoon and crew were negotiating the narrowing river, ominous black tribesmen seemingly appeared from nowhere. Fearful of another massacre, the crew started firing into the gathering tribe, wounding some of the startled natives. They immediately retaliated by propelling their long spears towards the boat, fatally wounding one of the oarsmen. Willem shouted

frantically to his men to turn about as he fired off his
pistols. With all speed they made it back to the *Duyfken*.

Enough was enough for Janszoon. With nine of his crew now
dead and two apparently wounded, he decided he must leave
this coast and sail back to the Aru Islands as quickly as possible.
His biggest challenge now was to encourage his remaining
crew to draw on all their strength to ensure the ship remained
safe, no matter the conditions.

It could be surmised that, if this latter incident had not
occurred, Janszoon would have continued north along the
coast and discovered Torres Strait. The tip of Cape York
would then have mystified him: just where did that coast,
which was seen to be disappearing to the south and into the
Pacific, go? Had he rounded the cape, turned to starboard and
continued south, then it is distinctly possible that the Dutch
would have initiated another expedition as soon as possible,
aimed at uncovering the secrets of the coast that Janszoon
would have put on the map. This might well have confirmed
the existence of the east coast of Terra Australis Incognita, the
Unknown South Land.

The course of history as we know it would have changed
dramatically.

Yet the reality was quite different. After many exhausting
months at sea, the tiny *Duyfken* finally reached the island of
Banda. Once again, it was the notes of Captain Saris that
confirmed this for the history books:

Nockhoda Tingall, a Tamil from Banda, in a Javanese junk, laden with mace and nutmegs, which he sold to the Gujaratis; he told me that the Dutch pinnace that went to explore New Guinea had returned to Banda, having found it: but in sending their men on shore to propose trade, nine of them were killed by the heathens, who are man-eaters: so they were forced to return, finding no good to be done there.

Diminutive *Duyfken* must have looked a sorry sight as she limped into Bantam with her sails draped forlornly from the yards. Aside from being bearded and generally dishevelled, the faces of her captain and crew would have reflected the harrowing times they had experienced. With nine of their shipmates having been killed, it would hardly have been the time to celebrate their discoveries: in fact there was little to celebrate anyway because, as Janszoon would have told his superiors, while they had found a previously unknown coast, it was of little or no value to the VOC. Sadly though for Janszoon, he would never know that he had taken such a prominent position in what would be the first page of European history in Australia: that he would one day be recognised as the first European to have stepped onto the shore of the great continent.

There was an ironic sequel to the Dutchman's discovery: a case where the Spanish deliberately suppressed details of new discoveries they had made. In December 1605, explorer Pedro

Fernandes de Quirós left Peru with three ships in search of Terra Australis Incognita. Later, after Quirós's ship was separated from the other vessels, Luís Vaz de Torres assumed command of the expedition, and sailed along the southern coast of New Guinea, proving the existence of the 80 nautical mile wide Torres Strait just eight months after the end of the *Duyfken* expedition. However, it appears that no one shared that information with the Dutch, or the rest of the world, including most of the cartographers who were continually upgrading their maps in this energetic era of exploration.

Though a few would have their suspicions, it would be 156 years after Torres's expedition before the English and Dutch became aware that a strait might exist and that, if it did, it separated New Guinea and the coast Janszoon had charted. It was in 1762, when Scottish cartographer Alexander Dalrymple (later the Royal Navy's first hydrographer) was translating a document captured from the Spanish into English, that he realised the southern coast of New Guinea and the coast revealed by the Dutch could be two distinct landmasses. It was then left to Captain James Cook to prove this correct.

The Spanish were not alone in suppressing news of such discoveries. It was standard practice during this era for seafaring nations to withhold valuable information from their rivals. Sir William Temple, British Ambassador to the Netherlands during the reign of Charles II, informed his government that 'a southern continent had long since been found out' by the Dutch, but that they had decided against 'any further attempts at discovering that continent, having already more trade than could be turned to account, and fearing that some more populous nation might make great establishment of trade in some of these unknown regions'. This was, in fact, more or less what the English were able to do.

In 1770, when Cook verified the existence of the east coast of Australia while sailing north, he eventually reached the tip of what is now Cape York and turned to the west, unimpeded. He knew from that moment that the coast he had discovered was that of Terra Australis Incognita, and that it was separated from the southern coast of New Guinea.

Intriguingly, there could well have been a totally different outcome if Torres had sailed through the strait on a westward course that was just 45 nautical miles further south than his actual track. On that course he would no doubt have discovered the east coast of Australia.

CHAPTER THREE

The Brouwer Route and the Roaring Forties

1610

Janszoon's attempt to discover the Great South Land might have been deemed a failure, but the VOC were going from strength to strength. Year by year, the ships grew larger, as did the profits.

Even so, the prevailing weather patterns made the outbound voyage from Europe unbearably slow. It took up to twelve months to sail the 12,000 to 14,000 nautical miles around the Cape of Good Hope, up the east coast of Africa, then east to Madagascar or Mauritius and on to India or the Spice Islands. The average speed of the ships between the numerous ports of call along the way was probably only 5 knots.

It took the skill of one VOC captain, Hendrik Brouwer, to find a way to more than halve the duration of this passage from Europe to Java. His new route would unexpectedly lead to the discovery of a large portion of the west coast of Terra Australis Incognita.

In 1610, Brouwer departed Europe aboard *Rode Leeuw* (*Red Lion*) as the commander of a three-ship convoy heading to the Spice Islands. It was on this voyage that he devised a way to dramatically shorten the duration of the outbound voyage, thanks to an unexpected discovery relating to the weather systems deep in the South Atlantic. The weather pattern that prevailed while the small convoy was en route to Cape Town caused them to sail further south than ususal – to a latitude of around 40 degrees south. As they sailed south, Brouwer and his men would have been wondering when the wind would turn in their favour and allow them to change course to the east towards their destination. When that change did eventually come the wind clocked to the west and increased in strength, driving the ships on a fast and boisterous downwind slide, right on the preferred course. The westerly continued unabated for day after day: perfect sailing conditions for a square-rigged ship. But the ride would soon have to come to an end and the course change to north of east, otherwise the ships would sail straight on and below the southern tip of the African continent.

Realising his course was well to the south of the norm, the mind of the mariner, Brouwer, was set wondering: might this weather system be a high latitude version of the almost ever-present tradewinds in the tropics? The thought obviously occupied his mind after *Rode Leeuw* reached the anchorage in Table Bay, off Cape Town, because, when the time came to set sail once more, Brouwer decided to abandon the accepted course to the Spice Islands and the East: instead of having to contend with the meandering winds that were experienced on the traditional north-easterly course across the Indian Ocean he would head south once more, down to the latitudes where they had found the westerlies on the previous leg.

It was a brave call – a gamble: sailing on a capricious whim into uncharted waters and against the normal practice, just in the hope of pioneering a new passage to Asia and the East. An air of uncertainty and concern would have spread across the crews of the three ships; they were sailing into an unexplored region of unknown dangers. Also, instead of the temperature rising and the winds becoming warmer, which was the norm on the usual course that took VOC ships north-north-east towards the equator, the wind was becoming frigid and the seas considerably larger as they headed south-east. But Brouwer remained unconcerned. The three ships continued to surge and roll their way south-east within sight of each other. Within days, though, the strong vein of westerly wind that Brouwer was hoping to find was with them. In no time the course had changed to the east, the sails were bosoming forth, and the speed increased. The loads on the mast, spars, sails and rigging were increasing in proportion to the rise in wind strength, so, before long, men were seen high in the rigging, their task being to furl sails and ease the pressure on their ships.

From that moment the captain must have been experiencing a high level of satisfaction as he watched his flotilla carving a swathe of white across the sea surface on what he hoped would be a non-stop passage to the East Indies. Regardless, there was no cause for celebration just yet: they had to proceed with great care as islands, reefs or a landmass might be lying anywhere along their course.

Brouwer's three ships arrived in Java inside six months: half the duration of the traditional route. A much-satisfied Brouwer penned a letter to his superiors at the VOC in the Netherlands, to inform them of his achievement. The decision to sail this course was a daring move on his part, but obviously one which his instincts convinced him would be successful. It was all that and more, as what became known as the Brouwer Route would soon be saving the VOC an inordinate amount of money annually due to the considerably shorter time the ships were at sea. Brouwer's letter to the VOC would prove to be his first step in what was an impressive ascent through the organisation to the point where he eventually became Governor-General of the Dutch East Indies.

He explained that by staying in the high latitudes when rounding the cape, the three ships had experienced a steady following wind for twenty-eight days, which had made for excellent speed. When they had reached what they believed to be the appropriate longitude (calculated by the Dutch at that time from the island of Tenerife), they had turned north and headed towards the Spice Islands, still in good sailing conditions.

The route had added benefits – in particular the fact that it avoided the calms and adverse currents that plagued the accepted course. The cooler weather conditions also meant that food did not spoil nearly as quickly as on the old route, which further benefited the health and fitness of the crew.

Within a short time the majority of VOC ships sailing to the Spice Islands and India were sailing the Brouwer Route, harnessing the benefits of a weather system that would become known as the Roaring Forties (because it generally lay between 40 and 50 degrees latitude). On 14 August 1616, this course became compulsory for VOC ships. That day, the company issued a directive that read in part: 'all ships, having revictualled at the Cape of Good Hope, have to lay their course east at the bearing 35, 36, 40 to 44 degrees Southern Latitude ... having the westerly winds, the ships will keep an easterly course for at least 1000 *mijlen* [Dutch miles]'. With this directive, there came a valuable incentive: the captains and helmsmen of the ships adopting this course were told they would receive bonuses of up to 600 guilders should they reach their destination within nine months, depending on which port they were sailing to.

There was another consequence of the adoption of the Brouwer Route. Due to either adverse weather, a navigational error, or both, this edict would lead to the discovery of the west coast of what would, a few decades later, start being referred to as New Holland.

Navigation, particularly when it came to the calculation of longitude – the east-west position of a ship at sea – was often more like a guessing game than a precise deduction, even for the best navigators. The possibility of human error in dead-reckoning navigation was forever present. The navigator's art was laden with ambiguities, and would remain that way for nearly one and a half centuries ... until Englishman John Harrison invented the marine chronometer. The challenge of calculating longitude is said to date back to the era of Greek mathematician and astronomer, Eratosthenes, who lived from approximately 276 to 194 BCE. He is credited with being the first person to calculate the circumference of Earth (incredibly to within four percent accuracy) and how to establish longitude, but his method was still not precise.

It was not until the mid-1730s that Englishman John Harrison presented to the world his marine chronometer, an ingenious device that revolutionised navigation through the virtual elimination of dead-reckoning for the calculation of longitude. When Captain James Cook set sail aboard *Resolution* in 1776 on his ill-fated final voyage, he stated that the most notable and exciting piece of equipment aboard the ship was the Larcum Kendall K1 chronometer, which was a replica of the acclaimed Harrison H4.

Brouwer's original letter to the VOC noted: 'On this route you do not have to fear any encounter with shallows or dangerous islands.' Yet over the next century, this statement would prove far from true. Had Brouwer sailed only a few hundred nautical miles to the east before turning north, he would have come across the west coast of New Holland and its hidden dangers.

In time, as an increasing number of VOC ships sailed this course, that element of danger became increasingly apparent – so obvious, in fact, that hundreds of sailors would lose their lives when their ships ran aground, taking to the bottom cargoes worth millions of guilders.

CHAPTER FOUR

Hartog: Blown into the History Books

January 1616

It was in the first year that the VOC ordered its fleet to sail the Brouwer Route that land loomed unexpectedly over the eastern horizon for one of its captains, thirty six year old Dirk Hartog.

Hartog was – literally but unintentionally – blown into the history books.

Born in Amsterdam in 1580, Hartog was apparently the second son of four children born to a seafarer, Hartych Krynen, and his wife, Griet Jans. On 20 February 1611, at the age of thirty-one, he married eighteen-year-old Meynsgen Abels. There is no standard practice for the spelling of Dutch names, so his surname appears in many forms – Hartogszoon, Hartogsz, Hartoogs, Hatichs and Hertoghsz. Existing documents do reveal that he signed his name on a number of occasions as Dyrck Hartoochz, but as far as Australian history is concerned, he is simply Dirk Hartog.

He followed his father into the life of a mariner, and by 1615 was the captain and owner of *Dolphyn* (*Dolphin*), a small coastal trader that sailed primarily out of the Netherlands, moving cargo between European ports. His vision was obviously set towards more distant horizons, because just one year later, he took up an offer from the VOC to become captain of *Eendracht* (*Concord*) for what would be her maiden voyage around the Cape of Good Hope and on to Asia and the East Indies.

Eendracht set sail on 23 January 1616 from the Dutch port of Texel as part of a small convoy of company vessels, probably two or three in total.

Eendracht's dimensions are unknown, but it is believed she was of 700 tons burthen, featured the standard three-masted rig configuration of the day, and had a high and steep sloping castle at the stern that was made up of five tiered decks. (The castle would become less pronounced in ships built during the following decades as designers and builders began to concentrate more on cargo-carrying capacity and design efficiency than on appearance.) *Eendracht* was fitted with thirty-two guns for protection and may have carried a crew of 200.

After being launched and rigged, she was moved 60 nautical miles north to the island of Texel, on the southern shores of the North Sea. (Nearly two centuries later, Texel would become famous in military history as the site where the Dutch Navy was captured by men on horseback: it became ice-bound and surrendered to Napoleon's army without a single shot fired.)

Winter had an ugly grip on Texel and surrounding regions when Hartog declared his ship ready to put to sea and had the pennant of the Chamber of Amsterdam (the Amsterdam branch of the VOC) hoisted to the masthead.

However, he didn't expect what occurred during his final preparations. Twenty-one crew and eight soldiers couldn't cope with the thought of sailing in such frigid conditions, so they deserted by walking ashore across the solid sea ice. Regardless, on 23 January 1616, when the ice had thawed and the wind and weather was suitable for departure, the small flotilla of which *Eendracht* was part prepared to set sail.

While some crew operated the windlass to weigh anchor, others clambered up the web of ice-laced ratlines and rigging to unfurl the sails from the yards. Meanwhile, men on deck manned the capstan so these sails could be hauled down and trimmed along with the braces and sheets, the intention being to have the yards and sails set to suit the prevailing offshore breeze. The helmsman was equally busy: he was on the steering deck within the confines of the aftcastle, constantly moving the hefty whipstaff steering lever athwartships to change the rudder angle and keep *Eendracht* on course. Once safely into the North Sea, the ships then headed down the English Channel before sailing out into the North Atlantic. Jacatra was the ultimate destination, but Cape Town's Table Bay was an important stopover.

The cargo *Eendracht* was carrying for this outbound passage was small in volume, but high in value: in the holds were an estimated 80,000 pieces-of-eight (Spanish dollars worth many millions in today's Australian currency). This would pay for the cargo to be transported back to the Netherlands. Additionally, *Eendracht* would have been carrying stone ballast in her bilge to provide stability when under sail: a burden that would be dumped once she was at her destination, to be replaced by weighty cargo.

At some stage during the arduous passage of around 8000 nautical miles to the Cape of Good Hope, *Eendracht* was hit by a powerful storm, and because of this, visual contact with the rest of the convoy was lost. Hartog had no option but to press on towards the anchorage in Table Bay, which he reached during the first week of August 1616. *Eendracht* lay at anchor there for three weeks while she was readied for the voyage of more than 6500 nautical miles to Jacatra. The captain hoped the other ships would arrive during this time, but they didn't, so he decided to go it alone.

Within a matter of days, Table Mountain, the backdrop to the bay, was merging into the distant horizon, and *Eendracht* had left Cape Town in her turbulent white wake. She then headed south towards the Roaring Forties; once conditions were suitable, there would be a call for a change of course to the east along a chosen latitude. From that point *Eendracht* could ride the strong westerly winds and big seas of the Brouwer Route.

It was calculated that ships sailing this route would need to cover about 4000 nautical miles before starting a long, curved course to the north towards Java: a requirement that meant there was considerable pressure on each ship's navigator to accurately calculate longitude by dead reckoning.

At this time no one sailing the Brouwer Route knew what lay east of the Cape of Good Hope. Was it a wide expanse of uncharted ocean, or did it contain land – an island, islands, or maybe even Terra Australis Incognita? Because each VOC voyage was a commercial venture, getting the ship safely to the Spice Islands and back to Europe was all that mattered.

Though determining longitude was difficult, there were two 'safety nets': the navigator, and the lookout, who stood on his platform while clinging to the rigging high up the mainmast, which was forever arcing through the air in response to wind and wave action on the ship.

It was 25 October 1616 when the lookout would have been the first to see it: land off the starboard bow, long and low in profile. It must have been an exciting moment for Hartog and his men as they observed a chunk of terra firma that no European knew existed. It certainly was not on any contemporary map. Suddenly, these commercial sailors were also discoverers, and they made the most of it.

With the leadsman standing in the chains so he could constantly plumb the depths with the leadline, Hartog directed that a new course be cautiously taken towards the shore of what appeared to be an island. It would prove to be just that: more than 40 nautical miles (80 kilometres) long and generally flat. Its western coast, which they were observing, seemed to be an endless strip of 150 metre high sandstone cliffs.

Eendracht was soon gliding north parallel to the shore, until a sheltered beach suitable for landing the ship's boats was located near the northern tip of the island. Hartog and some crew then went ashore to investigate their find, thus creating history: their footprints in the sand would be the first of any Europeans on what would, much later, be confirmed as the westernmost point of Terra Australis Incognita. Incredibly, though, had *Eendracht* been on a course just another 10 or so nautical miles to the west, it is probable that no land would have been seen.

Hartog, knowing there was no record of land in this part of the world, thought it essential that he leave evidence of his visit. He had one of his men flatten a pewter dinner plate and engrave onto it details of their presence. When completed, the plate, with its coarsely written message, was nailed to an oak post and set firmly in a fissure in the rocks, at the top of the cliff above the beach where they had landed. Translated into English, the message read:

1616 THE 25 OCTOBER IS HERE ARRIVED THE
SHIP EENDRAGHT OF AMSTERDAM THE
UPPERMERCHANT GILLIS MIEBAIS OF LIEGE
SKIPPER DIRCK HATICI IS OF AMSTERDAM.
THE 27 DITTO [we] SET SAIL FOR BANTUM THE
UNDERMERCHANT JAN STINS, THE FIRST
MATE PIETER DOOKES VAN BIL. ANNO 1616

*

The durable qualities of pewter saw the plate survive, despite being exposed to the ravages of the weather for eighty-one years, although the post had rotted. On 4 February 1697 it was found lying on the ground of the clifftop by Michiel Bloem, upper steersman on Dutch commander Willem de Vlamingh's expedition, which was in the region searching for survivors of the ship *Ridderschap van Holland* (*Knighthood of Holland*). The vessel was thought to have been lost in that part of the world two years earlier while on her fifth voyage to the East Indies. (The most recent theory is that she was wrecked on Pelsaert Island, 175 nautical miles south of where *Eendracht* anchored.)

There were three ships in de Vlamingh's convoy: *Geelvinck* (*Yellow Finch*), *Nijptang* (*Pincers*) and *Weseltje* (*Little Weasel*). On 29 December 1696 they made their first landfall on the coast of an island that de Vlamingh named Rattennest, because of the large 'rats' are were found there. Today it is known as Rottnest Island; the large 'rats' are actually quokkas, native to the island.

Soon after, de Vlamingh and some of his men sailed to the mainland coast, where they discovered the entrance to a river that they navigated upstream for nearly 10 nautical miles, to a point close to where Perth is located today. Along the way they observed many black swans, so the river was given the name Zwaanerivier, the Swan River.

As the most frequent wind direction on this coast is from the south-west, the de Vlamingh convoy would have enjoyed ideal sailing conditions as it made its way north at a slow pace after weighing anchor on 13 January 1697.

Following a seventeen-day passage of more than 400 nautical miles, what is now known as Dirk Hartog Island hove into view. De Vlamingh was all too well aware of Hartog's discovery and the fact that he had left a pewter plate at the northern tip of the island – today appropriately named Cape Inscription – so the three ships headed for that point.

After finding Hartog's plate, Bloem took it aboard *Geelvinck* for de Vlamingh to see. Realising the historical significance of the weather-beaten piece of metal, de Vlamingh decided to take it to Batavia with him, and replaced it onshore with his own. This plate included the text from Hartog's plate as well as his own details:

1697 THE 4 FEBRUARY IS HERE ARRIVED THE
SHIP GEELVINCK OF AMSTERDAM, THE
COMMANDER AND SKIPPER WILLEM DE
VLAMINGH OF VLIELAND, ASSISTANT JOAN-
NES BREMER OF COPENHAGEN; FIRST MATE
MICHIL BLOEM OF BISHOPRIC BREMEN. THE
HOOKER NYPTANGH SKIPPER GERRIT
COLAART OF AMSTERDAM; ASSISTANT
THEO-DORIS HEIRMANS OF DITTO [the same
place], FIRST MATE GER-RIT GERITSEN OF

BREMEN. THE GALIOT HET WESELTJE, MASTER CORNELIS DE VLAMINGH OF VLIELAND, MATE COERT GERRITSEN OF BREMEN AND FROM HERE [we] SAILED WITH OUR FLEET TO FURTHER EXPLORE THE SOUTHLAND AND [are] DESTINED FOR BATAVIA – #12 [on the twelfth] VOC.

When de Vlamingh eventually arrived in Batavia, he presented Hartog's plate to the VOC. Soon afterwards, it was shipped to the VOC headquarters in the Netherlands. The plate, which is the oldest known evidence of a European landing in Australia, is now on display in the Rijksmuseum, Amsterdam. The de Vlamingh plate is in the Shipwrecks Galleries of the Maritime Museum in Fremantle, Western Australia.

*

While Hartog was on the island he discovered in 1616, he spent two days exploring it before continuing on his voyage towards the East Indies. Once under way on 27 October, he held *Eendracht* on a course close to the coast so he could chart salient features of the land. He did this for more than 225 nautical miles, all the way to what is now known as North West Cape. At that point the coastline disappeared to the north-east, before fusing into the distant horizon.

Despite any desire Hartog might have had, he knew he could pursue it no further. His was a commercial venture, not one of exploration. He did, however, give the coastline a name – Eendrachtsland – that remained in place until around 1644, when Abel Tasman and his talented navigator Frans Visscher charted nearly 1500 nautical miles of the same coast. For more than a century afterwards the still-unknown landmass beyond the coast was known as New Holland.

On abandoning his charting of the coast, Hartog set a course that would eventually lead him to one of the larger ports of the Spice Islands, Macassar, where the Dutch had established a settlement in 1607. *Eendracht* arrived there on 14 December 1616 – but any pleasure that might have come for the crew through reacquainting themselves with civilisation was quickly extinguished when a confrontation with local inhabitants resulted in the death of fifteen of Hartog's men. They were part of a contingent that went ashore unaware that the islanders held a hatred for the Dutch because they had killed a local leader during a visit about one year earlier. The visitors walked into a trap and the massacre befell before they could retreat to their longboat and escape.

Consequently, Hartog had *Eendracht* sail away from that port as soon as possible, but over the next twelve months he visited other trading ports throughout the region to negotiate the purchase of cargo. At the same time, he no doubt spread the word of his discovery of islands and a lengthy coastline to the south, his written comment being that he had found 'various islands, which were, however, found uninhabited'.

Eendracht's last port of call was Bantam, from where, on 17 December 1617, Hartog commenced that long voyage back to Zeeland, the south-westernmost province of the Netherlands. The passage took *Eendracht* ten months to complete, and she arrived home on 16 October 1618. Her highly valuable cargo comprised the aromatic benzoin resin, a considerable amount of silk cloth and, almost certainly, spices.

It appears that one passage to the East Indies was enough for Hartog, as he decided to return to coastal trading in Europe. Soon after his arrival home, he took up the position of captain aboard *Geluckige Leeu* (*Lucky Lion*).

Incredibly, he lived for only another three years. When he passed away in Amsterdam in 1621, aged just forty-one, he could have had no way of realising the importance of his discovery. He had become the first European to sight and set foot on the west coast of the mythical Terra Australis Incognita.

History would eventually reveal that this accidental discoverer had provided the second small piece in a giant jigsaw: a puzzle that became a continent.

CHAPTER FIVE

A Coast of Hazards, not Desire

1616 to 1622

During the Age of Exploration, the discovery of new lands across the world by daring seafarers created considerable excitement, and on many occasions fostered thoughts of commercial opportunity. But not when it came to Eendrachtsland (soon to be known as New Holland). For more than a century after Hartog nailed his pewter plate to a post on the island that today forms the western shore of Shark Bay, there was no real rush to search or settle the coast that owed its discovery to the Brouwer Route.

Those sailors and their ships were there for commerce, not discovery; they were on their way north to a region of known riches and had little time for anything else. The Dutch in particular gave this emerging landscape scant recognition because they had been quick to assume there were no trade opportunities along the shoreline.

This distinct lack of interest in exploration or colonisation had been evident since Willem Janszoon's discovery in 1606 of what would later prove to be the east coast of the Gulf of Carpentaria. The Dutch navigator must have returned to his base in Bantam with the news that he had found an unknown coast, but that there was nothing of interest there. There was no need to go exploring any further ... and the VOC didn't.

Twelve years later, when Janszoon made another discovery in Eendrachtsland, the same lack of interest was evident on the part of the Dutch, even though general curiosity about Terra Australis Incognita was as strong as ever. The interest in the pieces of coast that had been discovered, and the quest to go in search of Terra Australis Incognita were, to some degree, inspired by Marco Polo's reference to 'Beach', the land of immense riches, in his writings some 300 years earlier. Certainly, the Dutch finds to date gave no indication that wealth was there to be enjoyed, but at the same time they realised there would be more undiscovered land in the region. That inevitably caused speculation that Beach might soon be discovered.

This time, Janszoon, sailing aboard *Mauritius*, would find a piece of a western coast that would eventually prove to be some 2000 nautical miles long. But not even this tangible evidence of the existence of a southern landmass was enough to entice explorers into the region to look for land and consider its potential for settlement. Simply put, the coast was seen as nothing more than a serious navigational hazard for vessels sailing to the Spice Islands and India in pursuit of the riches to be found there.

In 1616 the Dutch made an abortive attempt to mount an expedition out of Ambon (the VOC's centre of operations from 1610 to 1619) to discover what land might be found in the south, particularly in the region of Janszoon's discovery in the gulf. That plan came in the same month as Hartog made his discovery in the west. The proposed voyage – promoted by the Dutch governor of the island of Ternate, in the northern Moluccas – called for Cornelis Dedel to fit out and command the fluyt *Jager* (*Hunter*) and the pinnace *Morgensterre*. Being a fluyt, *Jager* was part of an extensive fleet of dedicated cargo-carrying vessels, a design that contributed much towards making the Netherlands a great maritime power in this era. As a pinnace, the smaller *Morgensterre* was a multi-purpose design; she could operate as a merchant ship, small warship or pirate vessel.

Just as the two vessels were about to set sail, however, Admiral van der Haghen (ironically, the man who had recommended Janszoon in 1605) usurped the governor's authority and ordered Dedel to intercept two British trading ships, *Swan* and *Defence*, that were heading for Banda, and prevent them from taking on a cargo of nutmeg. Dedel's mission was successful, but when he returned to Ternate he was told the planned voyage of discovery would not proceed.

There was one other registered sighting of the coast that came after Hartog's historic landfall and just prior to Janszoon's voyage on *Mauritius* – but those involved did not know of Hartog's discovery, because they had received no communications about it from Europe. The ship concerned, *Zeewolf* (*Catfish*), was again sailing for the United East India Company; her captain was Haevik Claeszoon van Hillegom and the supercargo – *opperkoopman* (upper merchant), the highest authority on the ship – was Pieter Dirkszoon.

It was 24 June 1618 when Dirkszoon wrote to the VOC from Jacatra to report their observations:

Worshipful Wise Provident Very Discreet Gentlemen,
… by God's grace we soon got south as far as 37, 38 and 39 degrees, after which we held our course due east for a thousand miles before turning it northward … on the 11th of May [1618, we] reached 21° 15' S. Latitude, we saw and discovered … land about 5 or 6 miles to windward east of us, which in consequence we were unable to touch at. We observed it to be a level, low-lying shore of great length, and looking out from the top-mast we saw on both ends of it, to north as well as to southward, still other land which showed high and mountainous. [We] do not know whether it forms an unbroken coast-line, or is made up of separate islands. In the former case it might well be a mainland coast, for it extended to a very great length. But only the Lord

knows the real state of affairs. At all events it would
seem never to have been made or discovered by any one
before us, as we have never heard of such discovery, and
the chart shows nothing but open ocean at this place.
According to our skipper's estimation in his chart the
Strait of Sunda was then N.N.E. of us at about 250
miles distance.

The description of the land they saw, and the latitude, indicates
this was what the world now knows as North West Cape.

For Janszoon, his second discovery came accidentally,
when he was supercargo aboard the East Indiaman *Mauritius*,
which had Lenaert Jacobszoon as captain. The vessel is
believed to have been of similar dimensions to Hartog's
Eendracht. She replaced the original *Mauritius*, which sank off
Gabon, on the west coast of Africa, in 1609.

Dates suggest this was the ship's maiden voyage to the East
Indies, and, like other VOC ships in whose wake she followed,
she sailed the Brouwer Route after departing Cape Town's Table
Bay. She weighed anchor and put to sea again on 16 June 1618.

Janszoon would later detail his discovery in a letter to the
Managers of the VOC's Amsterdam Chamber dated 6 October
1618:

Worshipful Wise Provident Discreet Gentlemen,
The present serves only to inform you that on the 8th
of June last with the ship *Mauritius* we passed Cap de

Bonne-Espérance, with strong westerly winds, so that we deemed it inadvisable to call at any land, after which we ran a thousand *mijlen* [around 3000 nautical miles] to eastward in 38 degrees Southern Latitude, though we should have wished to go still further east.

On the 31st of July we discovered an island and landed on the same, where we found the marks of human footsteps – on the west side it extends N.N.E. and S.S.W.; it measures 15 *mijlen* in length, and its northern extremity is in 22° S. Lat. It bears Eendracht [Eendrachtsland] S.S.E. and N.N.W. from the south point of Sunda at 240 *mijlen* distance ... from there through God's grace we safely arrived before Bantam on the 22nd of August ...

Ironically, just as Janszoon had believed he was observing an extension of the coast of New Guinea when he discovered the east coast of the Gulf of Carpentaria, this time he believed he was on an island, when he wasn't. His descriptions of the coast, and the latitudes and longitudes mentioned, indicate he was sailing along a 60 nautical mile stretch of relatively flat land between today's Point Cloates and North West Cape, at the northern end of Exmouth Gulf.

Janszoon and Jacobszoon's conviction that their discovery was an island was perpetuated for the next 209 years. In 1719 a European mariner gave it the name Cloat's (or Cloate's) Island without having attempted a circumnavigation of it.

But it was not until after 1827, when Phillip Parker King (the explorer son of the third governor of New South Wales) declared it a peninsula, that it started appearing on maps in its true form.

After clearing North West Cape, *Mauritius* obviously sailed about 25 nautical miles north-east across Exmouth Gulf and closed on its eastern coast, because the entrance to what is now known as the Ashburton River was sighted. At that time it was given the name Willem's River, perhaps in honour of Janszoon.

The fact that *Mauritius* held a course so close to the coast suggests those on board might have maintained visual contact with the land for more than 800 nautical miles, possibly as far as the northernmost point of the Kimberleys. From there they turned north-west and headed for Sunda Strait in the Spice Islands.

A year later, former governor Frederik de Houtman encountered the same part of the coast as Dirk Hartog when in charge of two ships, *Dordrecht* and *Amsterdam*, which were on a course to Java. Seventy-seven years later, he sailed past the Swan River and Rottnest Island, but mistook the island for a mainland cape.

From there he continued sailing north, and discovered the now well-known Houtman Abrolhos Islands, a remarkable chain of 122 islands plus coral reefs nearly 50 nautical miles off the coast from where Geraldton is today. Houtman was sufficiently proud of this discovery to write to the VOC:

On the 29th [June,] deeming ourselves to be in an open
sea, we shaped our course north-by-east. At noon we
were in 29° 32' S Lat.; at night about three hours before
daybreak, we again unexpectedly came upon a low-
lying coast, a level, broken country with reefs all round
it. We saw no high land or mainland, so that this shoal
is to be carefully avoided as very dangerous to ships that
wish to touch at this coast. It is fully ten miles in length,
lying in 28° 46' ...

For many years it was believed that the word Abrolhos was
derived from the Portuguese expression *abre os olhos*, meaning
'keep your eyes open', but this is incorrect. It has subsequently
been translated to mean 'spiked obstructions' (referring to the
islands' reefs).

At this point in history, as little as 300, and certainly no
more than 1000, nautical miles of the more than 19,000
nautical miles of coastline of what would be known as
Australia had been sighted by Europeans. It would be almost
two centuries before the continent was circumnavigated in its
entirety.

*

With so little detail known of the western coast of the Great
South Land, it stood as a life-threatening obstacle to seafarers
plying the route between Cape Town and the Spice Islands

early in the seventeenth century. There would soon be more than fifty merchant ships making that journey annually.

Australia's western coast was a lee shore for much of the time, so the chances of shipwreck were inevitably high, but it was not until 1622 that the first vessel was snared by an unforgiving, rocky shore. Surprisingly, she was not a ship flying the flag of the VOC. She was an English vessel, and it remains Australia's oldest known shipwreck.

Named *Trial* (also spelled *Tryal* and *Triall*), she smashed onto a reef off the western coast of Eendrachtsland in the dead of night. The tragedy was due to a navigational error by a captain of highly questionable ethics and character, and the consequences were dire: more than 100 sailors died in distressing and controversial circumstances.

Trial appears for the first time in British maritime history in July 1621, when an English East India Company (EIC) document revealed the ship, of some 500 tons burthen, would 'very shortly be ready to put to sea from Plymouth'. It was also noted that it was time to secure a captain and crew.

Another document dated 10 July delivers an enlightening insight into the domestic issues that confronted some seafarers of the day. It reads: 'Mr. Newport ... who had formerly been named to the Company to go [as Captain] of the Triall cannot resolve whether to undertake the charge yet or not until he have first satisfied his wife, which he would do forthwith and then give his answer.'

Mrs Newport was obviously not impressed by the offer made to her husband, especially considering he would be away for such a long time, because the next time *Trial* was mentioned, one John Brooke had been appointed captain (master). The note advised that 'Mr. Brooke Master of the *Triall*, being now ready to go down to Plymouth desired allowance for the carrying down of himself and four servants. The Court ordered he should have 13 pounds.'

In a matter of weeks, *Trial*'s departure was confirmed. It was reported that, 'manned by 143 good men', she sailed from Plymouth on 4 September 1621. Brooke's son, John, was apparently with him. *Trial* was 'light ship' when she sailed – not carrying any significant amount of cargo – but in her hold was a considerable supply of silver that would be used for currency when trading in the East Indies, and as a gift for the King of Siam.

Once under way, and with her sails stretching in response to a steady breeze, the call was for a course to the south-west, which would see *Trial* clear the island of Ushant at the western tip of France, 120 nautical miles away, then enter the North Atlantic.

At some time before leaving, perhaps when he was appointed to the position of captain for the voyage, Brooke was advised by his superiors at the EIC that his course to the East Indies must be via the considerably faster Brouwer Route. More specifically, he was to follow the route established by Captain Humphrey Fitzherbert, who in 1620 became the first English captain to sail the Brouwer Route to the East Indies.

The course that Fitzherbert logged, which was close to that of Brouwer, was known to be free from hazards.

It could be suggested that Brooke was not comfortable with this directive, possibly due to a sense of doubt in his own ability to calculate longitude, a critical factor when sailing from west to east in the southern latitudes, across the bottom of the Atlantic and Indian Oceans.

When *Trial* reached the Cape of Good Hope there was another English vessel there, *Charles*, which was returning to Europe. Brooke made contact with the ship's master, Captain Bickle, and asked if any of his experienced crew might consider sailing to Batavia with Brooke, as there was no one aboard *Trial* with sailing or navigational experience in that part of the world. Bickle was happy to release any of his crew, but only one agreed to go: Thomas Bright, who was immediately appointed first mate.

Trial sailed out of Table Bay on 19 March and held a course towards 39 degrees south, or until she ran into the Roaring Forties. From there she would sail east into a barely known and challenging ocean.

Like every other seafarer entering this part of the world, Brooke was well aware that there had been numerous sightings of land, rocks and reefs along the eastern part of the course they would sail. Every one of these, and others yet to be discovered, was a potential threat to the safety of the ship and its crew if longitude was determined incorrectly. If a ship was too far east then trouble was brewing.

By the end of April *Trial* had completed her run in the Roaring Forties and was sailing towards the north. She had been on an arc out of the high latitudes from the time when Brooke believed she had achieved the correct longitude. On 1 May, at latitude 22 degrees south, land was sighted, something Brooke later said left his entire crew feeling 'very joyful at ye sight thereof'.

Unbeknown to them, this was a historic moment: they were the first Englishmen to sight what would, nearly two centuries later, become a British territory – Australia. However, as momentous as this sighting might have been, the worrying aspect was that they should not have been in sight of land – not if they were following Fitzherbert's course.

For the next five days, *Trial* battled north-easterly headwinds, then on 6 May, conditions turned more in her favour. That allowed Brooke to call for his ship to hold a course towards the north-east, somewhat parallel to the land they could see in the distance to the south-east. This was an incredible decision when he surely knew they were sailing in unknown and potentially dangerous waters.

That night, unbelievably, Brooke did not order a lookout to be on station high in the rig, even though land had been seen and his ship's position on the chart was far from certain, a neglectful action that was the beginning of an almost inexplicable series of events. It could be described as a dereliction of duty.

The following is Brooke's paraphrased version of how a tragic situation unfolded:

[On 24 May] ye great island with 3 small islands …
bearing S.E. 20 leagues from us … we steered N.E.
expecting to fall in with the western point of Java. [On]
ye 25th day at 11 o'clock in ye night, fair weather and
smooth ye ship struck. I ran to ye poop [deck at the
stern] and hove ye lead and found but 3 fathoms water …

Trial was doomed from the moment she struck. The jagged reef that had ripped into her bow tore her forward sections apart as if the planks were matchsticks. Her timbers literally exploded open on impact, and in no time her belly was awash with tons of water. The force of the collision would have sent most of the sixty crew on watch cascading across the deck like falling ninepins, while below, those who were asleep would have been jolted from serenity into nightmare.

The first realisation of what had happened, and the accompanying look of shock on every face, would have lasted only a few seconds. While Brooke's immediate reaction was to call for the helmsman and crew to try to tack the ship, shouts laden with fear coming from below deck would have suggested that *Trial* was already beyond help. Even if they had somehow been able to tack the ship and free her, she would have sunk almost immediately: the damage to the hull was much too severe for her to be refloated.

There was no hope of saving the ship. All was lost.

Brooke would later declare in his report that he immediately ordered the longboat – one of the two small open boats *Trial* carried – to be launched: 'I had gotten her out and hanged her in ye tackles on ye side … seeing the ship full of water and ye wind [strength increasing, I] made all ye means I could to save my life and as many of my company as I could.' However, other documents and statements would later claim that Brooke's obvious priority was to save his own life, with little regard for others.

The captain would claim that he stayed with the ship until 0300 hours, and when nothing more could be done he slid down a rope at the stern and into the skiff floating below. He said he then ordered the men in the skiff to release the painter holding the bow of the boat to the then wallowing ship and row away.

There were ten men aboard the skiff, including Brooke's son, and thirty-six aboard the considerably larger longboat, which Brooke claimed he ordered Bright to command. It departed the ship, according to some reports, at about the same time as the skiff. The remaining 139 men lining the deck could only watch on in disbelief, knowing they were being abandoned and that their fate was sealed.

According to Brooke's records, the inevitable came at 0430. Every man's fear then turned to terror: the forward sections of the ship broke up, and with that the remaining aft section began to capsize and slipped further beneath the surface with the surge of each turbulent wave. As the skiff and longboat were rowed away, those whose lives had been saved could only listen in horror to the grief-laden cries of their dying shipmates, and the roar of the pounding surf tearing at the disintegrating hulk.

The longboat was crammed to the gunwales with survivors and what supplies could be gathered, while the skiff, which had aboard its usual complement of men, was also carrying at least one trunk that Brooke had insisted on taking.

Brooke's subsequently challenged account of events from this moment suggests that once the two boats were within hailing distance of each other, it was decided to head for an island they could see about six nautical miles away. The plan was to regroup there and consider their predicament. Their supplies were meagre – mainly barricoes of water, some wine and bread – so they were no doubt hoping they might find additional food on the island.

It appears these essentials were not found. The only hope they had of survival was to try to sail their two open boats to Java, a 1000 nautical mile passage. The lack of food and water made this considerable challenge even more life-threatening.

The smaller skiff reached Batavia in forty days with all ten crew still alive. The longboat, which arrived three days later, had had one man die while at sea.

The fact that these two small boats reached their goal was remarkable. But these are voyages that history has essentially ignored – or taken for granted – possibly because Brooke was soon afterwards identified as a liar and a charlatan.

Brooke must have known from the moment *Trial* smashed onto the reef that he was at fault, because immediately after arriving in Batavia, he went on the defensive. His first action was to write to his superiors in London and lay the blame for the tragedy squarely at the feet of Captain Fitzherbert. Brooke claimed that Fitzherbert's chart, which he said he had been following, was inaccurate, and that *Trial* had been lost on a reef where Fitzherbert's chart had shown there were no dangers.

The truth is that Brooke had not been remotely close to following Fitzherbert's instructions: *Trial* was on a course some 200 leagues (600 nautical miles) east of that which Fitzherbert followed. This would be confirmed more than three centuries later when the wreck was finally found, and the true location of what is now named Tryal Rocks established.

That Brooke was lying is apparent when it is realised what course he sailed to reach Java in the skiff. For Brooke to have reached the eastern end of Java he would have had to sail due north from the wreck site, but in a desperate bid to exonerate himself, he claimed he sailed north-east. Had he steered to the north-east from where Tryal Rocks is located, as he maintained, he would have found himself east of Timor. So, to perpetuate the lie, he had to state that the reef that claimed *Trial* was 200 leagues to the west of the actual site of the wreck.

Before long, it was clear to many that Brooke was embroiled in a cover-up: he was lying to save his own skin. While his story appeared logical, it was a complete fabrication.

Even Brooke's first mate, Thomas Bright, turned on him. On 22 August 1622, Bright wrote a secret communiqué to

Andrew Ellam, one of the hierarchy at EIC headquarters in London. In it he stated that the reasons for the loss of *Trial* and the lives of more than 100 men were Brooke's incompetence as a navigator and his failure to post a lookout aloft throughout the day and night after land had been sighted. He stated that before *Trial* was wrecked, 'we always feared the ship to be beyond his reckoning', and this was proved to be the case.

Bright believed that at the time of the wreck *Trial* was hundreds of leagues further east than Fitzherbert's course, a circumstance that placed her in a region where no other English ship had ever sailed. Worse still, they were holding a course to the north-east when they struck, not towards the north-west, which was the true location of Sunda Strait.

Bright also contradicted what Brooke claimed were his actions after the ship crashed onto the reef. He alleged that Brooke abandoned his ship and his men almost immediately after she was grounded. He took to the skiff and had it rowed away from the wreck when men were already in the water and drowning nearby, even though there was ample room in the skiff to take them aboard. Bright said that Brooke and 'fellow consorts' were seen gathering provisions and the captain's possessions so they could be saved, while all the time 'promising us [Bright and another officer named Jackson] faithfully to take us along' with them. Bright continues:

… but like a Judas [while I returned to the great cabin, he] lowered himself privately into the skiff, only with 9

men, and his boy, [then] stood for the Straights of Sunda
that instant, without care and seeing the lamentable end
of ship, the time she split or respect of any man's life …

Bright said that he then launched the longboat with the
express intention of saving as many men as possible who had
been 'left to God's Mercy'. In no time the boat was
dangerously overcrowded, so he had no option but to guide
her to a point about a quarter of a mile out to sea. If he had
not done this, and more men had tried to clamber aboard,
then the longboat would have capsized.

At daylight, there was no sign of Brooke's skiff: it had
disappeared over the horizon to the north. Bright said he then
guided the longboat towards an island they could see about 5
leagues away to the north-west. They stayed there seven days,
then, before heading to Java, took the longboat back to where
the ship was wrecked, but there was 'nothing we could see of
ship or anything pertaining thereto'.

Further discredit was heaped on Brooke in subsequent
reports and documents, as well as through searches of the
wreck site after it was discovered in 1969 just north of Barrow
Island, 40 nautical miles off the West Australian coast. Brooke
was adamant that the ship's cargo, plus the silver and the ship's
papers, were lost in the wreck, but it now appears that he
secretly crammed what silver he could into at least one trunk,
got it aboard the skiff, and took it to Batavia without creating
any suspicion. Bright certainly accused the captain of theft.

Incredibly, Brooke's employers fell for fiction, not fact. They believed his story and cleared him of all blame. For the next two years he was employed aboard ships trading along the coast of Sumatra, then in 1624 he was appointed to sail aboard the East Indiaman *Moone*, one of five ships scheduled to return to England at that time, all laden with spices and possibly unique fabrics sourced in the region.

This voyage again left Brooke enmeshed in controversy. An incident on 15 September 1625 on the shores of Dover led to the following report: 'Four other ships arrived from the East Indies, but *Moone* was cast away up our coast.'

All indications were that the grounding, for no justifiable reason, was deliberate. As a result, Brooke and another senior officer named Churchman were arrested and charged with wilfully running the ship aground. They were then imprisoned in Dover Castle

Brooke declared that the poor condition of the ship, its sails and ground tackle, were the reasons for it going aground. He petitioned the House of Commons for his release, advising the East India Company that he was destitute and begging for their forgiveness. Almost a year after the incident the charges were dropped and both he and Churchman were released.

CHAPTER SIX

Charting, Mapping and Exploring the Gulf

1622

While the Brouwer Route to the East Indies had made trading in the region a far more profitable venture for all concerned, the loss of *Trial* sharpened the focus on the dangers associated with sailing these barely known waters. The precise location of the reef that caused the English ship's undoing remained unknown, and the coast skirting the eastern perimeter of the Brouwer Route was still largely uncharted. Not surprisingly, then, the directors of the VOC in Amsterdam hastened their plans to more accurately map the coast of Eendrachtsland and its associated islands and reefs.

The charts of the time revealed a yawning gap between the small stretch of shoreline that Janszoon had mapped in 1606 and the western coast of Eendrachtsland charted by the navigators of ships sailing the Brouwer Route. It was a gap that needed to be filled so that ships on the outbound passage from Europe could be guaranteed the safest possible course.

The urgent need for better mapping became more evident just one month after the loss of *Trial*, when the small (500 tons burthen) fluyt *Wapen van Hoorn* (*Weapon of Horn*) almost came to grief on the same stretch of coast. This was her second voyage from the Netherlands to the Spice Islands, and like so many before her she was too far east of the safe course.

There was a strong westerly wind, so the coast was a lee shore. Despite the best efforts of captain and crew, the little ship was no match for the conditions. She could not claw her way to windward, so the inevitable happened … she was blown onto the shoreline near Shark's Bay.

Fortunately, where she was grounded was not rocky, and the seas weren't large at the time. It can also be assumed that the tide was on the ebb, because eventually, with the use of a rising tide and anchors that were no doubt set offshore with the aid of the ship's boats, the crew was able to kedge the ship back into deep water without any great drama. It was a predicament that could have had a far worse outcome if the winds had been stronger and the seas higher.

After being refloated and checked for damage, *Wapen van Hoorn* continued on her passage to Batavia, where she arrived on 22 July 1622.

*

It was a mere six months after *Trial* was wrecked when Herman van Speult, the Governor of Ambon, implemented orders from the Governor-General at Batavia, Pieter de Carpentier, for two ships to chart the coastline to the south of where Janszoon turned back in what is now known as the Gulf of Carpentaria. The expedition would be under the command of Jan Carstensz (also spelled Carstenszoon).

Carstensz's journal of his voyage indicates that his planned course was structured around the chart that Janszoon had pieced together aboard *Duyfken* in 1606. But he was also instructed to refine the details of the known coast of New Guinea, and hopefully determine once and for all if the coast that Janszoon had discovered was an extension of the coast of New Guinea or part of a separate South Land. Most importantly, though, it was hoped that this expedition would be able to trace the coastline all the way to existing points on the west coast of Eendrachtsland and thus produce more accurate charts that would ensure safer coastal navigation – but a margin note in Carstensz's journal some weeks into the voyage revealed another purpose relative to the inhabitants of the region:

> If we should come upon any capes, bights or roads, [we shall] come to anchor there for one or two days at the utmost for a landing, in which we shall run ashore in good order with two well manned and armed pinnaces, to endeavour to come to parley with the inhabitants and

generally inspect the state of affairs there; in leaving we shall, if at all practicable, seize one or two blacks to take along with us.

On 21 January 1623 Carstensz's two ships set sail from Ambon on an expedition that would take nearly six months to complete. Carstensz was aboard *Pera*, while Dirk Meliszoon had been appointed captain of *Arnhem*. Their three-masted ships had been built as East Indiamen for the VOC. *Arnhem* is known to have been about 1000 tons burthen, and it is thought that *Pera* had a similar displacement.

Almost three weeks after departing their home port, the two ships were cautiously probing their way along the western shoreline of New Guinea. Their progress was hampered, particularly at night, because there were no detailed charts or general knowledge of those waters.

Carstensz directed his men 'to use great caution' whenever they went ashore. Yet it was a decree that Meliszoon obviously ignored, with fatal consequences. The two ships were anchored off the west coast of what is now Papua, at latitude 4° 20' S, when an incident occurred that a frustrated and saddened Carstensz recorded in his journal:

This same day [10 February] the skipper of the yacht *Arnhem*, Dirk Meliszoon, without knowledge of myself, of the subcargo [junior merchant] or steersman of the said yacht, unadvisedly went ashore to the open beach in the pinnace, taking with him fifteen persons, both officers and common sailors, and no more than four muskets, for the purpose of fishing with a seine-net. There was great disorder in landing, the men running off in different directions, until … a number of black savages came running forth from the wood, who first seized and tore to pieces an assistant, named Jan Willemsz van den Briel, who happened to be unarmed, after which they slew with arrows, callaways [spears] and with the oars which they had snatched from the pinnace, no less than nine of our men, who were unable to defend themselves, at the same time wounding the remaining seven (among them the skipper, who was the first to take to his heels); these last seven men at last returned on board in very sorry plight with the pinnace and one oar, the skipper loudly lamenting his great want of prudence, and entreating pardon for the fault he had committed.

The wounds Meliszoon suffered were extreme, and he could not be saved. He died in agony forty-eight hours later. Carstensz then had no option but to appoint a new captain so they could continue sailing south. After consulting with his senior men he selected 'a young man, named Willem Joosten van Colster [or Coolsteerdt], second mate in the *Pera*, as being very fit for the post'.

As fate would have it, this was the first of a litany of problems this expedition would face. It would turn out that van Colster was a poor choice for captain of *Arnhem*: he would prove to be a man who caused division among the men and a hindrance to the commander.

For the next week they continued south, the crew at one stage being surprised to see high snow-capped peaks inland to the east. It was something they struggled to comprehend, especially considering they were so close to the Equator. Carstenz was ridiculed on his return to Europe when he declared that he had seen a snow-capped peak in the tropics. However, time would reveal he was telling the truth: he and his crew were observing what is now called Puncak Jaya or Carstenz Pyramid, located in the Sudirman Range of the western central highlands of Papua Province, Indonesia and which, at 4884 metres (16,024 feet), is the highest peak in Oceania.

For safety reasons, *Pera* and *Arnhem* sailed only in daylight hours, which meant that on many occasions, due to adverse currents or calms, they would cover only 6 nautical miles between sunrise and sunset. On 23 February, however, there came a dramatic change in the weather: a howling south-westerly wind and violent rain squalls.

Carstensz called for the anchor to be dropped as quickly as possible, but by early afternoon he realised that had been a mistake. The motion of the ships in the high rolling seas was brutal; it would be safer to be under sail. Still, drama would follow even after the anchors had been weighed. The pressure exerted by the strong winds on *Arnhem*'s sails and rig proved too much: the hemp stays stretched alarmingly and the masts and spars bent. Suddenly a resounding crack was heard above, as if a bolt of lightning had struck. The fore-topmast was exploding into splinters and crashing down onto the foredeck. It was either incompetence on the part of the crew or a stroke of misfortune that caused this problem. Regardless, the damage had to be repaired as soon as practicable. When conditions improved, some crew went aloft and lowered the damaged spar to the deck, while the ship's carpenters began shaping and rigging a new fore-topmast.

As the two vessels continued south along the New Guinea coast towards Frederik Hendrik Island (today Yos Sudarso Island) – the westernmost point of land they were likely to encounter before steering east of south towards the territory Janszoon had explored – Carstensz was struggling to gather the information his superiors had requested:

> … we are unable to give any information as to what fruits, metals and animals [the coast] contains, and as to the manner of its cultivation since the natives whom we found to be savages and man-eaters, refused to hold parley with us, and fell upon our men who suffered grievous damage; after the report, however, of some of the men of the yacht *Arnhem*, who being wounded on the 11th [informed us] the natives are tall black men with curly heads of hair and two large holes through their noses, stark naked, not covering even their

privities; their arms are arrows, bows, assagays
[throwing spears], callaways and the like. They have no
vessels either large or small ...

Yet more problems were to follow. On 4 March, the mission
came close to being aborted when it was realised that the
damage *Arnhem* had suffered in the storm some two weeks
earlier was more extensive than first thought – the breaking of
the fore-topmast was only minor in comparison to the real
damage: the crew soon realised that the ship had come close
to foundering. And because so much water had cascaded into
the cargo hold, a considerable proportion of the rice,
gunpowder and matches she was carrying had been ruined.

Carstensz sent two of his senior officers aboard *Arnhem* to
assess the problem. They reported back that *Arnhem* was 'very
weak and disabled above the waterline'. They suggested that
the best way to ease the rig loads and associated stress on the
hull was for the main-topmast, which had also been lowered
to the deck so damage could be repaired, not to be reset until
the condition of the hull had been further assessed.

Meanwhile, if Carstensz's efforts to explore the coast
weren't being thwarted by natives – whom they continued to
encounter regularly – then they were frustrated by the
shoreline itself. On many occasions men would climb over the
gunwale of the pinnace and into the shallows, only to find
themselves waist-deep in mud. On one occasion, however,
they persevered, and again they were attacked by natives:

In ... the forenoon I rowed to the land myself with the two pinnaces well manned and armed, in order to see if there was anything worth note there; but when we had got within a musket-shot of the land, the water became so shallow that we could not get any farther, whereupon we all of us went through the mud up to our waists, and with extreme difficulty reached the beach ... [We] tried to penetrate somewhat farther into the wood in order to ascertain the nature and situation of the country, when on our coming upon a piece of brushwood, a number of blacks sprang out of it, and began to let fly their arrows at us with great fury and loud shouts, by which a carpenter was wounded in the belly and an assistant in the leg. All of us were hard pressed, upon which we fired three or four muskets at them killing one of the blacks stone-dead, which utterly took away their courage ... we, being so far from the pinnaces and having a very difficult path to go in order to get back to them, resolved to return and row back to the yachts.

In late March, misfortune struck the seemingly hapless *Arnhem* once more. Carstensz left the ships at anchor and took two pinnaces to a small island to explore. While he was there, a strong wind struck, which, coupled with a fast-flowing current, caused *Arnhem* to drag her anchor. Those remaining aboard could do nothing to control the situation, and in no time *Arnhem* 'ran foul of the bows of the *Pera*, causing grievous damage to both the ships ... and without God's special providence they would both of them have run aground'. *Arnhem*'s rudder was smashed beyond repair in the collision, and Carstensz brought the expedition to a halt until a makeshift replacement could be made. Timber was scarce, so carpenters from both ships used *Pera*'s main-topmast, and what little suitable timber they could find ashore, to get *Arnhem* sailing again. The job took three days to complete.

At 9°20' S – about 200 nautical miles east-south-east of Frederik Hendrik Island – Carstensz realised that they could no longer continue exploring this part of the New Guinea coast. Men sent out in the pinnaces to sound the depths to the east reported back that only shallow water lay ahead; there was no way through to deeper water. On hearing this, the expedition leader decided to retrace his course until he could find a safe passage to deeper water. From there, he would steer for the point to the south where Janszoon had made his first landfall on the coast of the gulf.

The shallowness of the water also led Carstensz to make an interesting assumption: 'the space between us and Nova Guinea seems to be a bight'. This comment confirms his thinking that the New Guinea coast he was exploring and that which Janszoon had found were part of the same shoreline. If he had been able to continue to the east he would almost certainly have realised that a strait existed between New Guinea and the known land to the south.

After five days of probing his way through the shallows, all the time trying to find a safe course that would take his ships into the depths of the Arafura Sea, success: 'we managed with extreme difficulty and great peril to get again out of the shallows aforesaid, into which we had sailed as into a trap, between them and the land, for which happy deliverance God be praised'. Very soon after clearing the banks, Carstensz's leadsman was confirming depths of between 14 and 26 fathoms.

On 11 April, *Pera* and *Arnhem* reached the latitude of the northern tip of Cape York, but they were too wide of the coast for the crew to see land. The wind was a 'fair breeze' from the north, which allowed the two ships to keep their desired course to the south–south-east. At last Carstensz noted that he was happy with their progress, even if it was only 22 nautical miles in twenty-two hours.

The following morning there was cause for celebration, as the captain logged in his journal: 'at sunrise we saw the land of Nova Guinea' – which, at their latitude of 11° 45' S, could only have been the west coast of Cape York. They were some 30 nautical miles north of where Janszoon had landed seventeen years earlier.

The first attempts to get to a beach were frustrated by extensive muddy shallows that were like quicksand, and it wasn't until 17 April that Carstensz found a place further south (about 20 nautical miles north of the mouth of the Mitchell River, as it is known today) where they could land. He subsequently reported that he had explored 'flat, fine country with few trees, and a good soil for planting and sowing, but so far as we could observe utterly destitute of fresh water'. The beach itself proved a bountiful source of fish.

At this time, there was increasing concern regarding the seaworthiness of *Pera*. She was beginning to take on water, probably as a result of the battering her hull had taken during the storm off the coast of New Guinea.

The first contact with the Indigenous population came the day after they arrived. Carstensz detailed the momentous event:

> The skipper of the *Pera* got orders to row to land with the two pinnaces, duly provided for defence. In the afternoon, when the pinnaces returned, we were informed by the skipper that as soon as he had landed with his men, a large number of blacks, some of them armed and others unarmed, had made up to them. These blacks showed no fear and were so bold, as to touch the muskets of our men and to try to take the same off their shoulders, while they wanted to have whatever they could make use of; our men accordingly diverted their attention by showing them iron and beads, and espying vantage, seized one of the blacks by a string which he wore round his neck, and carried him off to the pinnace; the blacks who remained on the beach, set up dreadful howls and made violent gestures, but the others who kept concealed in the wood remained there. These natives are coal-black, with lean

bodies and stark naked, having twisted baskets or nets round their heads; in hair and figure they are like the blacks of the Coromandel [Indian] coast, but they seem to be less cunning, bold and evil-natured than the blacks at the western extremity of Nova Guinea; their weapons, of which we bring specimens along with us, are less deadly than those we have seen used by other blacks; the weapons in use with them are assagays, shields, clubs and sticks about half a fathom in length ...

Just twenty-four hours later there was an unfortunate encounter. When men went ashore to find firewood they were surprised by more than 200 natives, all of whom challenged the presence of these never-before-seen white people. Greatly concerned for the safety of his men, who were outnumbered ten to one, *Arnhem*'s captain, Willem van Colster, had no option but to have two of his men fire musket shots in the general direction of the natives, one of whom was hit. The natives then literally disappeared into the scrub, so van Colster took his men 'farther up country'.

Carstensz noted that this excursion brought a surprising result:

During their march they observed in various places great quantities of ... human bones, from which it may be safely concluded that the blacks along the coast of Nova Guinea are man-eaters who do not spare each other when driven by hunger.

By 24 April, the two ships were at 17° 8' S, near the mouth of what Carstensz would name the Staten River (now the Staaten River), a significant waterway that weaves its way inland for almost 200 kilometres, its headwaters being to the west of where Cairns is sited today. Their plotted position placed them some 150 nautical miles south of Cape Keerweer, the southernmost point that Janszoon had reached. Also – obviously unbeknown to them – they were then only 80 nautical miles from the south-eastern corner of the Gulf of Carpentaria.

For some days, Carstensz had been considering his options for the future of the expedition – so much so that, on that same day, he decided to convene a meeting with his senior men so they could discuss their immediate plans. Should they continue south, go west, or return home? Most importantly, they had to decide what their safest option would be:

> I submitted to them the question whether it would be advisable to run further south, and after various opinions had been expressed, it was agreed that this would involve diverse difficulties, and that the idea had better be given up: we might get into a vast bay, and it is evident that in these regions in the east-monsoon north-winds prevail [and should that occur] we should thus fall on a lee-shore ...

The resolution from the meeting was that they should turn back 'and follow the coast of Nova Guinea so long to northward as shall be found practicable'.

There was no mention in Cartstensz's journal at this stage of the native captured earlier. However, since he had been ordered by the VOC to seize as many natives as possible, he also announced after the meeting that he was proposing 'to give ten pieces-of-eight to the boatmen for every black they shall get hold of on shore, and carry off to the yacht [so] our Masters may reap benefit from the capture of the blacks, which may afterwards redound [have a consequence] to certain advantage'.

Preparations for the return voyage were hastened when it was realised there was no fresh water to be found anywhere on the shore, but before departing, Carstensz made one symbolic gesture:

> ... since by resolution it has been determined to begin the return-voyage at this point, we have, in default of stone, caused a wooden tablet to be nailed to a tree, the said tablet having the following words carved into it: '*Anno 1623 den 24n April sijn hier aen gecomen twee jachten wegen de Hooge Mogende Heren Staten Genl.*'

The translation is: 'A.D. 1623, on 24 April there arrived here two yachts dispatched by their High Mightinesses the States-General.'

A margin note in Carstensz's journal detailing what was on the tablet added: 'We have accordingly named the river aforesaid Staten revier [Staaten River] in the new chart.'

Despite the decision to return to Ambon, a dilemma that had been developing with *Arnhem*'s captain and steersman now came to a head. Carstensz's frustration over this situation – exacerbated by problems with the soundness of his own vessel – was apparent in another margin note in his journal:

> … the yacht *Arnhem*, owing to bad sailing, and to the
> small liking and desire which the skipper [captain] and
> the steersman have shown towards the voyage, has on
> various occasions and at different times been the cause
> of serious delay, seeing that the *Pera* (which had sprung
> a bad leak and had to be kept above water by more than
> 8000 strokes of the pump every twenty-four hours) was
> every day obliged to seek and follow the *Arnhem* for 1, 2
> or even more miles to leeward.

But while it was *Pera* that was then taking on water, there was dissension developing within the expedition, as the crew of *Arnhem* wanted to be part of it no more, as Carstensz's journal entry of 27 April confirmed. He recorded that *Pera* had sailed slowly all day 'in order to wait for *Arnhem* which was a howitzer's shot astern of us'. That night he ordered that his ship anchor close to land, and that a lantern be placed in the rigging so van Colster and his men could see it. But at first light the next morning, there was not a sail in sight. Carstensz could then reach only one conclusion: 'on purpose and with malice prepense [premeditated] she away from us against her instructions and our resolution, and seems to have set her course for [the] Aru [Islands] to have a good time of it there'.

It would later be confirmed that van Colster and his crew had in fact decided to abandon the expedition and sail for home. They did, however, make one contribution to the chart of Eendrachtsland while heading that way. The weather conditions saw *Arnhem* set off towards the west-north-west, and after sailing for more than 300 nautical miles, a coastline was seen to emerge above the western horizon. Van Colster then navigated his way around the north-east corner of this never-before-seen shoreline before heading north towards the Aru Islands. Appropriately, the land that he had observed and put on the map took the name of his ship: Arnhem Land.

Meanwhile, Carstensz maintained a course to the north along the eastern coast of the gulf, his desire being to stop wherever it looked likely they would find much-needed water. On 3 May, after anchoring off the entrance of what is now the Mitchell River, the expedition leader and some of his men yet again went ashore in quest of water, but all Carstensz returned with was an abject opinion of the land:

I went ashore myself with ten musketeers, and we advanced a long way into the wood without seeing any human beings; the land here is low-lying and without

hills ... it is very dry and barren ... for during all the
time we have searched and examined this part of the
coast to our best ability, we have not seen one fruit-
bearing tree, nor anything that man could make use
of ... it may be safely concluded that the land contains
no metals, nor yields any precious woods, such as
sandal-wood ... this is the most arid and barren region
that could be found anywhere on the earth; the
inhabitants, too, are the most wretched and poorest
creatures that I have ever seen in my age or time. As
there are no large trees anywhere on this coast, they
have no boats or canoes whether large or small ...

Despite the poor appearance of the natives on this part of the
coast, the desire to capture one or more remained. That
opportunity presented itself on 8 May, when Carstensz again
took ten musketeers ashore. They spotted footprints in the
sand, and decided to follow them, but after covering some
considerable distance and not sighting anyone, they decided to
return to their small boats.

As they were boarding and preparing to row back to *Pera*,
two armed groups of men emerged from the woods. Carstensz
would later note:

By showing them bits of iron and strings of beads we
kept them on the beach until we had come near
them ... One of them who had lost his weapon, was by

the skipper [steersman] seized round the waist, while at
the same time the quartermaster put a noose round his
neck, by which he was dragged to the pinnace; the
other blacks seeing this, tried to rescue their captured
brother by furiously assailing us with their assagays; in
defending ourselves we shot one of them, after which
the others took to flight, upon which we returned on
board without further delay.

The latter part of this journal entry was directed to Carstensz's
superiors:

We cannot give any account of their customs and
ceremonies, nor did we learn anything about the
thickness of the population, since we had few or no
opportunities for inquiring into these matters
Meanwhile, I hope that with God's help Your Worships
will in time get information touching these points from
the black we have captured ...

There is no credible explanation as to what happened to either
one of these captured Aboriginals, although it has been
suggested that one died in Ambon, and the other made it to
Batavia. There is no reference to them in Carstensz's journal
apart from recording that they had been captured.

Carstensz also stressed in his writings that they had, by the
standards of the day, treated 'the blacks or savages with especial

kindness … hoping by so doing to get their friendship … but in spite of all our kindness and our fair semblance the blacks received us as enemies everywhere, so that in most places our landings were attended with great peril'.

His comments also left no doubt that he saw the natives of New Guinea and those of the gulf as living along a common coast. This was confirmed in a journal entry dated 14 May: 'From the 9th of this month up to now we have found the land of Nova Guinea to extend N.N.E. and S.S.W., and from this point continuing N. and S.'

It was on 15 May, when *Pera* was close to the northern tip of Cape York, that Carstensz decided that the navigational hazards were becoming too great. He then set a course to the west, and before long, no bottom could be found at 27 fathoms.

No doubt, had Carstensz been aware of an assumption by the VOC's highly respected official cartographer, Hessel Gerritsz, he would have done everything in his power to continue north with the coast still in view. The previous year Gerritsz had published a chart that included the part of the same coast that Willem Janszoon had mapped in 1606.

The chart treated Janszoon's find as being part of New Guinea, but Gerritsz obviously held some doubts. He made a notation alongside this part of the chart that read:

Those who sailed with the yacht of Pedro Fernández de Quirós in the neighbourhood of New Guinea to 10

degrees westward through many islands and shoals and
over 2, 3 and 4 fathoms for as many as 40 days,
presumed that New Guinea did not extend beyond 10
degrees to the south. If this be so, then the land from 9
to 14 degrees would be a separate land, different from
the other New Guinea …

The reasoning behind Gerritsz's theory can only be speculated upon. It was Gerritsz's role to analyse the charts of all VOC ships on their return from the East Indies and update his master copies when required. The VOC demanded that all ships departing Europe carry Gerritsz's most recent maps, but unfortunately for Carstensz, the chart with the above inscription had not arrived in the Spice Islands before his expedition departed. Had Carstensz been in possession of this chart, then there is no doubt he would have been ordered by his superiors to search for the strait. Even so, making this scenario more perplexing is the fact that no one actually went in search of the strait until Captain Cook's voyage in 1770. So *Pera* continued sailing west, away from the coast, until Carstensz considered it was safe to change course to the north, his desire then being to sail to the latitude of the Aru Islands. Once at that point *Pera* would again sail west, cruising along that latitude until the islands were sighted.

Pera reached the main island of Aru on 22 May, while *Arnhem* is reported to have arrived in the same port just a few days later.

Having replenished supplies, Carstensz set sail for his home port on the island of Ambon. Once there, he described his arrival in writing to his superiors:

> In the evening of the 8th we came to anchor before the
> castle of Amboyna, having therewith brought our
> voyage to a safe conclusion by the merciful protection
> of God Almighty, who may vouchsafe to grant
> prosperity and success in all their good undertakings to
> their High Mightinesses the States-General, to his
> Excellency the Prince of Orange etc, to the Lords
> Managers of the United East India Company and to the
> Worshipful Lord General and his Governors.
> Continuing for ever
>   Their High Mightinesses' etc obedient and
> affectionate servant
>   Jan Carstensz.

Carstensz added one last gesture to his report: believing that a gulf had been discovered, it would be named the Gulf of Carpentaria in honour of the then Governor-General of the Dutch East Indies, Pieter de Carpentier.

CHAPTER SEVEN

Morsels, Magnificence and a Massacre

1622 to 1629

After almost two decades of landings by European vessels in both the north and the west, the approach to mapping the basic outline of Terra Australis Incognita remained casual, to say the least. Although it was becoming clearer that there was a large chunk – or chunks – of land in that part of the world, it would be 165 years from the time when Janszoon made the first recorded discovery of what was a mere morsel of the coastline, to when Captain Cook returned to England in 1771 with news of his discovery of the entire east coast – all 2000-plus nautical miles of it. But even after that monumental discovery, it would be an additional thirty-two years before Matthew Flinders completed the first circumnavigation of Australia: a voyage that allowed him to add much of the minute, or missing, detail.

Yet for now, the British continued to remain conspicuous by their absence from this part of the world, despite having shown considerable interest in the early days of the spice trade. Part of the reason why they all but exited the spice trade was the Ambon Massacre of 1623.

The roots of this atrocity went back two decades, to 1603 when both the Dutch and English established factories under mutual agreement in Bantam. However, the English soon had their eyes on expansion across the region, their first desire being the stronghold of Ambon, where the Dutch had claimed the fortress of Victoria from the Portuguese in 1605.

At this time, the VOC refused to tolerate any expansion plans the English had in the East Indies; they were determined to retain the lion's share of the spice trade, and made sure the EIC knew it. Angst and apprehension developed between the two corporations and this spilled over into national politics, a consequence that threatened the congenial relations that the two allies had enjoyed over many years. The tension escalated to a point where, in 1619, King James I of England and the Netherlands States General were forced to negotiate a 'Treaty of Defence' between the two companies, a document designed to recognise cooperation between the two companies in the East Indies: it fixed the market share at two to one in favour of the Dutch, and gave each company a monopoly in their home market.

Soon after the treaty was signed it was apparent that the VOC and EIC placed different interpretations on the agreement: clarity was replaced by suspicion. The friction that existed prior to the creation of the treaty quickly resurfaced.

In late 1622, the Dutch were becoming increasingly suspicious of English activity in Ambon: the VOC's governor there saw signs which he believed indicated that EIC traders were undercutting VOC deals struck with the Sultan of Ternate, who represented suppliers in the region.

The situation erupted in February 1623 when a Japanese mercenary soldier apparently in the employ of the VOC was taken into custody by the Dutch for allegedly spying on the extent of the defences existing around the Victoria fort. The soldier was water tortured (waterboarding today) and soon confessed: acting on behalf of EIC authorities, he and other mercenaries were intending to overrun the fort and assassinate the governor. He implicated the senior EIC factor in Ambon, Gabriel Towerson, and other company representatives. All the named conspirators were quickly rounded up by the Dutch and taken into custody. Most of those arrested pleaded guilty (with or without torture) to the charge of treason. However, four Englishmen and two Japanese were subsequently pardoned. On 9 March 1623, ten Englishmen, nine Japanese mercenaries and one Portuguese employee of the VOC were beheaded. Towerson having been identified as the ringleader, his head was impaled on a stake and displayed in public for everyone to see.

The four Englishmen who were pardoned soon managed to get word of the massacre back to England, adamant that the men were executed as a result of trumped-up charges that were obtained under torture. National outrage ensued: it became a scar on English-Dutch relations for decades and influenced the three Anglo-Dutch wars that occurred between 1652 and 1674. Regardless, the Dutch domination of the spice trade in the East Indies continued for decades. Eventually the English were forced out; they closed their Bantam factory in 1683. The English then chose to do business in other parts of the world: in particular, they concentrated on developing trade with India and establishing opportunities in the West Indies, especially in sugar production.

*

Even as the United East India Company increased its dominance in the spice trade, its attitude towards the Great South Land remained essentially unchanged. In the years after Carstensz's venture into the Gulf of Carpentaria, there came a few intended and unintended encounters. Later in 1623, *Leijden*, a VOC ship captained by Claes Hermanszoon, made landfall south of Dirk Hartog Island while on a passage to the East Indies. There was little that was unusual about this event except for the fact that a child was delivered on board at the time, making the infant the first European born in what would become Australian waters. The ship's journal entry for the day, 27 July, read: 'Willemijntje Jansz., wedded wife of Willem Jansz, of Amsterdam, midshipman, was delivered of a son, who got the name Seebaer van Nieuwellandt [Sea Baby of the New Land].'

The same ship returned three years later, this time under the command of Daniel Janssen Cock. It was recorded that the coast was sighted – again south of Dirk Hartog Island – but no effort was made to anchor and go ashore. This was possibly because, when *Leijden* was 10 nautical miles from the coast, it was realised that a strong easterly current was carrying her towards land. This potential threat to safety saw Cock retrim the sails and put the helm down so *Leijden* could change course to the north-west, thus sailing away from possible danger. From that point the ship continued her passage to her destination.

*

But while numerous ships had visited the west coast of Australia by this time, occasionally a VOC vessel would find itself much further south on the same coast. In 1622 the crew of another Dutch ship, *Leeuwin* (*Lioness*), en route to the East Indies from Texel, had seen a substantial and never-before-sighted coast emerge unexpectedly above the horizon to the east. *Leeuwin* thus became only the seventh ship to be in sight of Eendrachtsland.

The land the crew sighted is today referred to as Cape Leeuwin, the south-westernmost part of the continent. A chart published in 1627 by VOC cartographer Hessel Gerritsz shows a distinct and clearly definable coast extending for approximately 100 nautical miles between what are today identified as Hamelin Bay and Point D'Entrecasteaux respectively, although Cape Leeuwin cannot be recognised. The Dutch subsequently referred to the region as 't Landt de Leeuwin (Leeuwin's Land), and in 1801, during his circumnavigation, Matthew Flinders gave the name Cape Leeuwin to this region's most south-westerly tip.

It was the same corner of the continent that another VOC crew gazed at in awe from the deck of *Gulden Zeepaard* (*Golden Seahorse*), on 26 January 1627. *Gulden Zeepaard*, part of a nine-ship convoy, was carrying 158 male passengers, six women and fifty-six soldiers; she was under the command of supercargo Pieter Nuyts and his captain, Frans Thijssen (or Thijsz). Their visit would make an even more important contribution to the unveiling of Australia's coastline.

Either the weather conditions or the intrigue of a new discovery made Nuyts and Thijssen set out to explore this alien stretch of coast, something they did for the next eight weeks. Over that time they guided *Gulden Zeepaard* along a significant part of the southern coastline of the continent: the longest stretch of Australia's coast encountered to date.

As Thijssen cruised the spectacular, towering, flat-topped coast of the Great Australian Bight, he continually took bearings and noted details of what he was observing. He displayed such accuracy and attention to detail that he was subsequently applauded by cartographers in the Netherlands, and much later by the likes of Matthew Flinders.

His map covered 1000 nautical miles along the southern coast from what would be Cape Leeuwin to what is now known as Fowlers Bay, 100 nautical miles west of Ceduna in South Australia. One thing quickly became apparent: the topography of this coast was dramatically different from what had previously been seen in the west and north. For much of the distance, sheer cliffs up to 200 feet high with rich ochre colours predominate.

After completing the return voyage across the Bight, *Gulden Zeepaard* cleared Cape Leeuwin, then was set on a course to the north towards Batavia. When she finally arrived there, those aboard had been at sea eleven months: more than twice the time most ships took to sail to Batavia from Europe. Her arrival was recorded in print in Batavia at the time:

On the 10th [April 1627] there arrived from the Netherlands the ship [*Gulden Zeepaard*] fitted out by the Zealand Chamber, having on board the Honourable Pieter Nuyts, extraordinary councillor of India, having sailed from there on 22 of May 1626 …

Surprisingly, a number of scholars and explorers of the era, all of whom were well versed in geography, became convinced that *Gulden Zeepaard*'s voyage disproved the belief that Eendrachtsland was attached to a landmass to the south, i.e. Antarctica, which was not discovered until more than 150 years later. Yet the reality was that this theory could not be fully discounted until Abel Tasman's first exploratory voyage fifteen years later.

Apart from detailing the coast, the chart Thijssen sent back to the VOC cartographers in the Netherlands revealed that he had named much of the land that had been discovered 't Landt van Pieter Nuyts. The captain saw this as a mark of respect for Nuyts, the highest-ranking VOC representative on the voyage.

Interestingly, Nuyts would later prove not to be the character he pretended. Soon after joining the VOC in the Netherlands he had decided he wanted to be part of the excitement in the East Indies, so he took up a senior position in Batavia, the reason for his being aboard *Gulden Zeepaard*. He took his elder son Laurens with him, but left his pregnant wife Cornelia and his other son, Pieter, at home, the arrangement being that they would join him at a later date. Sadly, both Cornelia and Pieter died soon after arriving in Batavia; there is no mention of the fate of the expected baby.

Before long, Nuyts was appointed the VOC's ambassador in Japan, so he moved there with Laurens. He proved to be totally incapable in that position, so he was transferred to Formosa (now Taiwan), where he eventually became governor. The *Australian Dictionary of Biography* states that Nuyts again failed, primarily because he was 'arrogant, haughty and dedicated to his own financial interests'. He was subsequently arrested, charged with fraud and jailed for six years. At one stage he married a Formosan woman and also had numerous affairs — which required an interpreter to be under his bed so amorous conversation could be translated!

*

During the same year as Thijssen and Nuyts were uncovering the southern coast of Eendrachtsland in relative safety, the west coast was continuing to offer up underwater traps for the unwary, or unfortunate.

One incident — in which the ship *Galias* went dangerously close to being pounded to pieces on the barely visible reefs that stand like sentinels around the Abrolhos Islands — involved the Governor-General of the Dutch East Indies, Jan Pieterszoon Coen.

The close call occurred when *Galias* was more than halfway through a passage from Cape Town to the Spice Islands, in company with two other ships, *Utrecht* and *Texel*. In a report penned when he reached Batavia to his directors in Amsterdam, Coen explained that after leaving Cape Town a powerful southerly wind made it impossible for the three vessels to clear the Cape of Good Hope. Try as they did for eight days, they made no progress towards the east. Finally, when the wind went in their favour, they were able to get to 37°15' S — about 180 nautical miles south of the cape — where they found the Roaring Forties in full song.

They made impressive progress across this latitude for more than a week, until 10 August, when the winds became stronger and the waves larger. The crew of *Galias* was kept busy as sails were either hauled up to the yards or lowered to the deck in proportion to the increasing force of the wind. But busiest of all was the steersman: he was continually struggling to keep the ship on a downwind course without going anywhere near beam-on to the then huge waves. By day and night, they peaked then roared like thunder as they broke into masses of churning foam, leaving shrouds of white water behind them.

Suddenly, a moment of dread arrived when the pressure on the planks of the wooden rudder became too much and it broke. In an instant *Galias* was out of control, her sails flogging violently. She was completely at the mercy of the wind and waves.

Coen would later report:

> The ship became ungovernable, and the sails were dashed to pieces, in consequence of which she got separated from the other two ships, who had failed to observe the accident of the *Galias* owing to the darkness. The next day, the rudder having been repaired, we continued our voyage with the *Galias*.

Coen's ship was now going it alone, which placed far greater emphasis on the need for accurate navigation. There was no longer the security that came from having two other ships tracking in company along the same course.

After twenty-five more days of sailing, *Galias* had exited the band of westerly wind she had been riding and was set on a curved trajectory north towards Batavia. On 5 September it was either alert eyes on the part of a lookout up the mainmast, or someone on deck, that averted tragedy. Coen's report to his 'Most Noble Wise Provident Very Discreet Gentlemen' in Amsterdam continued:

> ... in the afternoon of the 5th of September in 28½ degrees S. Lat. came upon the land of d'Eendracht. We were at less than half a mile's distance from the breakers before perceiving the same, without being able to see land. If we had come upon this place in the night-time, we should have been in a thousand perils with our ship and crew. In the plane charts the reckonings of our steersmen [indicated we] were still between 300 and 350 miles from any land, so that there was not the slightest suspicion of our being near any ...

Coen went on to ask his directors for anomalies in the plane charts to be addressed and corrected 'as a matter of the highest importance, which if not properly attended to involves grievous peril to ships and crews (which God in his mercy avert)'. He concluded by saying that on the plane chart aboard *Galias*, 'the south land lies fully 40 *mijlen* more to eastward than it should be'.

The VOC hierarchy obviously took notice: soon afterwards, instructions for VOC ships sailing the Brouwer

Route directed captains and navigators to use extreme caution when nearing the west coast of Eendrachtsland, and to use their leadline constantly to plumb the depths at night and in stormy weather when visibility was reduced.

*

Despite the new precautions, the coast of Eendrachtsland remained a serious navigational hazard, as would be proved in a horrendous way in 1629 by a newly launched VOC ship, *Batavia.*

Before that, there were two other unplanned encounters with this treacherous coast, and each led to the uncovering of a little more of the Eendrachtsland shoreline.

In 1627 the small fluyt *Wapen van Hoorn* (*Weapon of Horn*), captained on this occasion by David Pieterszoon de Vries, returned to this coast – and this time she managed not to run aground. Instead, de Vries, having come into visual contact with the mainland near Dirk Hartog Island, was able to chart a further stretch of that coast. He reinforced Coen's assertion, later reporting to the VOC that the plane chart he was using 'involve[d] serious drawbacks' when it came to navigation. He added: 'By estimation the land of d'Eendracht is marked in the chart fifty miles too far to eastward, which should also be rectified.'

In 1628 the area saw the first known grounding of a VOC ship on its return voyage to Europe. The ship was the 400-ton fluyt *Vianen*, on her first return trip to the West Indies, and the incident came after she was hammered by brutal headwinds, having departed Batavia on 14 January then sailed south into the huge expanse of the Indian Ocean.

Vianen, captained by Gerrit Frederikszoon de Witt, had been due to sail on 6 January as part of a seven-ship fleet under the command of the departing Governor-General of the Dutch East Indies, Pieter de Carpentier. She was, however, held back at the last minute so she could take on additional cargo that had arrived late from China. When she finally put to sea it was quickly realised she was dangerously out of trim: the new cargo had been put aboard incorrectly and the ship's stability had been compromised. So, with his home port more than 11,000 nautical miles away, de Witt quite logically returned to port and put aboard 5000 ingots of copper as trim ballast.

By the time *Vianen* departed Batavia again on 20 January, the monsoon season had arrived. This made the usual passage into the Indian Ocean via Sunda Strait too dangerous to negotiate, so de Witt steered his ship to the east and through another strait, one that placed her closer to the coast of Eendrachtsland.

Once *Vianen* was clear of that strait, the strong headwinds soon created an insurmountable predicament. She was unable to be held on a course to the south-west towards the Cape of Good Hope; instead, she was being driven relentlessly to the south, towards the west coast of Eendrachtsland. As de Witt later explained in his report to VOC headquarters in

Amsterdam, nothing could be done to prevent his ship from
going aground 'in the latitude of 21 degrees', believed to be
somewhere in the region of Barrow Island:

> She was by head-winds driven so far to south-ward that
> she came upon the South-land beyond Java where she
> ran aground, so that [we were] forced to throw
> overboard 8 or 10 lasts [10,000 to 12,500 kilograms] of
> pepper and a quantity of copper, upon which through
> God's mercy she got off again without further
> damage …

Having experienced the coast first-hand, de Witt then decided
to turn a negative into a positive: he would chart it to the
north as far as practicable, which was about 200 nautical miles.

De Witt's exploration is believed to have ended near where
Port Hedland is today. The section of coast he and his men
observed soon became recognised on charts as 'de Witt's
Land'. The crew of *Vianen* also reported sighting Indigenous
people near the location of present-day Roebourne. It is
highly probable that this was the first sighting of Aboriginal
people in Western Australia. De Witt's report to his superiors
left no doubt that he was not impressed by what he saw: 'a foul
and barren shore, green fields; and very wild, black, barbarous
inhabitants'.

Vianen was not so fortunate on her second voyage to the East
Indies. After departing Texel for Batavia on 7 May 1629, she was

snared by an adverse current and treacherous winds while trying to negotiate Sunda Strait, less than 100 nautical miles from her destination. It was a hopeless situation: despite the best efforts of the captain and crew, nothing could be done to save her. The VOC's register of ships records that *Vianen* was driven onto rocks and sank in Sunda Strait on 14 November 1629.

CHAPTER EIGHT

Treachery, Mutiny and Murder

June 1629

On the night of 4 June 1629, the newly launched pride of the VOC East Indiaman fleet, the 186-foot *Batavia*, was under full sail, heading north-east off the west coast of Eendrachtsland. Her bow was being pressed up and over long and loping swells that were constantly being brought alive by shimmering and stippled splashes of silver: reflections of the light from a magnificent full moon. This was a superb time to be at sea, but only those few on watch among the 322 passengers, soldiers and crew — most of whom were sleeping below in cramped and stifling conditions — could appreciate the serenity and beauty of the moment.

It was then two hours before sunrise, and the conditions were far from rough. The commander, François Pelsaert, was still confined to his bunk in the great cabin, having fallen ill soon after the ship departed Cape Town many weeks earlier. It is not known what role, if any, he had played in navigation in preceding days, but it is apparent that those on board had no real concern for the safety of the ship on the course she was holding. The navigator would have been checking the ship's position by dead reckoning and sun sights on a regular basis, and pricking the chart [marking the ship's position on the chart] accordingly. Were there any sudden thought that danger lurked, it would be easy to call for a course change towards the west. But the greatest comfort for Pelsaert that night probably came from the knowledge that there was a lookout stationed high up the 55 metre tall mainmast, and that his captain Adriaan Jacobsz (whom he knew to be capable, despite their personal animosity) was at the helm.

Nothing could have prepared Pelsaert for what happened next. As he later wrote in his journal:

I … felt suddenly, with a rough terrible movement, the
bumping of the ship's rudder, and immediately after that
I felt the ship held up in her course against the rocks, so
that I fell out of my berth. Whereon I ran up and
discovered that all the sails were in top [the yards
askew – one end higher than the other], the wind south
west, the course north east by north during that night,
and [we] were lying right in the middle of a thick spray.
Round the ship there was only a little surf, but shortly
after that one could hear the sea breaking hard round it.

I said, 'Skipper, what have you done, that through your reckless carelessness you have run this noose round our necks?'

He answered, 'How could I do better? I did not sleep, but watched out very well, for when I saw the breakers in the distance I asked Hans the gunner, "What can that be?" Whereupon he said, "Skipper it is the shine of the moon, upon which I trusted."'

Pelsaert barked another question at the captain: where did he think they were relative to the coast? His journal recorded Jacobsz's reply: 'He said, that only God knows, this is a shallow that must be lying quite a distance from the unknown land, and I think we are just on the tail of it.'

The commander's immediate and logical thought was to get the ship back into deep water. In the rapid analysis he then made of their predicament, he realised that the only way to achieve that was to launch one of the boats and have an anchor set some distance off the stern. This would then enable the crew to 'wind her off' using the capstan.

Then a second, more cogent thought rushed through his mind: as the depth of the water behind the ship was unknown, the anchoring manoeuvre might waste precious time. So he considered another option: lighten the ship in the hope that she might (with the aid of the surging waves, and a rising tide, if it was on the flood) float off the reef and into deep water.

With that new priority, he had his men start by throwing overboard the ship's twenty-four cast-iron cannons.

The scene on deck by this time must have been mayhem. Almost everyone aboard, all 300-plus of them, would have scurried up the companionway ladders and onto the deck like ants abandoning a disturbed nest. While orders were being shouted from one end of the ship to the other, those who were not part of the crew would have cowered in corners not knowing what to do. Others would have run in every direction in a state of hysterical panic.

Pelsaert's next move would have been to get as high as he could on the aftcastle, behind the helm station. This would allow him to get a better appreciation of the danger confronting *Batavia*. It would then be possible for him to decide on a salvage plan.

But once high up on the aft-castle, he didn't like what he saw:

> … we found ourselves then surrounded by rocks and
> shallows on every side, and very suddenly by the fall of
> the waters (for we had sailed there by high tide) it began
> to surf and foam around the ship, so that through the
> bumping of the ship [pounding on the reef], one could
> not stand or walk [on deck] …

Each time all 650 tons of *Batavia* were lifted by the surge of a wave then dropped onto the reef, the chance of salvage decreased. The hull was being weakened to the point where its heavy oak planks would soon prove no match for this destructive force of nature.

Compounding the problem was the massive, solid-pine mainmast, which was the height of a giant tree. With every shuddering thump onto the reef, the mast was hammering its way through the bottom of the ship like a giant pile driver.

Pelsaert responded to this threat by shouting an order for the mast to be chopped down. Armed with axes, large saws and knives, crewmen took to the towering piece of timber, which was more than 50 centimetres in diameter. Some hacked away at deck level, while others either cut or released the rigging that held it in place.

Pelsaert would have realised that success might bring a twofold benefit. By casting the mast and rigging overboard, they would, at least for the short term, be lessening the risk that the hull would be smashed open. They would also be making the ship substantially lighter, further improving the chances of saving her.

Unfortunately though, chopping down the mast only made matters worse: 'when it was cut down we found that it caused much damage, for we could not get it [overboard]'.

The felled mast smashed its way through the deck and topsides. The time for the commander to call 'Abandon ship' was rapidly approaching.

A glimmer of good fortune came soon after sunrise. The expanding daylight brought a sight that might provide some form of salvation. Two low-lying islands could be seen not far from where the still-writhing *Batavia* was trapped. Pelsaert immediately ordered the ship's captain and some oarsmen to take one of *Batavia's* small boats to the islands and investigate what, if anything, these rocky outcrops offered in the way of sanctuary.

The report came back that it appeared the islands would remain above water at high tide. This was what the commander wanted to hear. He could then make the call to abandon ship:

> Because of the great wailing that there was from the
> ship, by women, children, sick, and anxious people, we
> decided to put most of the people on land first and
> meanwhile to get ready on deck the money and the
> most precious goods, for which I did my utmost. But
> God the Lord chastised us with many rods, for in spite
> of all the zeal we made to cant the vessel to leeward or
> to fall, it turned out exactly the opposite because of the
> uneven reef upon which it was set, which so caused it
> that the people could only come out of the ship very
> slowly ...

By this time *Batavia's* fate was terminal. The hull planks had burst apart and a torrent of foaming water was washing through the bilge. The plan now was all about saving souls: hastily ferrying passengers and as much bread and water as possible to one of the islands (now Beacon Island), which was only 1 nautical mile away to the west–north–west.

Pelsaert began issuing new orders, but with them came another realisation. Many of the men were only interested in saving themselves and had abandoned any respect for his authority:

> Our goodwill and diligence were impeded by the
> godless unruly troops of soldiers, as well as sailors, and
> their likes whom I could not keep out of the hold on
> account of the liquor or wine, so that one could not get
> there [to retrieve food and water] … in the meantime
> the entire hold became flooded …

But, concerned as Pelsaert was about the men's dismissive attitude, this mini-rebellion was nothing compared with what would follow.

Since leaving Cape Town, some of the men had been plotting to overrun the ship. The current insubordination was merely one step in a grand scheme that history would view as one of the most gruesome and brutal maritime atrocities of all time: a mutiny led by a religious zealot that culminated in the torture, rape and murder of the majority of the survivors.

*

When *Batavia* was launched in Amsterdam in 1628, her shape and construction reflected every recent advance in naval architecture when it came to building a ship most suited for the East Indies trade. She fulfilled both the VOC's demands for commercial viability, and a seafarer's desire for seaworthiness and structural integrity.

The most obvious feature of Dutch ships in the early seventeenth century was their heavily pronounced sheerline, and *Batavia* certainly boasted that. It was not there for aesthetic reasons, but to create the safest possible seagoing vessel.

The sweep of the sheerline – the upwards curve of the deck towards the bow and stern – was one of the secrets of the success of VOC ships. As vessels became longer, the structural strength required to counter the enormous loads exerted by wind and sea when they were under sail increased dramatically. If the ship's construction wasn't strong enough then the hull would soon hog or sag – bend either upwards or downwards at the bow and stern – when the loads on the structure became too great. The combination of an accentuated sheer and a horizontal deck meant that ships of Dutch design were well capable of coping with these stress loads: they were 'pre-tensioned'.

It has been estimated that 800 cubic metres of timber, much of it sourced from the highlands of northern Europe, was used in the construction of *Batavia*, while the combined length of her standing and running rigging exceeded twenty-one kilometres. The area of the ten sails she carried totalled more than 1180 square metres.

Batavia sailed from Texel on her maiden voyage on 27 October 1628, as part of a seven-ship flotilla, bound for the town that had given its name to the ship – Batavia. Pelsaert held the position of supercargo, or *opperkoopman* – the senior merchant on board. His highest ranking officers were captain Adriaan Jacobsz, and a somewhat mysterious character, Jeronimus Cornelisz, whom the VOC had put aboard as the *onderkoopman* – subcargo, or junior merchant. In fact he was a bankrupt pharmacist from Haarlem, west of Amsterdam, who was apparently fleeing the Netherlands.

Apart from his financial woes, there might have been another reason why he wanted to leave the country: fear of being arrested because of the heretical beliefs he held, influenced by Torrentius, otherwise known as radical artist Johannes Symonsz van der Beeck, a still-life master. Van der Beeck's hard-held philosophy was: 'All traditional religions restrict pleasure. In doing so they are contrary to the will of God, who put us on earth that we might, during our brief existence, enjoy without hindrance everything that might give us pleasure.' These religious views did not sit well with the conventional Christianity of Dutch society. Van der Beeck was arrested for airing his beliefs, and after being accused and found guilty of being a blasphemer, he was tortured, imprisoned, and later exiled to England following the intervention of Charles I, who employed him as a court painter.

There were three interesting and very valuable lots of cargo aboard on *Batavia*'s outbound voyage: a number of chests laden with silver coins; two rare artefacts owned by famous Flemish artist Peter Paul Rubens, which were intended to be sold to an Indian Mogul ruler; and a mass of sandstone blocks destined to form a portico at Batavia Castle.

Officially, there were 341 people on the manifest for the voyage, but a few last-minute desertions were noted, something that was relatively common at the time. Of those who actually embarked, slightly more than two-thirds were the officers and men sailing the vessel. Then there were about 100 soldiers, while the smallest group comprised civilian passengers, many of them women and children – either families or servants of VOC employees.

Before the ships even entered the English Channel – barely 200 nautical miles into the voyage – they were dealt a pummelling by a typical North Sea gale. It blew them in all directions, to the extent that when the rain and sea mist cleared, only three of the seven remained in visual contact – *Batavia*, *Buren* and *Assendelft*.

During what was then a relatively fast passage to Cape Town, animosity began to brew between Pelsaert and Jacobsz, due mainly to the fact that the captain became exceedingly drunk on numerous occasions.

In sensing this rift, Cornelisz saw an opportunity to ensure he made the ultimate escape from Europe – one where he, and anyone who wanted to join him, would live an idyllic lifestyle and never be found. His plan started with befriending the disgruntled Jacobsz before *Batavia* reached Cape Town, gaining his confidence then concocting with him a plot to orchestrate a mutiny.

By the time *Batavia* sailed out of Table Bay and south towards the Roaring Forties, the recalcitrant Cornelisz – who was also described as being cunning, manipulative and charismatic – had gained the support of Jacobsz and a small number of the crew: enough to execute the scheme he had devised.

The first move was to lose contact with the other two ships so there could be no outside interference, something Jacobsz would achieve with ease by simply steering away from them in the dead of night. The conspirators would then take control of *Batavia*, determine who would support them, and dispose of all opposition. The commander would be thrown overboard, and the soldiers, along with anyone else challenging the mutiny, killed.

With that achieved, *Batavia* would disappear over the horizon to a far-off destination, possibly somewhere beyond the Spice Islands, where the mutineers would establish their own community, inspired by Cornelisz's heretical beliefs. This utopia would be financed by the huge amount of silver stacked in *Batavia*'s hold. Once their colony was established onshore, the ship would more than likely be scuttled so that their presence there would not be evident.

Pelsaert's confinement to his cabin soon after *Batavia* left Cape Town came as an unexpected bonus for the would-be mutineers. His absence from the deck and the everyday management of the ship saw discipline among the crew become increasingly lax, a slide that was no doubt accelerated by Cornelisz and Jacobsz as they continued to recruit supporters for their planned treachery.

By the time *Batavia* was well into the Roaring Forties, contact with the two other ships had been lost as planned. The would-be mutineers initiated the next stage of their plot. This involved a physical assault on the high-ranking, twenty-seven year old Lucretia van den Mylen, who was travelling to meet her husband, a senior VOC employee in Batavia.

The Western Australian Museum's authoritative report on the loss of *Batavia* tells the story:

> The potent mix of many men and few women without
> the firm hand of control led to a very ugly incident …
> Lucretia van den Mylen's social standing meant that she
> had her own alcove and was accompanied by her maid.
> Jacobsz resented her, since she had spurned his advances.
>
> In mid-ocean Lady van den Mylen was assaulted by
> masked men who proceeded to 'hang overboard by her
> feet the Lady van den Mylen and indecently maltreat
> her body'. She later claimed to have recognised the
> voice of Jan Evertsz, a man devoted to the commander.

Cornelisz and Jacobsz had hoped that Pelsaert would mete out severe punishment to the perpetrators of the assault, thus turning more of the crew against their commander. But that did not happen, probably because the offenders were not identified.

Had this part of the plot gone as planned it is possible the mutiny would have occurred soon afterwards. Alternatively, the conspirators might have been planning to take charge of the ship when they were closer to the East Indies. Whichever is correct, Pelsaert was still very much in command of *Batavia* when she thundered onto the reef with violent force and shuddered to a halt.

Unbeknown to anyone on board, *Batavia* was little more than 30 nautical miles off the coast of Eendrachtsland when she struck what is now known as Morning Island, part of the Houtman Abrolhos group. As fate would have it, if she had been just 2 nautical miles to the east, sailing parallel to the course she had been holding, she would have missed the reef altogether and sailed on safely in deep water towards the coast, the outline of which would have become apparent not much later as dawn broke.

For the conspirators, the need for survival suddenly outweighed any thoughts of insubordination – but rebelliousness was not completely erased from their minds.

With the surge of the waves and the jagged reef combining to tear the ship asunder, a yawl and a small skiff began ferrying survivors to one of the two nearby islands, both of which Pelsaert had decided were suitable refuges. It was a slow process, and each time a boat laden with men, women and children cleared the ship, all had ample time to look back at what must have been a dismal sight: a once proud new ship that now looked as though she had been blown apart. The mainmast was smashed and hanging over the side, while the fore- and mizzenmasts remained erect amid a tangle of heavy rope rigging. With the tide rising and the hull settling deeper and deeper into the water as it broke up, waves were beginning to crash over the poop deck in a mass of white water.

Twenty-four hours after *Batavia* had gone aground, rising seas meant the seventy men who had remained aboard overnight – including Cornelisz – had still to be rescued. It was an exercise fraught with danger, but was finally completed with success. By that afternoon, it was apparent that all seventy were fortunate to have been transported to safety as *Batavia* continued to disappear beneath the waves.

An accurate count of survivors does not exist, but it appears that some sixty people died when the ship was wrecked. It is possible that many of those who died were trapped below deck and drowned when the hull flooded. Of the survivors, it was later suggested by Pelsaert, who was obviously speculating, that there were 'about 40 people' on the smaller of the two islands – later named Traitor's Island – and 180 on the other.

The immediate problem was a lack of food and, even more urgent, water. The fear of dying from either starvation or thirst generated an upsurge of discontent, to the point where, after much debate, Pelsaert initiated the only logical plan for survival:

[it was decided] that we should go in search of water on the islands most nearby or on the vast mainland to keep them and us alive, and if we could find no water, that we should then sail with the boat without delay to Batavia, with God's grace there to inform of our sad unheard of, disastrous happening.

Pelsaert and his officers were on Beacon Island, and it was his intention to first go by boat to the smaller island and inform the survivors there of his plan. But on hearing this, Jacobsz strongly advised against it, saying, 'They will keep you there and you will regret it.' As the yawl approached the second island with Pelsaert, his bosun and oarsmen aboard, all were quick to realise that Jacobsz's warning had been well judged. The threat was obvious: the survivors were desperate to come aboard. Pelsaert could only order his boat to turn around and head back to the other island.

It was then imperative that a group of them sail for the mainland to search for the precious water as soon as possible.

Pelsaert knew that the 30-foot yawl he intended taking had shortcomings when it came to crossing the open ocean to the barely visible coastline 30 nautical miles away. The freeboard needed to be increased to make the hull more seaworthy, and leeboards (wooden fins) had to be fitted to each side to minimise leeway when sailing upwind. One of the ship's carpenters, Jan Egbertsz, swiftly made these modifications using timber he had salvaged from the wreck.

Four days after *Batavia* had been lost, Pelsaert set sail, taking with him his captain, Jacobsz. First they stopped at two islands where searches for water proved fruitless, and next they headed for the coast. Once there, they were surprised to see *Batavia*'s sloop come over the horizon and join them. It was commanded by third steersman Gillis Franssz Halffwaack, who, with ten others, had decided to join the search.

Back on Beacon Island, where Cornelisz was in charge as the most senior officer remaining, there was already a level of discontent: many of the survivors felt Pelsaert had abandoned them and might never return. This made it easier for Cornelisz to influence some forty or so men to follow him as leader. He wanted them to see him as the man who gave them hope, the person who offered them the best chance of survival.

Deep down, though, his own plan to make good his intention never to return to the Netherlands was evolving. His prime intention was to take control of any rescue ship that might come their way, then either establish his own colony or take to a life of piracy on the high seas. If those schemes failed, the island group where he and the remaining castaways were gathered would become his safe haven: he would live life to the full, following the philosophies of Torrentius by seeking happiness and sensual pleasures.

Both goals had one common denominator: he needed supporters and believers. Those who wouldn't help him would have to be eliminated.

*

Meanwhile, Pelsaert's quest to find a source of water sufficient to support the castaways was being frustrated by a high-running surf. This prevented him from landing his boat on the shore, so he had no option but to have men swim to the beach and explore the surrounds. No water was found, but on one occasion they did report back that they had seen:

> ... four men creeping towards them on hands and feet, when our folk, coming out of a hollow upon a height, approached them suddenly, they leapt to their feet and fled full speed, which was clearly seen by us in the boat. They were black people, entirely naked, without any cover.

Pelsaert's principal observation on the coast was: 'level rocky land without trees, about as high as Dover in England'.

On 16 June, eight days after departing Beacon Island, Pelsaert's arduous quest for water continued without success, as his journal detailed:

> ... it appeared it had not rained there for a long time, nor was there any sign of running water, for beyond the heights the country was flat again, without trees, foliage or grass, except for high anthills thrown up of earth ... there was also such a host of flies, which came to sit in the mouth and the eyes, that they could not be

beaten off … we were forced to take a resolution,
because we were more than 100 miles away from the
people left by us and had up to now not found water to
assist them, as for ourselves only, that we might have
the benefit of 2 *mutskens* [1 cup] daily, to do our utmost
in the name of God to further our journey to Batavia as
quickly as possible in order that through the Hon. Lord
General some order or means might be set to work
towards succour.

Pelsaert decided that there was no alternative but to let
Halffwaack and his men sail their own boat alongside his yawl
to Batavia. In all, there would be forty-eight men making the
journey, covering more than 1500 nautical miles, to Sunda
Strait then east to Batavia. Despite agreeing to sail in convoy,
the two open boats, one large and the other small, somewhat
understandably lost sight of each other (probably at night) in
the early days of the passage.

On 26 June, ten days after departing the shores of
Eendrachtsland, Pelsaert and his men had reason to celebrate
when they sighted Java. It had been a frustrating journey, in
conditions that had ranged from almost calm, when Pelsaert's
yawl had averaged considerably less than 1 knot, to high seas
and near-gales. At times, their progress under sail had been so
slow that it had been faster to row. It had been an epic voyage.

Pelsaert noted that they reached land forty-eight hours
later:

… we rowed ashore to seek fresh water, where to our
luck we found a running streamlet. Thanks and praise
the Lord, for we could quench our great thirst at last,
here we filled our casks and before noon were again
under sail …

After twenty-two days, their gruelling endeavour was over:
'we arrived at night at the fall of darkness in the roads of
Batavia. God be praised and thanked.'

Halffwaack's boat arrived just a few days later.

Pelsaert's first priority was to meet with the Governor-
General of the Dutch East Indies, Jan Pieterszoon Coen, to
explain what had happened to *Batavia* and stress that there
were survivors in dire need of rescue. His meeting also led to
the indictment of two of the men who had been with him on
the yawl: the bosun, Jan Evertsz, and the captain, Jacobsz. The
bosun was charged with outrageous behaviour – being
implicated in the assault on Lucretia van den Mylen – and for
his negligence leading to the wreck of *Batavia*, while Jacobsz,
who had been at the helm when the ship struck the rocks, was
also charged with negligence. Both were found guilty. Evertsz
was executed while Jacobsz is believed to have died some years
later in a dungeon in Batavia.

Meantime, Coen ordered that the small VOC inter-island
trading ship *Sardam* be prepared and sent on a rescue mission as
quickly as possible, under Pelsaert's command. Unfortunately,
once *Sardam* was under way, unfavourable weather conditions

thwarted any chance of a fast passage south. It was not until 13 September – more than fourteen weeks after *Batavia* ran aground – that the rescuers arrived at the scene of the tragedy.

What Pelsaert was then confronted with was far worse than anything he could have imagined. It was a scene of mass murder, the consequence of Cornelisz's reign of terror.

*

While the commander was absent, Cornelisz held to his scheme to disappear with his supporters into oblivion. But before that could happen, he needed to reduce demand on the meagre food supply and silence all opposition to his plan. That meant dramatically decreasing the number of survivors on Beacon Island. It was a circumstance that brought out the evil side of his psychopathic nature.

In frenzied attacks, victims were stabbed, strangled, bashed, drowned, raped and tortured – a murderous orgy that showed no respect for human life. Cornelisz did not involve himself directly. Instead, he acted as the puppeteer, manipulating his supporters into carrying out atrocities beyond comprehension.

The brutality was such that the island became known, among the few survivors, as Batavia's Graveyard. The graves of victims are still being discovered there to this day.

Cornelisz began introducing the 'pleasurable' lifestyle associated with the philosophies of Torrentius: he claimed

Lucretia van den Mylen for himself, and allowed his closest supporters to take other women as sex slaves.

Before the atrocities began, in another move to shore up his authority, Cornelisz declared that he was in charge of all weapons and discipline. He ordered a group of twenty unarmed soldiers, commanded by twenty-one year old Wiebbe Hayes, to be transported to what they would name High Island – today West Wallabi Island – 4 miles west of Beacon Island. He did this on the pretext of asking them to search for water, and send up a smoke signal should it be found; in fact, he was abandoning them to eliminate another potential threat, his belief being that they would die of thirst.

Twenty days after arriving on the island, which covered 2.4 square miles, Hayes – who despite his young age had been made commander due to his exceptional leadership qualities – and his men found water, so they did as directed and sent up a smoke signal. Much to their surprise, there was no response. They did this twice more, but there was still no sign that Cornelisz was coming to collect them.

Hayes and his men realised they had been conned and would have to fend for themselves. Fortunately, there was no reason for immediate concern, as they had also found food: sea lions and wild birds were so plentiful that the twenty men were self-sufficient.

They did not realise that Cornelisz had a further ulterior motive. That awareness came only when small bands of survivors managed to escape Cornelisz's island by making rafts and crossing the lagoon to where Hayes and his men were exiled. Before long, there was a total of forty-five people on West Wallabi Island: more than Cornelisz had with him.

The runaways told Hayes of the atrocities that were occurring under Cornelisz's hand and warned him that Cornelisz and his men were planning an attack. The reason Cornelisz had given for this attack was simple: 'If the [rescue] yacht comes through the inside passage [Hayes] will warn them, and our plan will not succeed, therefore they must be killed.'

On hearing this, Hayes and his men immediately set about building a small stone fortress – which still stands today, and is seen as the oldest European structure existing in Australia. They then armed themselves with whatever they could.

It has been suggested that around this time, Cornelisz also sent a messenger to Hayes's island with a letter addressed to the French soldiers who were part of Hayes's contingent. It was designed to influence the French into betraying the Dutch soldiers with the promise that they would receive favourable treatment as a pay-off. The French saw through this and continued to stand with Hayes.

When that ploy failed, Cornelisz sent men to attack and kill Hayes and his men, but the invaders were repelled each time with improvised weapons such as cudgels, pikes and planks. Totally frustrated, Cornelisz decided to mount his own attack, supported by four of his murderous henchmen. This, too, was unsuccessful – but in even more spectacular fashion. All five were captured. Cornelisz was bound and kept alive, while the others were promptly executed.

A fourth attack followed, led by Wouter Loos, on 17 September. He had been made captain of the rebel group following Cornelisz's capture. But while Loos's raid was under way, Hayes saw the magnificent sight of *Sardam* coming over the northern horizon, her sails billowing as she headed towards the island. Still, salvation was not certain; Loos might well be able to reach *Sardam* first and concoct a story in his favour, one which could have led to him and his men taking control of the ship. Hayes and his supporters could only hope that luck would bring the ship their way.

Pelsaert later wrote of *Sardam*'s approach:

Before noon, approaching the island, we saw smoke on
a long island 2 miles West of the Wreck, also on another
small island close by the Wreck, about which we were
all very glad, hoping to find great numbers, or rather all
people, alive. Therefore, as soon as the anchor was
dropped, I sailed with the boat to the highest island,
which was nearest, taking with me a barrel of water,
ditto bread, and a keg of wine; coming there, I saw no
one, at which we wondered. I sprang ashore, and at the
same time we saw a very small yawl with four Men
rowing round the Northerly point; one of them, named
Wiebbe Hayes, sprang ashore and ran towards me,
calling from afar, 'Welcome, but go back aboard

immediately, for there is a party of scoundrels on the islands near the wreck, with two sloops, who have the intention to seize the Yacht.'

On reaching Pelsaert, overwhelmed by relief, Hayes quickly explained in broad terms what had happened during his absence: that the miscreants had remorselessly murdered more than 125 men, women and children. He also revealed that, two weeks earlier, he and his men had had the good fortune of capturing Cornelisz, 'the chief of the scoundrels', and that he was being held on West Wallabi Island. With that, the commander straightaway ordered Hayes to sail back there and retrieve Cornelisz, then returned himself to *Sardam* and waited for the reprobates to approach:

When they came near the ship, it could be seen that they were dressed mostly in red cloth, trimmed with golden lace. I called to them, why for do you come aboard armed? They answered me that they would reply to that when they were on the ship. I ordered them to throw their weapons into the sea before they came over, which at last they did. When they came over, we immediately took them prisoner, and we forthwith began to examine them, especially a certain Jan Hendricxsz from Bremen, soldier, who immediately confessed that he had murdered and helped to murder 17 to 20 people, under the order of

Jeronimus [Cornelisz]. I asked him the origin and circumstances of this, why had they practised such cruelties. Said he also wished to explain how it had been with him in the beginning – saying, that the skipper [Adriaan Jacobsz], Jeronimus Cornelisz, the Highboatswain [Jan Evertsz] and still more others, had it in mind to seize the ship *Batavia* before it was wrecked; to kill the Commander and all people except 120 towards whom they were more favourably inclined, and to throw the dead overboard into the sea and then to go pirating with the ship.

With those men and their leader Cornelisz in custody, Pelsaert moved swiftly. The next morning he took a yawl to West Wallabi Island and armed Hayes and ten of his men with muskets and weapons. All of them then sailed to Batavia's Graveyard, 'where the rest of the scoundrels were':

When they saw us coming they lost their courage, and said to each other, now all our necks are in the noose, thinking that they would be killed immediately, and when I came ashore I had them bound hand and foot and so secured.

Pelsaert had been shocked by the murderous actions of Cornelisz and his principal villains, so retribution was swift. As Pelsaert's journal revealed, Cornelisz was not given the chance of a trial back in Batavia. Instead a court martial was initiated on Batavia's Graveyard that afternoon:

> The question has been put by the Commander, whether one should take such a gruesome villain (who is with all thinkable misdeeds and horror besmirched) in captivity on our ship to Batavia to bring him before the Hon. Lord General, who could give him the justly deserved punishment, or whether, because according to the strict order of our Lord Masters, villains and criminal evil-doers must not be brought to Batavia, in order not to put ships and men in further danger (should be punished here).

Pelsaert's report on the proceedings when Cornelisz appeared read in part:

> First there will follow the examinations of Jeronimus Cornelisz, from the day when he was brought to us as a prisoner until today ... as well as his freewill confession, concerning the great, evil, misdeeds done and intended by him. Whereupon follow the sentence that has been pronounced on him, as well as on his accomplices ...

> Jeronimus Cornelisz, brought in, has been asked ... why through the devil he has denuded himself of all humanity, and why he was more evil than if he had

143

been changed into a tiger animal, so that he had to let flow so much innocent blood, and also has had the intention to do that with us.

Pelsaert then pronounced Cornelisz's sentence:

Jeronimus Cornelisz, of Haarlem … [shall be taken] to Seals Island, to a place made ready for it in order to exercise Justice, and there firstly to cut off both his hands, and after shall be punished on the Gallows with the Cord till Death shall follow, with confiscation of all his money, gold, silver, monthly wages …

Cornelisz's immediate subordinates, who were also condemned to be hanged, had their right hands cut off before going to the gallows. The other mutineers, who were deemed to be less threatening, were to be transported to Batavia to face court.

Before *Sardam* sailed from the islands and headed back to Batavia, her commander had the ship's captain, Jacop Jacopszoon, and four crew go by small boat to all the nearby islands and search for the treasures that *Batavia* had carried, which were known to have been put ashore after the ship ran aground. The men and boat disappeared. It can only be assumed that the boat capsized close to a rocky shore and the men drowned. However, a considerable amount of the booty, mainly in the form of gold, silver and coins, was recovered.

While a considerable amount had been accumulated by Cornelisz on the island, more was retrieved from what remained of the shattered wreck, which was then barely visible above the waves surging across the nearby reef. Pelsaert's men managed to dive into the hold and bring treasure to the surface.

Surprisingly, during the voyage back to Batavia, it was decided by Pelsaert that twenty-four year old Wouter Loos and a cabin boy, Jan Pelgrom de Bye, eighteen, were only minor offenders, so they should suffer a lesser fate than the other rebels, who were expected to be executed. Loos and de Bye were put ashore near what is now named the Hutt River, east of the Houtman Abrolhos Islands, given meagre supplies and left to fend for themselves. Pelsaert explained the action in his journal:

> Therefore after the council has … debated the case of
> the foresaid Wouter Loos we have decided to sentence
> him, preferring grace in place of rigour of the Justice
> and also the service of the General East India Company,
> that he, together with Jan Pelgrom de Bije van
> Bemmel … who on account of his youth obtained by
> entreating to be put on an island, they shall be put with
> a small yawl on the foresaid land as scoundrels and
> death-deserving delinquents, in order … to become
> familiar with the people there and to get to know and
> find out what there be of material in those lands, be it

145

gold, silver, or anything of value, and if at any time
some ships come to that coast, or yawls come ashore,
that they may then be rescued by those and report the
opportunities of those lands

The pair were never seen again, although some early British settlers in that region are said to have seen abnormally light-skinned Aboriginal people. If true, that might suggest the pair became part of a local Aboriginal tribe and adopted their lifestyle. Regardless, Loos and de Bye could be considered the first European settlers in Australia.

On arriving in Batavia aboard *Sardam*, Wiebbe Hayes was hailed as a hero by the new governor-general, Jacques Specx, who immediately promoted him to the rank of sergeant in the VOC. Unfortunately for Pelsaert, his superiors saw him as guilty of negligence in relation to the loss of *Batavia*. As a punishment, all his belongings and financial wealth were confiscated. He died a shamed and ruined man within a year.

Of the mutineers who faced court in Batavia, five were sentenced to be hanged while those deemed to be lesser offenders were flogged. The most severe punishment possible was handed down to Cornelisz's subordinate, Jacop Pietersz: death on the torture wheel. He was strapped to something resembling a wagon wheel which was slowly turned, and as it revolved the torturer smashed his limbs using an iron club, the gaps between the spokes allowing the limbs to easily give way and break. He was then left to die.

The Dirk Hartog plate, which marked the accidental Dutch discovery of the west coast of Australia by the crew of *Eendracht* in 1616. The message translates as: '1616 The 25 October is here arrived the ship Eendraght of Amsterdam; the uppermerchant Gillis Miebais, of Luyck; Skipper Dirck Hatichs of Amsterdam. The 27 ditto [we] set sail for Bantum; the undermerchant Jan Stins, the first mate Pieter Dookes van Bil. Anno 1616.'
Rijksmuseum NG-NM-825

The Torture of the English by the Dutch in Ambon in 1622, Anonymous, 1673. The Governor of Ambon believed a group of English, Japanese and Portuguese had plotted his assassination, to take control of the Dutch garrison of Fort Victoria. Many were tortured, and twenty – including ten Englishmen – were beheaded, leading to a deterioration in Dutch–English relations.
Rijksmuseum_RP-P-OB-68.279

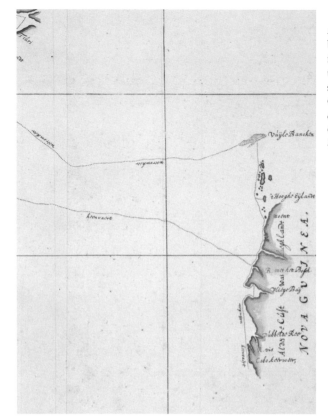

A detail from the map created by Willem Janszoon, the first European to set foot on the Australian continent. It shows the section of Gulf of Carpentaria shoreline that he charted and labelled 'Nova Guinea' in 1606.
State Library of Queensland 769146

Australian-built replica of the *Duyfken*, first launched in 1999. The 'jacht' has since sailed to the Netherlands and back.
Fairfax Syndication / Angela Wylie

View of Batavia by Hendrick Dubbels (1640–76), showing the fort known as Batavia Castle, the residence of the Governor-General of the Dutch East Indies.
Rijksmuseum SK-A-2513

Victory over the Portuguese Fleet, Bantam, 1601, Anonymous. The *Duyfken*, already under the command of Willem Janszoon, is believed to be shown at the centre of the sea battle between the Dutch and Portuguese fleets.
Rijksmuseum RP-P-OB-75.315

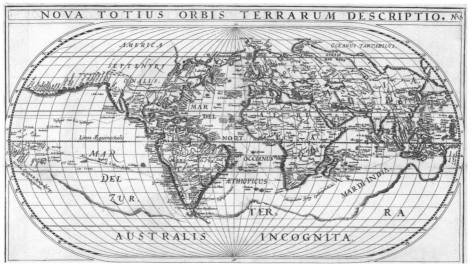

A 1593 Dutch map by Cornelius de Jode, showing East New Guinea, the Solomon Islands and imaginary coast of Australia with mythical beasts.
National Library of Australia nla.map-rm389

The belief in a great southern landmass dates back to the days when the world was first understood to be round; it was assumed that it existed to balance the large land mass in the northern hemisphere, otherwise the globe would topple over. This early seventeenth-century map shows a huge southern continent, labelled *Terra Australis Incognita* (Unknown South Land).
Rijksmuseum RP-P-OB-75.472

Three engravings from *The Unlucky Voyage of the Ship Batavia* by
Francois Pelsaert (1649 edition). TOP: The murders and massacre
on Batavia's Graveyard (today Beacon Island). MIDDLE: Wiebbe
Hayes and his men row out to warn Commander Pelsaert of the
mutiny. BOTTOM: Hand amputation and execution of Jeronimus
Cornelisz and other mutineers on Seals Island.

[All] Mitchell Library, State Library of NSW V/42 / a1528388

Abel Tasman with his wife and daughter, painted by Jacob Gerritsz Cuyp in 1637.
National Library of Australia nla.pic-an2282370

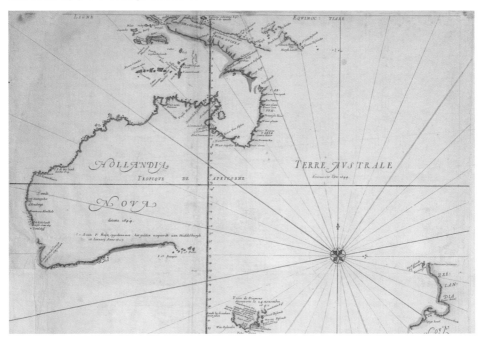

Hollandia Nova detecta 1644 (New Holland discovered in 1644). This map, published in Melchisedech Thevenot's *Relations de Divers Voyages Curieux (Tales of Various Strange Voyages)* in Paris in 1663, revealed the extent of Tasman's discoveries in print for the first time.
National Library of Australia nla.pic-an2272869

Portrait of William Dampier by William Charles Thomas Dobson, circa 1850, copied from a portrait painted by Thomas Murray just after the publication of *A New Voyage Round the World* made Dampier suddenly famous.
National Library of Australia nla.pic-an2272869

Prince Giolo [Jeoly], Son to the King of Moangis or Gilolo, etching by John Savage, circa 1692. William Dampier purchased Jeoly in the Philippines in 1690 and took him to England, where he was sold and exhibited as a curiosity. In *A New Voyage Round the World* (1697), Dampier wrote of 'Romantick stories' that Jeoly's tattoos repelled poisonous creatures. Fleeing snakes and scorpions can be seen at his feet.
Mitchell Library, State Library of NSW V/42 / a1528388

Meeting of Sailors with the Inhabitants of New Holland, illustration from Dampier's *A New Voyage Round the World* (1697).
Rijksmuseum RP-P-1896-A-19368 1316

William Dampier in a Small Open Canoe Travelling to Aceh (Indonesia), illustration from Dampier's *A New Voyage Round the World* (1697).
Rijksmuseum RP-P-1896-A-19368-1317

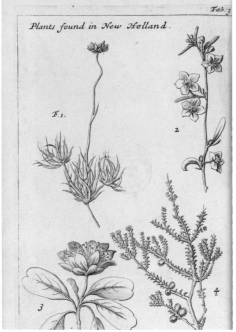

'Some Birds of New Holland', in Dampier's *A Voyage to New Holland* (1703). In his journal, Dampier noted, 'we saw … 5 or 6 sorts of small birds. The biggest sort of these were not bigger than larks; some no bigger than wrens, all singing with great variety of fine shrill notes'. *Dixson Library, State Library of NSW 70/9 / a2736004*

'Plants found in New Holland' in Dampier's *A Voyage to New Holland* (1703). Dampier was the first explorer to properly detail Australian flora and fauna. The botanical drawings that accompanied his journal notes were, it is believed, created by Dampier's clerk, James Brand. *Dixson Library, State Library of NSW 70/9 / a2736006*

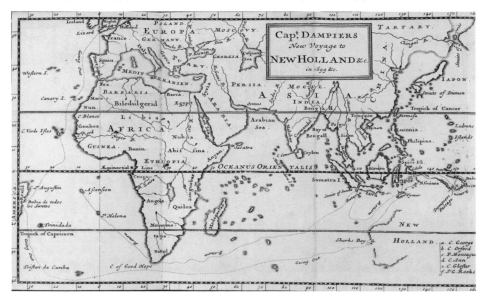

Map tracking Dampier's 1699 voyage, from *A Voyage to New Holland* (1703). This voyage was England's first ever expedition into the southern seas, dedicated to both scientific research and exploration. *Dixson Library, State Library of NSW 70/9 / a2736001*

Only sixty-eight of the 322 people believed to have been aboard *Batavia* when she departed the Netherlands ever reached their destination.

*

Following the loss of *Batavia*, there was little Dutch exploration in the region of Eendrachtsland for more than a decade. In 1635, the ship *Amsterdam*, under the captaincy of Wollebrand Geleynszoon de Jongh, did cruise the coast in the vicinity of Shark's Bay. De Jongh was able to create more detailed charts of this region for the benefit of future voyagers. The following year, VOC commander Gerrit Thomasz Pool and merchantman Pieter Pieterszoon led a two-vessel expedition (*Klein Amsterdam* and *Wesel*). Their mission was to chart what they could of the coast while looking for any signs of Wouter Loos and Jan Pelgrom de Bye who had been abandoned on the coast as punishment for their part in the loss of *Batavia*.

*

Intrigue relating to the *Batavia* tragedy crossed the centuries, but the actual site of the wreck was not confirmed for more than 300 years.

The first suggestion that it might have been found came when Lieutenant John Lort Stokes, who was conducting

Admiralty surveys around the Abrolhos Islands in 1840 aboard the famous HMS *Beagle*. Consequently he named the islands he was charting the Pelsart Group. However, it is now believed he confused the wreck of *Zeewyk* with that of *Batavia*. The Pelsart Group is more than 20 nautical miles south of the *Batavia* wreck.

In the 1950s novelist Henrietta Drake-Brockman, who gathered information relating to *Batavia* while visiting the Abrolhos Group, became convinced that the wreck was somewhere in the vicinity of the Wallabi Group of islands.

The breakthrough came when a local lobster fisherman, Dave Johnson, revealed to a group searching for the site that he had seen a large anchor close to the sea surface while setting his lobster pots off Morning Reef, near Beacon Island. On 4 June 1963 Max and Graham Cramer and Greg Allen dived on that location, and discovered a significant part of Australian maritime history: the wreck of *Batavia*.

Parts of *Batavia*'s hull and numerous other items, which have since been recovered from the site, now form a remarkable centrepiece at the Western Australian Museum in Fremantle.

CHAPTER NINE

Land of Gold

August 1642

In the seventeenth century, the world's most southern ocean was the domain of a vast and varied array of wildlife and little else: soaring seabirds large and small, massive whales on their annual migratory passage, diving dolphins ... and marauding storms that often bred satanic seas.

Since time immemorial, little had changed, until one particular day: 6 November 1642.

It was a horrid, miserable day, like many others in what is all too often a barbarous wilderness. A howling, icy wind propelled hail and snow almost horizontally at more than 50 knots across a leaden sea – laced with long streaks of off-white spume: the aftermath of huge, breaking wave crests, which, though sometimes a mile apart, peaked at more than 15 metres.

One thing that set this day apart: history was about to be made. Amid the giant, wildly careering waves were two relatively small ships, each running downwind and carrying the minimum amount of heavy canvas sail. Just about anywhere else in the world this sight would not have been out of the ordinary – except, possibly, for the powerful nature of the storm – but these two ships were traversing an ocean where no man or vessel had previously ventured. Both were three-masted and square-rigged: the 105-foot *Heemskerck*, and the 80-foot *Zeehaen*, a bulky Dutch fluyt designed as a cargo carrier.

This expedition into the unknown was being led by successful seafarer Abel Janszoon Tasman, who would note the severe conditions in his journal entry for that day:

> We had a storm from the west with hail and snow, and ran on before the wind with our foresail barely halfway [up] the mast; the sea ran very high and our men begin to suffer badly from the severe cold. At noon Latitude estimated 49° 4', Longitude 114° 56'; course kept east by south, sailed 49 miles …

Often, while the helmsman fought with the cumbersome whipstaff steering system while trying desperately to hold a course to the east, a cloud of snow, hail and flying spray from the west would strafe the deck from stern to bow. Making the situation even worse were the giant pursuing waves. Every time one of these combers slammed into the port or starboard quarter, and lifted the stern skywards amid a churning mass of white foam, *Heemskerck* and *Zeehaen* would roll heavily like lumbering elephants, then surge forward while being driven 20 or 30 degrees off course. At the same time, the bitterly cold spray was cutting like razor-sharp knives into any exposed flesh, chilling the bones of the already soaked crewmen on deck.

Not surprisingly – considering the ships were in a no-man's land in the Southern Ocean – all aboard had rarely, if ever, seen a storm of such ferocity. Visibility was next to nothing, and the captain and his men had no real idea of where they were headed, or what they might discover.

For Tasman, there was added concern: he knew their predicament could well get worse, because he was under instruction from his superiors to sail even further to the south, out of the Roaring Forties and into the Furious Fifties. He had been ordered to travel to 54 degrees latitude – just 12 degrees to the north of what is now known as the Antarctic Circle! This was a region so distant from, and alien to, the rest of the known world that, only a few centuries earlier, these sailors could have been forgiven for thinking they might sail off the edge of the Earth.

It was late spring, with the promise of warmer weather still weeks away. Tasman was mindful of the welfare of his men and the security of his ships while sailing through such high latitudes.

So, on this storm-sodden day, Tasman and his senior officers made a decision of historic significance. They resolved that they could no longer follow the VOC's orders and remain safe. In an effort to escape the wrath of the Roaring Forties, Tasman called for a change of course:

> In the morning, the wind still westerly with hail and snow so that we had to run on with a furled foresail as before, and as we could not make any progress in this way, we deemed it best to alter our course to northward upon which ... we resolved first to our course north-eastward, running on to 45 or 44°; having reached the 45th or 44th degree, to direct our course due east ...

Just eighteen days later, on 24 November 1642, Tasman and his men sighted land:

> Good weather and a clear sky. At noon Latitude observed 42° 25', Longitude 163° 31'; course kept east by north, sailed 30 miles ... In the afternoon about 4 o'clock we saw land bearing east by north of us at about 10 miles distance from us by estimation; the land we sighted was very high; towards evening we also saw, east-south-east of us, three high mountains, and to the north-east two more mountains, but less high than those to southward ...

Had *Heemskerck* and *Zeehaen* remained in higher latitudes and continued on their intended course to the east, they would have sailed on into the wide open space of what is now the Tasman Sea.

The wind was then very light, enabling the two ships to close to within a mile of this spectacular and rugged coast. It was the foreground to a series of high, undulating mountains, two of which would later take the ships' names.

This was a scene of wonder that excited everyone from captain to cabin boy. They were observing a part of the world that no Europeans had ever seen.

Well aware of the unpredictable nature of the weather, and that a westerly gale like those already experienced would make the coast a forbidding lee shore, Tasman called for his ships to change course to the south. *Heemskerck* and *Zeehaen* skirted the coastline of a land that he would name just twenty-four hours later:

> This land being the first land we have met with in the South Sea and not known to any European nation, we have conferred on it the name of Anthoony Van Diemenslandt in honour of the Honourable Governor-General, our illustrious master, who sent us to make this discovery ...

This was a find that would add yet another fragment of detail to the ever-expanding world map, but right then it remained unknown what piece, if any, it might be in a puzzle that could one day lead to confirmation of the existence of Terra Australis Incognita.

Accordingly, it was Tasman's intention to discover where this coast would lead him. It was time to re-trim the sails and follow the lie of the land towards the south.

*

Abel Janszoon Tasman was born in 1603 – the year after the VOC was founded – in the tiny Protestant village of Lutjegast, in the far north of the Netherlands. This part of the world is so flat that it is almost beyond comprehension; the highest point of land is just 35 feet above sea level. The town is little more than 10 miles from the coast, and highly vulnerable to the ravages of the North Sea when in its foulest mood; Lutjegast and the entire region are protected from flooding by a series of huge dykes, built in those days from stone and timber. Back then, the local populace was made up of either sea beggars (privateers or pirates), or farmers who prospered handsomely from fertile fields.

It is likely that Tasman had a modest upbringing. It is not even known how he came by the surname Tasman, as family names did not exist in that era. It was certainly not unusual for a son to have his christian name added to the christian name of his father; thus, Abel, who was the son of John, became Abel Janszoon; and it is by this name that Tasman often appears in historic records. Nicknames, which often originated from a feature of someone's life, were also quite common. This could explain the name Tasman; it might have been derived from the word Taschman, which was possibly the name of a boat belonging to the family.

Young Abel's love for the ocean was probably fostered by vibrant stories from the beggars – tales of the beggars' own adventures or the heroic deeds of kindred folk in their epic sea battles against the Spanish forces. He set himself on a life as a seafarer, and in doing so he had one advantage over so many of his young friends: he had achieved some level of education, and because of that, he knew how to write.

Where, or how, he first ventured onto the open ocean is unknown, but the spirit of adventure that was part of his life soon saw him looking to a world beyond the lowlands and dykes: he headed 80 miles to the south-west, to Amsterdam, which was then the cornerstone of world commerce, thanks in no small way to the VOC.

The fact that Tasman took up residence in one of the poorest canal-front parts of the city, Teerketelsteeg, indicated he had little money. His name first appears on official Amsterdam records on 11 January 1632 when, aged twenty-seven, he married Jannetjie Tjaers (also known as Tjaerts, Tjercx, Tiercse or Tjercks). She was his second wife; his first, Claesjie Heyndricks, had given birth to a baby girl, Claesjen, but died before the child was two years old. Jannetjie came from a poor working-class family, a circumstance confirmed by the fact that she was unable to sign her name on the marriage certificate. Documents relating to this second marriage provide some insight into Tasman's life at that time: he was officially described as being a *vaerentgesel* — a common sailor — meaning that he was yet to achieve any qualified position.

He soon found more distinguished employment with the Dutch East India Company, as he sailed on his first voyage to the East Indies not long after he was married. He must have impressed the management of the company from the outset, because within two years he had progressed from being a deckhand to first mate of a ship, *Weesp* (*Wasp*), which was trading between Batavia and the surrounding islands. Such ventures had two additional purposes besides trade: to protect the company's ports and shipping from foreign attack, and to deal with any islanders who were considered to be not acting in the best interests of the VOC.

By 1634 Tasman was very much on the ascendency in the VOC: on 18 May of that year he was appointed captain of *Mocha*, an inter-island trader that sailed out of Batavia as part of a fleet carrying cargo to Ambon and Banda and back. That return voyage would prove to be Tasman's first taste of exploration: the fleet had been tasked with searching for a safe course through the seas to the north of Ceram (now Seram) Island. It was found: a discovery that meant Ambon could be reached by a safer route during the monsoon season.

It was an exercise not without fear and frustration for Tasman. At one stage *Mocha* became separated from the rest of the fleet, and as supplies were running low the captain decided he and some of his men should venture onto one of the islands and inquire if anything could be procured by way of barter. Supercargo de la Salle wrote in his diary of what followed:

> Having spoken with the blacks, and being amicably
> received by the same, at length at our departure, Fiscal
> Balthzar Wijntjes and Sub-merchant [Subcargo]
> Abraham van der Plasse were barbarously murdered,
> chopped into small pieces, and three persons very
> grievously wounded ...

While escaping the slaughter, Tasman managed to get the three wounded men back aboard the pinnace and row them to the ship, all the time 'in great peril of being all of them killed together'.

Word of Tasman's bravery, his contribution to the Ceram Sea expedition, and his skill as a seafarer and leader of note filtered through to the VOC's governor-general and councillors in Batavia. This led to his appointment as captaining Mocha on a run carrying rice between Macassar and Ambon. However, the most important part of this voyage was transporting reinforcements to gather intelligence about the activities of smugglers, who were prolific in the region. The confidence the hierarchy held in their man was evident in their instructions for the voyage:

> ... we shall not by the present determine what course
> the aforesaid fluyt shall have to follow from Macassar to

> Amboyna, since in this matter we entirely rely on the
> skill and experience of skipper Abel Janszoon Tasman,
> whom we have instructed by word of mouth …

It appeared Tasman could do no wrong: his life was heading in the right direction. But he ran into a hurdle in September 1636 when, having reached Batavia after yet another cargo run between the islands, he was confronted by an uprising among his crew. The men claimed to the Chief Magistrate's Court that Tasman had not provided them with their full allowance of rations during the voyage. There is no written finding from the court, so it can only be assumed that the case was dismissed. Adding weight to this conclusion is the fact that Tasman's ascendancy within the VOC continued unimpeded.

Having now been absent from his wife in the Netherlands for some four years, Tasman decided it was time to return home − at least for a brief time. To do this he had to step down in rank and take the position of mate on board another VOC vessel, *Banda*, which was the flagship for a fleet preparing to head back to Europe.

Nothing out of the ordinary occurred during this passage, until they were crossing the North Atlantic towards Europe. The commander of the fleet, Matthys Quast, decided that, to minimise the risk of attack by Spanish men-of-war or privateers sailing out of Dunkirk, they would not pass through the English Channel. Instead, they would sail a looping course around England, Ireland and Scotland then approach home waters through the North Sea. Finally, after being at sea seven months, *Banda* arrived safely in Texel on 1 August 1637.

Tasman never wavered in his desire to pursue a career under sail in the East Indies, so it is probable that the reason for his return home was to encourage his wife to start a new life with him in Batavia. Fortunately, the VOC's Heren XVII – the company's seventeen governing commissioners – had recently decided that senior officers would be permitted to take their lawfully wedded wives to the East Indies with them ... but only if they signed a ten-year contract with the company.

This was the ideal arrangement for Tasman, so on 15 April 1638, having been appointed the captain of the fly-ship (a small, manoeuverable and inexpensive three-masted vessel of between 70 and 200 tons suitable for both mercantile and naval activities) *Engel* (*Angel*), he sailed from Texel bound for Batavia with Jannetjie and Claesjen on board. They arrived there on 11 October.

Within a short time, Tasman was back at sea, expanding a career that would eventually see his log book recording visits, for either commercial or exploratory reasons, to Formosa, Japan, Cambodia and China.

*

During Tasman's absence from Batavia, a gradual shift in the official Dutch attitude towards the Great South Land was at last emerging. Terra Australis Incognita, so long perceived as a myth or mystery, was still largely seen that way more than a quarter-century after it was first linked with Dirk Hartog's discovery of Eendrachtsland. But the winds of change were coming.

The VOC's relentless desire to establish new trade opportunities was drawing their attention more and more towards the land to the south, whose outline was becoming increasingly apparent on charts. The Dutch were well established as the dominant European power in the East Indies, but it was now imperative that they looked to extend that supremacy, maybe all the way to 'Chyly' (Chile). It was considered a logical extension of their existing areas of operation.

Frans Thijssen had, by this time, confirmed the presence of around 800 nautical miles of a possible southern coastline of a continent, while parts of a western coastline had been mapped by several others. But no one yet knew if, or how, these finds might be connected.

In early 1642, a meeting of the Council of the Indies – the Governor-General of the Dutch East Indies, Anthony van Diemen, plus Pieter Boreel, Cornelis van der Lijn, Joan Maetsuycker, Justus Schouten, Salomon Sweers and Cornelis Witsen – considered a Memoir Concerning the Discovery of the Southland, which Frans Visscher had prepared. They decided on 1 August 1642 to send two ships to explore what they called 'all the totally unknown provinces of Beach'.

In the sixteenth and seventeenth centuries, 'Beach' was a name given to the northern coast of the yet-to-be confirmed Great South Land. It derives from *Marco Polo's Travels*, in which the author wrote of Locach, a kingdom in the southern latitudes where gold was 'so plentiful that no one who did not see it could believe it'. (In reality this land was probably southern Thailand or Cambodia.) Somehow, in the 1532 edition, the word 'Locach' was corrupted, through poor transcription, to become 'Beach'.

Even Gerardus Mercator – arguably the greatest cartographer of all time, and the first person to use the word 'atlas' to describe a collection of maps – fell under the spell of Marco Polo's writings. A globe that he produced in 1541, and his world map of 1569, showed 'Beach the gold-bearing province, whither few from other countries go because of the inhumanity of its people' as the northern part of Terra Australis Incognita, in accordance with Marco Polo's text.

Obviously van Diemen and his council thought that, if Marco Polo's Beach did exist, the coast that was emerging to the south of Java just might be it – and there was only one way to find out. That this idea had been in discussion for some time is suggested by the enthusiastic response van Diemen received from VOC headquarters in the Netherlands, dated 25 September 1642:

We trust that the intended further discovery of the South-land, which we have urged in diverse letters, has by this time been carried into effect, in consequence of the opportune arrival of fitting vessels for the purpose; but if this should not be the case, we hereby once more recommend the project to your serious attention; seeing that many are of opinion that great profits for the Company might accrue thereby, as perhaps time will show ...

The position of commander for this expedition called for a first-rate seafarer and an exceptional leader, which was why he chose Abel Tasman. He also enlisted the Netherlands' most capable theoretical geographer and cartographer, Frans Visscher, who would be involved in the planning and would also accompany Tasman on the voyage.

Visscher immediately set about reviewing details that had emerged from every known discovery in the region of Eendrachtsland, then proposed a course that would most likely lead to the finding of new lands.

Visscher continued with his extensive appraisal of maps, so he could further develop his concept for the voyage. He decided they should sail into the never-before-sighted latitudes to the south of the coast that Thijssen and Nuyts had mapped in 1627. After setting out from Batavia, the expedition should actually start its search from Mauritius – more than 3000 nautical miles to the south-west of Batavia, and a similar distance west of the already discovered west coast of Eendrachtsland. The reason for this was that, on departing

Mauritius, the two ships could ride the prevailing westerly wind down to somewhere between 52 and 54 degrees south latitude before tracking east. From that point three options were to be considered:

- If, after sailing along the proposed latitude, no land had been encountered by the time the known longitude of the east coast of New Guinea was reached, then the ships should sail north-west until reaching New Guinea, then return to Batavia.
- Alternatively, Tasman might consider sailing towards the Solomon Islands. This would be a point of navigation for him: should they not encounter any unknown land on that course, then, on reaching the Solomons, they would be able to return home via the northern coast of New Guinea.
- Or, thirdly, he might continue sailing east towards Cape Horn, and on reaching that coast, explore the lands to the north before returning to Batavia.

Van Diemen had two ships prepared in Batavia for the expedition. *Heemskerck* was Tasman's flagship. The word translates to 'home church', but she was named in honour of earlier Dutch explorer Jacob van Heemskerk (1567–1607). Manned by a crew of sixty, she was a heavily armed, three-masted 'war-yacht' with a burthen of 120 tons. *Zeehaen* (*Gurnard* or *Sea Robin*) was a fast three-masted fluyt which, although smaller in dimensions than the flagship, was estimated to be 80 tons heavier in burthen. She had a complement of fifty men.

If there was a similarity between the two ships, it was that both hulls featured the traditional high sweeping sheer and bulging tumblehome of that era. Ide Tjaerts Holleman was the captain of *Heemskerck* and Gerrit Jansz the captain of *Zeehaen*.

With the southern hemisphere summer approaching, it was imperative that the expedition would leave as close to the scheduled date as possible. The comforting factor was that the jobs that would not be completed would not jeopardise the safety of the ship, so they could sail to Mauritius as planned, and complete the work on the ships while there.

*

'May GOD ALMIGHTY be pleased to give His Blessing to this Voyage. Amen.' Having taken his ink-tipped quill and penned those thirteen words with swirling flair, Tasman commenced his account of a voyage of exploration that would take him beyond the known world, and forever into the annals of maritime history.

By the time the voyage was completed, he would have sailed some 16,000 nautical miles – the equivalent of two-thirds of the Earth's circumference – on a mission that would be recognised as the most valuable voyage of exploration in more than a century, since Ferdinand Magellan's expedition circled the globe between 1519 and 1522.

Even so, there would be a dubious honour associated with this voyage: Tasman would become the first explorer to circumnavigate what is now Australia without sighting the mainland.

CHAPTER TEN

The Land that Wasn't Found

August 1642

After some frenetic weeks of toil by shipwrights and the crews, *Heemskerck* and *Zeehaen* finally weighed anchor and sailed clear of the port of Batavia on 14 August 1642. Conditions were ideal for them to clear the land, and the two ships ran seaward on a gentle north-east breeze with all sails set. Their plotted course saw them destined to arc to the west towards Sunda Strait, then once clear of the strait to sail 3000 nautical miles south-west to Mauritius.

Unfortunately, this great historic adventure got away to an inauspicious start, as recorded in Tasman's journal:

> ... in the evening the *Zeehaen* ran aground near the island of Rotterdam but got afloat again in the night

without any notable damage, after which we continued our voyage to the Straits of Sunda.

For much of the time under sail, Tasman would have dedicated himself to planning for the all-important voyage beyond Mauritius. It was vital that the men and ships were prepared in the best possible manner for a venture that was impossible to predict. Their course would cover an indeterminate number of nautical miles – thousands upon thousands – perhaps without stopping. When it came to the weather, they needed to be prepared for the worst quite possibly worse than they had ever experienced in their lives at sea.

Three weeks after departing Batavia, the lookout aboard *Heemskerck* called out that land had emerged over the horizon to the west: Mauritius. The 2000 square kilometre island, 500 nautical miles east of Madagascar, had been a Dutch outpost since 1598, when a squadron led by Admiral Wybrand van Warwyck landed on the east coast. He named the island Mauritius after the then stadtholder of the United Provinces of the Netherlands, Maurice van Nassau.

On 6 October, with both ships safely at anchor, Tasman and his officers organised work details and set them about their tasks. Problems had been detected on both ships while sailing from Batavia, but until he reached Mauritius, Tasman hadn't realised just how bad they were.

A report written on the condition of the ships by the island's governor, Adriaan van der Stel, mentioned 'how hopelessly unsatisfactory was the outfit of the ships for a voyage of such a nature, so that we have been compelled to provide them with firewood, canvas, cordage and various other necessaries'. He added that *Zeehaen* 'had put to sea with her upper work half-rotten, so that a great part of it had to be repaired and renewed'.

Much of the activity was now concentrated aboard the ships, but some men still had to be sent ashore to procure food:

> We were engaged nearly all day repairing our ropes and
> tackle; considering that our rigging was old, weak and
> not much to be depended on we added three more large
> ropes to the rigging on both sides of the main and
> foremast in order to steady the same; towards evening
> we got 8 head of goats and one pig from shore. In the
> morning we sent to the *Zeehaen* four out of the 8 goats
> received yesterday …

While the hunting party went away to do its job, the carpenters were kept busy. Some were dedicated to caulking the hulls and filling deck seams with pitch to minimise leaks, while those with ship-building skills were sent into the forests to gather all the timber they believed would be necessary to maintain the hulls, masts and spars for the duration of the voyage. The teak growing on Mauritius was superior to what was then available in Batavia; this timber, which would become a ship-builder's favourite, would not be introduced to Java from India until some decades later.

When it was confirmed that *Heemskerck* and *Zeehaen* were close to being ready for sea, Tasman sent details of men onto the island to collect two essential items: water and firewood. For hour after hour, pinnaces heavily laden with both items ran a shuttle between shore and ship. At the same time, other small boats were sent out with nets to fetch as many fish as possible. The catch from their first effort was enough to feed all 110 men.

Finally, after a month of work, the two ships were ready to put to sea, with the men 'strong and in good liking'. So, on 8 October, despite heavy rain and the presence of waterspouts, Tasman sent the signal up the mainmast that called for anchors to be weighed and a course set towards the beckoning expanse of wide open ocean:

> We shaped our course to the south-south-east, having the wind north-east, a weak top-gallant gale [meaning full sail was set]; at noon we turned our course to the south by east ...

Only four days into the passage, every man was made aware of the vulnerability of their ships. Despite Tasman's best endeavours to have the masts strengthened and reinforced with the addition of extra rigging, there was a failure.

It came just before daybreak, 'when the sea began to run high from the south': a splintering sound high up the mizzenmast of *Heemskerck* sent men ducking for cover. Fortunately, weakened as the mast was, it remained erect, no doubt thanks to quick action by the crew, who took the pressure off the rig by easing the sails. Soon afterwards, when it was decided that it was safe to go aloft, carpenters went up and strengthened the splintered section on both sides with the addition of fish plates – short lengths of timber.

After that, they continued without incident until 24 October, the day when these daring adventurers got their first real taste of a barbarous storm. Both ships canted alarmingly from side to side each time a massively powerful wave burst over the bulwark and surged like surf across the deck. Tasman later detailed the maelstrom in a seemingly nonchalant manner, even though he thought at the time there was every chance they might not survive:

> In the morning we took in our bonnets [strips of canvas attached to the foot of the fore-and-aft sails to increase their area], lowered our foresail down to the stem, and ran on before the wind with our mainsail only …
> because of the strong gale blowing. This gale was attended with hail and rain to such a degree that we feared the ship would not live through it, but at noon the storm somewhat abated … We could not see the

Zeehaen, for which reason we hauled to the wind to [wait] for her. At noon ... the wind south-west and south with a violent storm; we kept a sharp lookout for the *Zeehaen* but could not get sight of her. In the morning we sent a man to the masthead to look out for our partner whom he saw astern, of which we were full glad; the weather getting slightly better we again set our bonnets and drew up the foresail. Towards noon the *Zeehaen* again joined us.

The two ships were now in the middle of a maritime desert, where no man had been before. Tasman decided a cautious approach to navigation was essential. As a consequence, he sent a flag signal aloft, directing *Zeehaen*'s captain and senior officers to launch a pinnace and come aboard *Heemskerck* so a council of the expedition's hierarchy could be held to discuss matters.

Of principal importance was the sighting that day of rock weed and seagrass, signs that land might be close by. Accordingly, a key decision needed to be made: should a lookout be positioned at the masthead around the clock? If the vote was yes, then another decision would be necessary: 'what sum had best be fixed upon as a reward to be given to him who should first see land'. Tasman later noted in his daily record that the decision was 'to give three pieces-of-eight and a can of arrack [a coarse sugar-cane spirit] to whoever shall first see and observe land, shoals, sunken rocks, etc'.

Their caution also extended to reducing speed at night: they would either progress slowly under greatly reduced sail, or lie a-hull. Then another problem arose unexpectedly: dense fog. Suddenly visual contact between the ships was lost, so they adopted their only alternative: audible contact via occasional musket or cannon fire. It turned out that their concern about being near land was unwarranted: despite the sighting of even tree limbs and seals, these natural signs were a false alarm. They had been carried there by a swirling ocean current of a wide radius.

On 6 November, after a second mighty gale hammered the two ships, Tasman made the crucial decision to abandon their planned course and head north-east. Conditions were too rough for Captain Jansz and his officers to go aboard *Heemskerck* for another briefing, so Tasman used the seafarer's alternative method of communication:

Towards evening we dispatched to the officers of the *Zeehaen* the letter following, the said papers being enclosed in a wooden canister-shot-case, duly waxed and closely wrapped up in tarred canvas, which case we sent adrift from the stern part of the poop; the letter duly reached its destination and ran as follows:
To the officers of the Zeehaen
… We resolved with the members of our council and our second mates to shape our course north-east as far as 44° South Latitude, and then keep a due east

course as far as 150° Longitude; should you agree to this resolution then be pleased to hoist a flag at your stern as a sign of approval that we may duly ratify the resolution *Farewell. Actum* Heemskerck ... *this day November 9, 1642.*

Signed,

ABEL JANSZ TASMAN

Tasman subsequently recorded: 'After reading the above, those of the *Zeehaen* hoisted the Prince-flag [the state flag of the provinces of the Low Countries] in sign of approbation of our resolution.'

Two days later, at another meeting, it was agreed 'to run on in the parallel of about 44° South Latitude from our present longitude as far as 195° Longitude, being the meridian of the east side of New Guinea'.

This would lead to the discovery of the west coast of Tasmania soon afterwards, on 24 November 1642.

A frustrating few days followed the discovery as Tasman and his men tried to keep the land in sight while remaining a safe distance from an obviously inhospitable shore. Some time later, having rounded the south-eastern extremity of the land mass and turned north, they had to abandon their hopes of finding respite in a picturesque, east-facing and beach-lined bay:

In the evening about 5 o'clock we came before a bay which seemed likely to afford a good anchorage, upon

which we resolved with our ship's council to run into it.
We had nearly got into the bay when there arose so
strong a gale that we were obliged to take in sail and to
run out to sea again under reduced sail, seeing that it
was impossible to come to anchor in such a storm; in
the evening we resolved to stand out to sea during the
night under reduced sail to avoid being thrown on a
lee-shore by the violence of the wind ...

The following day, 30 November, Tasman signalled that another
attempt should be made to reach the anchorage. But again a
howling wind and rough seas prevented an approach. It is not
surprising that he would later name this place Storm Bay. More
than 150 years later, it would provide safe haven for the likes of
Captains James Cook, William Bligh and Tobias Furneaux
during their respective passages to that part of the world. It was
Furneaux who, in 1773, gave it the name of his ship, *Adventure*.

After forty-eight hours of trying to reach the shore,
Tasman surrendered to the power of the elements when the
raging wind blew *Heemskerck* and *Zeehaen* even further
offshore. Finally, conditions eased to the point where a course
could be held that would take them back towards the coast,
just to the north of the now suitably named Tasman Island, at
the northern seaward entrance to Storm Bay. The ships were
eventually steered up the coast and into a suitable anchorage
to the north of the bay. Tasman recounted in his journal what
happened after the ships came to anchor:

In the morning, the weather having become somewhat better, we set our topsails, the wind blowing from the west-south-west [and] made for the coast ... course kept north-north-west. In the afternoon we hoisted the white flag upon which our friends of the *Zeehaen* came on board of us, with whom we resolved that it would be best and most expedient, wind and weather permitting, to touch at the land the sooner the better, both to get better acquainted with its condition and to attempt to procure refreshments for our own behalf. We then got a breeze from eastward and made for the coast to ascertain whether it would afford a fitting anchorage; about one hour after sunset we dropped anchor in a good harbour, in 22 fathom, white and grey fine sand, a naturally drying bottom; for all which it behoves us to thank God Almighty with grateful hearts ...

They were anchored just to the north of what charts now identify as Cape Frederick Hendrick, on Tasmania's east coast, 24 nautical miles north of Tasman Island.

The next day, 2 December, Tasman sent *Heemskerck*'s pinnace and *Zeehaen*'s cock-boat (small rowboat) to investigate a bay that could be seen about a mile to the north-west of where the ships were anchored. The pinnace was under the command of *Heemskerck*'s Pilot Major, François Jacobsz (who, because of numerous names that could be applied to Dutch citizens, would become better recognised as Fransz Jacobsz Visscher) and manned by four musketeers and six rowers; the cock-boat was commanded by the second mate of *Zeehaen*. The men were directed to 'ascertain what facilities (as regards fresh water, refreshments, timber and the like) may be available there'.

Visscher and the second mate of *Zeehaen* returned to *Heemskerck* and provided the first ever European report on the flora, fauna and natural attributes of Van Diemen's Land:

> They found high but level land covered with vegetation
> (not cultivated, but growing naturally by the will of
> God), abundance of excellent timber, and a gently
> sloping watercourse in a barren valley, the said water of
> good quality ... they had heard certain human sounds
> and also sounds nearly resembling the music of a trump
> or a small gong not far from them though they had seen
> no one ... they had seen two trees about 2 or 2½
> fathom in thickness measuring from 60 to 65 feet from
> the ground to the lowermost branches, which trees bore
> notches made with flint implements, the bark having
> been removed for the purpose; these notches, forming a
> kind of steps to enable persons to get up the trees and
> rob the birds' nests in their tops, were fully 5 feet apart
> so that our men concluded that the natives here must be
> of very tall stature, or must be in possession of some sort
> of artifice for getting up the said trees ... on the ground
> they had observed certain footprints of animals, not
> unlike those of a tiger's claws ...

The most historic moment on this part of the mission came the following day. The story is best told by Tasman:

> In the afternoon we went to the south-east side of this bay [North Bay] in the boats; we carried with us a pole with the Company's mark carved into it, and a Prince-flag to be set up there, that those who shall come after us may become aware that we have been here, and have taken possession of the said land as our lawful property. When we had rowed about halfway with our boats it began to blow very stiffly, and the sea ran so high that the cock-boat of the *Zeehaen*, in which were seated the Pilot-major and Mr Gilsemans, was compelled to pull back to the ships, while we ran on with our pinnace. When we had come close inshore in a small inlet … the surf ran so high that we could not get near the shore without running the risk of having our pinnace dashed to pieces. We then ordered the carpenter aforesaid to swim to the shore alone with the pole and the flag; we made him plant the said pole with the flag at top into the earth, about the centre of the bay near four tall trees easily recognisable and standing in the form of a crescent. Our master carpenter … performed the work entrusted to him, we pulled with our pinnace as near the shore as we ventured to do; the carpenter aforesaid thereupon swam back to the pinnace through the surf. This work having been duly executed we pulled back to

the ships, leaving the above-mentioned as a memorial for those who shall come after us, and for the natives of this country, who did not show themselves, though we suspect some of them were at no great distance and closely watching our proceedings …

As if nature were doing its best to repel this 'intrusion', a violent storm swept in from the north-west just on sunset, not long after Tasman and his men had returned to the ships. With the wind howling through the rigging, the anchor cables drawn alarmingly taut, and night approaching, Tasman demanded a rapid response from his crew: a second anchor was released as added security, and the yards on each mast were lowered to the deck to reduce windage.

Fortunately, by the time first light was beckoning a new day, the wind had abated, so Tasman signalled that both ships should put to sea. When they hove *Heemskerck*'s second anchor, set for added security during the storm, it became apparent that they had been very fortunate: 'When we had weighed the said anchor and got it above the water we found that both the flukes were broken off so far that we hauled home nothing but the shank.' Luckily, the main anchor had held throughout the night and the ship remained safe.

The next day, 5 December, the weather once again changed the course of history. The two ships were about 6 nautical miles offshore, sailing in a west-north-west breeze that saw them holding a northerly course. They soon realised that the coastline they were observing was starting to sweep away to the north-west, which meant that in the prevailing conditions the ships could not hold a course that would keep them in contact with the land. It was decision time for Tasman.

Keeping in mind the directions for the expedition that had been issued prior to sailing from Batavia, Tasman signalled *Zeehaen* to steer as close to *Heemskerck* as Jansz dared so he could be informed of Tasman's decision. Tasman's journal reveals the formal version:

> … pursuant to the resolution of the 11th *ultimo* [to head
> for the east coast of New Guinea] we should direct our
> course due east, and on the said course run on to the
> full longitude of 195° or the Salomonis [Solomon]
> islands. At noon we then shaped our course due east for
> the purpose of making further discoveries …

With *Heemskerck* and *Zeehaen* no longer sailing north, the chance of further discoveries in this region had been erased. As a result, the east coast of the land of many titles – Terra Australis Incognita, Eendrachtsland, the Great South Land – would lie in wait for discovery for a further 128 years.

*

It was a rough but rapid trip across the sea that would one day bear Tasman's name: the strong wind and large following seas saw *Heemskerck* and *Zeehaen* average 6 knots for the more than 1000 nautical miles they covered before land was again sighted.

It was on the seventh day – 13 December – that the expedition provided Europe's cartographers with another exciting addition to their charts: a second history-making discovery in less than three weeks. Tasman recorded the event:

> Towards noon we saw a large, high-lying land, bearing south-east of us at about 15 miles distance. We turned our course to the south-east, making straight for this land, fired a gun and in the afternoon hoisted the white flag, upon which the officers of the *Zeehaen* came on board of us, with whom we resolved to touch at the said land as quickly as at all possible …

The spectacular high peaks on this mysterious west coast caused the commander to comment in his journal, '*groot hooch verheven landt*', meaning 'a large land, uplifted high'.

As the ships closed on the coast, the lookout at the masthead confirmed it would not be safe to land anywhere that could be seen, because of 'the high open sea running there in huge hollow waves and heavy swells'.

Interestingly, while Tasman had proved through the discovery of Van Diemen's Land that the southern coast of Eendrachtsland did not sweep towards the apparently ice-laden ocean to the south, he thought this new land he was observing was more than likely a part of Staten Landt (now

Staten Island), which was known to be at the southern tip of South America:

> To this land we have given the name of Staten Landt, in honour of Their High Mightinesses the States-General, since it could be quite possible that this land was connected with Staten Landt, although this is not certain. This land looks like being a very beautiful land and we trust that this is the mainland coast of the unknown south land ...

Three years later, after word of this discovery by Tasman reached VOC headquarters in Amsterdam, Dutch cartographers decided to recognise it as 'Nova Zeelandia' on their charts, a tribute to the Dutch province of Zeeland. Eventually it became New Zealand on British maps.

While impressions of the spectacular coast were noted and sketches continually created, *Heemskerck* and *Zeehaen* made slow progress north for more than 150 nautical miles. On 18 December, after spending forty-eight hours in a near calm, they entered a large, open bay and dropped anchor in 15 fathoms. Soon after this, as the sun descended, Tasman had his first contact with the Maori when two twin-hulled 'prows' approached the ships:

> The men in the two prows began to call out to us in the rough, hollow voice, but we could not understand a

word of what they said. We however called out to them
in answer, upon which they repeated their cries several
times, but came no nearer than a stone shot; they also
blew several times on an instrument of which the sound
was like that of a Moorish trumpet; we then ordered
one of our sailors (who had some knowledge of
trumpet-blowing) to play them some tunes in answer.
Those on board the *Zeehaen* ordered their second mate
(who had come out to India as a trumpeter and had in
the Mauritius been appointed second mate by the
council of that fortress and the ships) to do the same;
after this had been repeated several times on both sides,
and as it was getting more and more dark, those in the
native prows at last ceased and paddled off ...

This first ever communication between Maori and Europeans
was completely uneventful, but even so, Tasman decided he
should take added precautions while at anchor overnight. The
number of men on watch was doubled, and weapons were
prepared and placed on deck at the ready.

It was an incident-free evening, but not so the next day:
the Maori made a gruesome attack on the visitors, which
Tasman later described in great detail:

Early in the morning a boat manned with 13 natives
approached to about a stone's cast from our ships; they
called out several times but we did not understand them,

their speech not bearing any resemblance to the
vocabulary given us by the Honourable Governor-
General and Councillors of India, which is hardly to be
wondered at, seeing that it contains the language of the
Salomonis islands. Their boats consisted of two long
narrow prows side by side, over which a number of
planks or other seats were placed. The paddles [they use]
are upwards of a fathom in length, narrow and pointed
at the end. We repeatedly made signs for them to come
on board of us, showing them white linen and some
knives that formed part of our cargo. They did not come
nearer, however, but at last paddled back to shore. [A
while later] we saw 7 more boats put off from the shore,
one of which (high and pointed in front, manned with
17 natives) paddled round behind the *Zeehaen* while
another, with 13 able-bodied men in her, approached to
within half a stone's throw of our ship. The captain of
the *Zeehaen* now sent out to them his quartermaster with
her cock-boat with six paddlers in it … Just as the cock-
boat of the *Zeehaen* had put off from board those in the
prow before us, between the two ships, began to paddle
so furiously towards it that, when they were about
halfway slightly nearer to our ship, they struck the
Zeehaen's cock-boat so violently alongside with the stem
of their prow that it got a violent lurch, upon which the
foremost man in this prow of villains with a long, blunt
pike thrust the quartermaster, Cornelis Joppen, in the

neck several times with so much force that the poor man fell overboard. Upon this the other natives, with short thick clubs and with their paddles, fell upon the men in the cock-boat and overcame them by main force, in which fray three of our men were killed and a fourth got mortally wounded through the heavy blows. The quartermaster and two sailors swam to our ship. After this outrageous and detestable crime the murderers sent the cock-boat adrift, having taken one of the dead bodies into their prow and thrown another into the sea ...

It's little surprise that Tasman gave the scene of this slaughter the name Murderer's Bay. Today it is known by the more pleasant name of Golden Bay.

With the commander convinced that there was 'not hope to enter into any friendly relations with these people', and that the 'detestable deed of these natives ... must teach us to consider the inhabitants of this country as enemies', Tasman ordered that anchors be weighed and the two ships continue to sail north. On departing, they observed twenty-two prows on the beach which, it appeared, were being prepared to give chase. So, as a parting gesture, two cannon shots were lobbed in the natives' direction from *Heemskerck* to quell any thoughts of aggression. It worked.

Because of the lie of the land that was visible as the ships headed offshore, and considering the run of the current and the form of the seas, Tasman was convinced they were in a large bay, which accordingly he named Zeehaen's Bight. In fact, as Captain Cook would prove years later, it was the western entrance to what became known as Cook Strait, separating New Zealand's North and South Islands. Golden (Murderer's) Bay is located on the north-westernmost corner of the South Island. The cape to the north of the strait, Tasman named Kaap Pieter Boreels; it was renamed Cape Egmont by Captain Cook 126 years later.

Heemskerck and *Zeehaen* next continued on a course north along the coast, which stretched as far as the eye could see. Before long, though, the new year of 1643 delivered a welcome no sailor would desire: one of the storms for which the Tasman Sea is today infamous began to brew. It came just after the ships had anchored close to the coast, and its ferocity was such that Tasman called for the yardarms to be lowered to the deck to reduce windage and thus take pressure off the already strained anchor hawser. That still wasn't enough: it was apparent to the commander that there was every chance his ship would soon drag anchor and be washed onto the shore, so he urgently ordered that the topmasts be lowered and another anchor deployed. Relief came the following morning when the storm abated and the ships were able to get under way unscathed.

By 5 January, there was a pressing need aboard both ships for water supplies to be replenished. Eventually a bay was sighted where there might be a source of fresh water, so Tasman called for the ships to come to anchor as close as possible to the shore.

A detail of men was sent off in the pinnace to investigate. Some time later they returned and reported that while they had seen a stream, the boat had not been able to get to the beach because of the surge of the surf. Even if they *had* got there, the men would have been concerned for their own safety, because 'they saw in several places on the highest hills from 30 to 35 persons, men of tall stature ... armed with sticks and clubs'.

The same circumstance arose the next day when the pinnace from *Zeehaen* was sent in search of water. The sight of hostile natives onshore caused the captain, Gerrit Jansz, and the pilot major to agree 'to abstain from exposing the small craft and the men to such great peril, seeing that there was still a long voyage before them and the men and the small craft were greatly wanted by the ships'.

Frustration loomed for all. Tasman could only call for a gathering of the ships' council to decide what course of action to follow. With little hesitation it was resolved that they would continue north along the coast they were currently skirting, until it was possible to turn east into the Pacific Ocean and continue with the voyage as directed by van Diemen and his associates in Batavia.

After a few days the two ships reached what was believed to be the northernmost tip of 'Staten Landt', sailing along its western shore between 4 and 6 January. They observed that the land comprised mainly hummock-like hills and sand dunes. Tasman named the very conspicuous, north-westernmost headland Cape Maria van Diemen, in honour of the wife of the governor-general. He also provided cartographers with an additional name for their charts: Three Kings Islands, a group of thirteen islands 30 nautical miles north of the cape.

The two ships anchored near the cape for a short period, and while there Tasman saw his first indication that he might have found the much-desired access into the Pacific Ocean:

> Here we found ourselves in a very strong current,
> which set us to eastward, while at the same time a
> strong sea came running from the north-east, which not
> a little rejoiced us, because we hoped thus to find a
> passage [into the South Seas].

There was cause for more excitement the following day when the two ships began sailing, unimpeded, into the wide blue ocean then lying off *Heemskerck*'s bow. With the helmsman holding a course to the north-east, Tasman commenced the next stage of his voyage, one that would take them into warm tropical waters:

> The sea runs very strongly from the eastward, so that
> there is no ground for us to suppose any great mainland
> to lie east of us … The heavy swells are now running
> from the south-east. This water-route from Batavia to
> Chyly [Chile] is a very smooth one, so that there is no
> objection to making use of it …

Heemskerck and *Zeehaen* were then at the start of a 7500 nautical mile anti-clockwise loop, first to the north-east then north and west. The commander was no doubt satisfied by what had been achieved to date, even though he had been unable to pursue the coast of Van Diemen's Land to the north due to the unfavourable weather.

Had he managed to do so, one can only wonder what the consequences might have been. What if he had ventured just an additional 200 nautical miles north from the north-east corner of Van Diemen's Land and discovered the eastern side of what would later be known as New Holland? It could well have caused world history to be very different from what it is today: 'New Holland' might have become just that.

The need for fresh water was becoming increasingly pressing as they headed into the Pacific, even though rainwater could be captured by sails suspended horizontally above the deck during the now all-too-infrequent storms. For Tasman, there was only one solution to this problem: sail towards a group of islands, 1000 nautical miles to the north-east, that had been discovered by Willem Schouten and Jacob Le Maire twenty-seven years earlier – now part of Tonga. On 19 January, a relieved Tasman wrote of his approach to this group:

About two o'clock in the afternoon we saw land bearing from us east by north, at about 8 miles distance. We held our course towards it but could not make it owing to the sharpness of the wind. This island bears a

resemblance to two women's breasts when it bears from
you east by north at 6 miles distance ... We should have
greatly liked to sail close along it in order to ascertain
whether we should have any chance of getting fresh
water or refreshments there, but we could not get nearer
to it ...

They had no option but to sail on towards other islands they
could see in the distance – islands in the group that Schouten
and Le Maire had not sighted, in particular Tongatapu, Eua
and Nomuka, which are in the southern region of the group.

Tasman would later describe the interaction between his
men and the natives, who had obviously never encountered
Europeans before. When the ships were at anchor there was
initially much bartering between the two sides, then, when a
comfortable rapport was established, the islanders dared to
venture aboard the ships:

We filled a rummer of wine for them, from which we
first drank ourselves lest they should think we were
going to poison them or do them other harm; having
taken the rummer they poured out the wine and took
the rummer onshore with them. After some time an
aged man came on board of us to whom all the others
paid honour, so that we concluded him to be one of
their chiefs. We conducted him to the cabin; he did us
reverence by inclining his head down to our feet; we

paid our respects to him in return after our own fashion, and showed him a cup with fresh water which he showed us by signs to be obtainable onshore; we then presented him with a knife, a small looking-glass, and a piece of dungaree [a coarse calico]. As they were leaving the cabin one of the natives was caught in the act of stealing the skipper's pistol and a pair of slippers. We took these articles from him again without showing the least dissatisfaction …

With cordial relations established – which explains why Captain Cook years later identified these as the Friendly Isles – Tasman directed men to go onto the island and collect water and provisions, something that had not been done since they had left Mauritius. Much to the delight of the crews, they were able to go ashore in complete safety for the first time since departing Van Diemen's Land. At one stage a single expedition onshore was able to collect eight casks of water and was provided with 'four live hogs and a number of fowls, coconuts, bananas, etc'.

On 1 February, when Tasman decided that they had been 'provided with plenty of refreshments and that we [had] got nearly all our casks filled with water', it was time to continue the voyage. The new course that would take the ships to the northern side of New Guinea was to the north-west … and it would lead to yet another important discovery a few days later: the islands in the northern archipelago of Fiji.

However, this was a discovery that came close to bringing this expedition to a dramatic end. On 6 February both ships appeared trapped in a minefield of reefs. Tasman wrote:

> In the morning we saw land, to wit three small islets, on all sides surrounded by shoals and reefs; we tacked about to the south and saw a large reef to westward stretching as far as the south, which we sincerely regretted; this land is fully 8 or 9 miles in length; straight ahead there were also breakers which we were unable to pass. Seeing that we could clear neither the reef straight ahead nor another which lay north of us we observed to leeward a small space about two ships' lengths wide where there were no breakers; for this we made since there was no other way of escape; we passed between the rocks in 4 fathom, though not without great anxiety; all about here there are reefs and 18 or 19 islands, but the shoals which abound here and are very dangerous render it impossible for ships to pass between them

It was an incredibly lucky escape, and as it became increasingly apparent that they were surrounded by reefs, any desire to anchor and take time to investigate the numerous islands they could see was promptly eliminated. They would simply record the first sighting of these islands by Europeans.

Visscher suggested that they take up a course to the west, but Tasman disregarded the advice. However, had he adopted his pilot major's recommendation and sailed due west on the same latitude as Fiji, they would have discovered the Great Barrier Reef and the east coast of the Great South Land at a point around 500 nautical miles south of the tip of what is known today as Cape York. By sailing north from there, they would have proved the existence of a strait between New Guinea and the Great South Land. These discoveries would have come some 130 years before Captain Cook's historic achievement.

Instead, Tasman's decision was to continue to the north-west towards New Guinea. Even that passage was not without its share of danger. His journal entry for 9 February recorded:

> The wind blowing from the north with rain and a strong gale. We kept sailing with our mainsail set, the sea being very rough and running very high from the north and north-west … For the last five days past we have been without seeing either sun, moon or stars. In the evening we lowered the foresail down to the stem and lay-to with mainsail and mizzen-sail.

With the Fijian Islands and their navigation hazards merging into the watery horizon astern, Tasman decided it was time to head home – which was still some 5700 nautical miles, and more than three months, away. In his own mind he had done everything possible that had been asked of him, so from this point, there was little if any exploration to be done.

If there was one lasting memory of the arduous and slow passage towards the north coast of New Guinea, it was the thirty or so days during which, due to the monsoon season, it rained every day, often torrentially.

Heemskerck and *Zeehaen* were navigated safely through the chains of well-identified islands, large and small, scattered between New Guinea and Batavia.

In the second week of June 1643, as the two ships were gliding along the north coast of Java towards their home port, Tasman could contemplate what he had achieved during the previous ten months. It was a history-making voyage, inasmuch as he had discovered new lands and shown that the Great South Land was separated from any hypothetical continent in the far south. He could also take pride in the fact that the voyage had gone virtually without incident, and that only ten of his initial crew of 110 had died, including the four who had been murdered at the hands of the Maori in New Zealand.

The final entry in his journal was dated 15 June 1643:

In the morning at daybreak I went to Batavia in the pinnace. God be praised and thanked for this happy voyage. Amen.

CHAPTER ELEVEN

Success and Failure

Late 1643

Incredibly, when Tasman returned to Batavia with what he believed was remarkable news relating to the discovery of previously unknown lands, his superiors, including van Diemen, were far from impressed. Yes, they rewarded him and his crew with the usual 'handsome' financial bonus for their success – Tasman and his officers received two months' additional pay, and the sailors one month's – even though the commander had failed to achieve what had been expected of him.

The Governor-General and the Heren XVII in Amsterdam recorded this disappointment:

> [Tasman] had been to some extent remiss in investigating the situation, conformation and nature of the lands and peoples discovered, and left the main part of this task to be executed by some more inquisitive successor …

They were firm in the belief that Tasman should have been more thorough in his efforts to ascertain if there was any possibility of trade opportunities in these newly discovered territories which, it was hoped, might be rich in gold and silver and inhabited by civilised people who cultivated fertile lands. He was also deemed to be neglectful in not having gone ashore so he could explore those lands more thoroughly and search determinedly for Torres Strait.

Fortunately, it wasn't long before van Diemen's disappointment, and his intention to employ a 'more inquisitive successor', were on the ebb. Tasman and Visscher were summoned to headquarters to be told they were being re-assigned to complete their previous commission. Tasman would again be the commander, and Visscher the pilot major and cartographer, for a three-ship expedition. The mission statement from the governor-general read:

> [We] intend to have the unknown land situated between Nova Guinea and the unknown South-land discovered and surveyed by way of Banda by Commander Tasman and Pilot-major Frans Visscher with two yachts and a pinnace [in this case a galiot, a small, shallow draft coastal trading vessel fitted with leeboards], in February next; the said exploration to begin from Cape Keer-weer ... and with God's aid to end at Willems River (being the northernmost extremity of the known South-land), in which

intervening region (extending to a length of fully 400
miles) there are likely to be found sundry lands and
islands, not far distant from Java; this expedition being
also charged with the task of ascertaining whether the
two large lands aforementioned are connected with
each other, or are separated by channels; certainty about
this point being highly desirable with a view to the
further exploration of the newly discovered South-
lands, and of the passage to the South Sea and to Chili;
on which account it is expedient that the said point
should be investigated as soon as possible, the more so
since such investigation can be conveniently completed
within the space of five or six months ...

An entry from van Diemen's diary at the time implied his
confidence in Tasman's success, and the company's eagerness
to pursue profit-making ventures in the region, and maybe
even discover the legendary land of Beach:

By September next, when the projected discovery of the
north coast of the South-land is likely to have been
successfully effected, we also intend to dispatch two or
three yachts for the further exploration of the newly
discovered South-lands, with express orders to ascertain
what advantages for the Company may be obtained
there. They will especially have to inquire whether in
these vast regions there are any silver, gold or copper-

mines, which we deem very likely, seeing they are situated under a climate especially adapted for such mines, and resembling that of the silver and gold-bearing regions of Peru, Chili, China and Japan …

In elaborating, van Diemen declared that, should a passage to 'the great South Sea' be discovered, it would no doubt provide a 'short and convenient route to Chili', something that would be 'a matter of the utmost importance and of great advantage to the company'. It would enable the VOC 'to form trade connections with the vast and renowned country of Chili', and present the opportunity for 'important dealings with the Chilese, and by means of this route to snatch rich booty from the Castilian [Spanish], who would never dream of our ships coming that way'. He intended to prove this point by immediately sending a flotilla of cargo-laden ships to 'Chili', should the route be found.

The three vessels chosen for the expedition came from the existing VOC fleet in the East Indies. They were *Limmen*, with a burthen of 60 lasts (about 120 tons) and carrying a crew of forty-five sailors and eleven soldiers; *Zeemeeuw*, 50 lasts (100 tons), with thirty-five crew and six soldiers, and the considerably smaller pinnace or tender *Bracq*, which had only fourteen crew. The ships were loaded with provisions that it was anticipated would last eight months, although additional supplies would be taken aboard wherever possible during the voyage. *Limmen* and *Zeemeeuw* also carried in their holds a wide range of items for bartering should trading opportunities be found.

Although it was the monsoon season, official records reveal that on 30 January 1644 – just three weeks after the VOC's formal resolution was declared – the small flotilla 'put off to sea in the name of God … after due muster', with Tasman's house flag, which had been hoisted to the top of *Limmen*'s mainmast, wafting proudly in the breeze.

While Tasman no doubt penned details of the voyage into his hard-bound journal on a daily basis, that account has disappeared. Even so, much of what occurred can be gleaned from snippets of information from the period.

Tasman's directions from the VOC instructed him to first sail 750 nautical miles east to Macassar, but while there no mention of the then secret mission's objectives were to be revealed for fear that word might reach ships of other nations. Next, they were to proceed to Ambon and Banda and take on fresh provisions. Tasman and Visscher were directed to visit the governors at these ports and seek 'special information they might possess touching the lands and islands east of Banda'.

With Banda behind them, the commander and his pilot major were confronted by a wide range of challenges as they traversed the waters towards the coast of New Guinea. They knew that fast-flowing tidal currents and the proliferation of shallows close to the coast could wreak havoc, possibly causing them to run aground. Caution when under sail and an ever-alert lookout at the masthead made for the best forms of protection. The most seasoned sailors – those with years of experience in the region – would also have been keeping an eye on the weather. They knew all too well of the fearsome and ferocious winds a monsoon could deliver – storms that could blow the three ships into oblivion.

Nearly forty years after the voyage of Luís Vaz de Torres, the Spanish had still managed to keep the existence of Torres Strait a secret. But – no doubt influenced by the suspicions of cartographer Hessel Gerritsz – there was some level of belief within the VOC that 'Nova Guinea' and 'the unknown South-land' might be separated by a strait. One of the directives issued to Tasman ordered him to sail south off the coast of New Guinea, to approximately 8 degrees latitude. Once there he should:

> ... cautiously cross the shallow bay situated there
> [before] sending off the galiot *Bracq* into the bay for the
> space of two or three days, with the object of finding
> out within this vast bay any eventual passage to the
> South sea ...

It was here that Tasman went close to making a monumental discovery – one that could, quite possibly, have changed the course of history. Had *Bracq*'s passage east gone a little further, then it is very likely that Torres Strait would have been found. To hypothesise: should that have happened, Tasman would have followed another of his directions from the VOC, to sail east and then south, the hope being he would reach Van Diemen's Land. Such a discovery would have made Captain Cook's search for Terra Australis Incognita in 1770 irrelevant.

Interestingly, Tasman's sailing instructions for this voyage did refer to Van Diemen's Land: should New Guinea be found to be 'divided from the large known South-land', he was then to sail to 17 degrees south – the farthest south that Carstensz had sailed – then continue 'as far as the newly discovered Van Diemens land'.

The Dutch obviously thought it possible that the east coast of the Gulf of Carpentaria might extend all the way south to the west coast of Van Diemen's Land, which Tasman had already discovered. In short, all possibilities were being considered.

Regardless, should he get to 17 degrees south, he was to follow that coast to wherever it led, possibly Willems River (now the Ashburton River), discovered by Janszoon and Jacobszoon on the west coast of Eendrachtsland.

Here, once again, Tasman could be seen to have failed by not fully investigating the 'bay' they were crossing. At its narrowest point, Torres Strait is only 80 nautical miles wide, and there are ample islands to be observed as well, yet it is obvious that the commander decided to turn south before 'finding out within this vast bay any eventual passage to the South sea'. What makes this decision even more curious is that, on his previous voyage of discovery, Tasman demonstrated an innate skill in deciphering his surroundings simply through observing the run of the ocean swells and the direction and strength of currents, factors that indicated for him the presence or absence of land in the vicinity. It is common knowledge for sailors today that one of the key challenges when navigating Torres Strait is the strength and direction of the currents, which flow to and from the Coral Sea, in the western sector of the Pacific Ocean.

Obviously convinced there was no strait to be found, Tasman would have signalled through the hoisting of a large flag that the three vessels should set a course for the known coast along which Janszoon (in 1606) and Carstensz (in 1623) had sailed.

On reaching 17 degrees south, where the Staten River enters the Gulf of Carpentaria, Tasman continued on for around 100 nautical miles before realising the coast took a 90-degree turn to the north-west. This observation must have led to much speculation by the commander and his officers: just where did this coast go, and what form did this land mass take? The one thing they did know was that they were again discovering a new coast.

It appears that much of the exploration was carried out from some distance offshore, possibly because of the suspected presence of shallows and reefs. As a result, on three occasions Tasman named conspicuous points of land that he believed were part of the mainland, but as Matthew Flinders would prove 158 years later, all were located on islands in the gulf. These are known today (respectively) as Cape Van Diemen on

Mornington Island, Cape Vanderlin on Vanderlin Island, Observation Island, and Cape Maria on Maria Island in the south-western corner of the gulf.

If Tasman struggled to distinguish the coast from islands, he was probably even more confused by the tides in the gulf. This is one of the few places in the world where only one high tide a day can occur, instead of the usual two. This is because the gulf is such a great distance from the tidal influences of the Indian Ocean, and also due to the narrowness of Torres Strait, which tends to dam tidal flows coming in from the Coral Sea and Pacific Ocean. It was not until forty-three years later, when Sir Isaac Newton explained the tidal phenomena in his classic work *Philosophiae Naturalis Principia Mathematica* (*Mathematical Principles of Natural Philosophy*), that there came a better understanding of the cause and timing of tides. The famous 1687 publication explained the laws of motion and universal gravitation.

Having sailed along the southern coast of the gulf for some 300 nautical miles, Tasman called on his three ships to anchor in the south-western corner at a destination he named Limmens Bocht (Limmen's Bight). From there, he set a course north along the west coast of the gulf, leaving today's Groote Eylandt on his starboard side, then onwards to what we know as Arnhem Land, discovered by Carstensz's expedition of 1623.

Once there, Tasman could be satisfied that he had completed one part of his mission, and that he could now report on the basis of his observations – after going ashore at times – that there was no reason for the VOC to consider establishing any form of operation along this coast.

His next challenge was to navigate a way around the reef-strewn Wessel Islands north of Arnhem Land, then return south-west to the mainland coast so he could conduct further exploration. The ships would have been making remarkably slow progress at this time because of the danger from the numerous reefs that lurked just below the sea's surface. Adding to this challenge was the enormous tidal range along the north-western coast of the mainland: in some places up to 10 metres.

From here, Tasman completed his mission as directed, sailing along Australia's northern coast, to the known coast of Eendrachstland that began at Willems River, before returning to Batavia. All three ships completed the voyage unscathed and arrived at their home port on 4 August 1644, after an absence of six months, and having sailed more than 5500 nautical miles, more than 2000 nautical miles of which was along Australia's northern coast.

While fine details are scarce, this voyage can be recognised as a momentous achievement by Tasman and his expedition, especially when the dangers they faced from navigational hazards, like reefs and fast-flowing unpredictable tides are considered. His charts confirmed that the entire western and northern coasts of a land that would soon be recognised officially as 'Nieuw-Holland' had been observed and mapped. However, because the expedition had failed to venture further into the 'bay' between New Guinea and the land to the south, these two shorelines would continue to be identified as a single coast, the southern part of which appeared on Dutch charts as the South Land.

Once again, the Governor-General and his councillors weren't happy with the results of the voyage, as they made clear in a General Missive dated 23 December. Tasman and his crews

> had found nothing that could be turned to profit, but had only come across naked beach-roving wretches, destitute even of rice, and not possessed of any fruits worth mentioning, miserably poor, and in many places of a very bad disposition ... We are left quite ignorant what the soil of this South-land produces or contains, since the men have done nothing but sail along the coast; he who wants to find out what the land yields, must walk over it in every direction; the voyagers pretend this to have been out of their power, which may to some extent be true ... [We intend] to have everything more closely investigated by more vigilant and courageous persons than have hitherto been employed on this service; for the exploration of unknown regions can by no means be entrusted to the first comer ...

Regardless of this harsh reaction, Tasman's career continued to flourish. Three months after returning to Batavia, he became a member of the Court of Justice there, and then spent the next five years leading VOC trade missions through Asian waters. In late 1649, he was charged with having hanged one of his crew without fair trial. Having been found guilty, he was suspended from his rank of commander, fined and ordered to pay an appropriate compensation to the family of the dead sailor. He was reinstated to his post just eighteen months later, however, and spent his remaining years in Batavia, where he became a wealthy trader. He died on 10 October 1659, aged fifty-six, and was survived by his second wife Jannetjie and daughter Claesjen.

Tasman had carried his nation's flag further than any other Dutchman of that era: more than 21,000 nautical miles. Yet his second expedition would later be recognised as representing the end of major Dutch exploration across the entire region during the seventeenth century.

The wording of the General Missive leaves no doubt that the Dutch were by then realising the land Tasman and others had explored offered little in the way of long term commercial benefits for the VOC. Consequently, there was a waning of interest in further exploration to the south. The death of Anthony van Diemen in Batavia in 1645 closed out any thoughts the Dutch might have had of further extensive exploration in the region, at least for the time being. He had been the driving force behind these investigative endeavours, whereas his successor, Cornelis van der Lijn, held no such interest.

Despite this, the Dutch are known to have made contact with the west and north coasts on at least ten occasions over the next four decades, some in passing while others led to additional mapping and sketching of coastal features. The most noteworthy came on 28 April 1656 when the VOC ship *Vergulde Draeck (Gilt Dragon)*, captained by Pieter Albertszoon, was wrecked on shoals 50 nautical miles north of the Swan River, near what is Ledge Point today.

Vergulde Draeck was carrying a cargo that included eight chests of silver, worth near 800,000 guilders, and 193 passengers, only 75 of whom reached shore. To their good fortune one of the ship's small boats was salvaged, which enabled seven of the crew to sail to Batavia and raise the alarm. Two ships, *Goede Hoop (Good Hope)* and *Witte Valcq (White Falcon)*, were immediately despatched south to rescue the survivors, but when they reached the scene of the wreck all had disappeared. Eleven men from the rescue ships were also lost during this unsuccessful mission. On three further occasions, ships were directed to the coast in a bid to find survivors from *Vergulde Draeck*, but their quests were also fruitless. Now it was time for the British to enter the arena and look to solving the remaining mysteries of the Great South Land.

CHAPTER TWELVE

Enter the Pirate

July 1687

Some forty-three years after Tasman's second voyage of discovery, a British vessel was traversing the Pacific Ocean with very different purposes in mind. The ruffians who made up the crew of *Cygnet* led the carefree life of pirates – yet as they approached the port of Mindanao in the southern Philippines, their thoughts were full of mutiny, not plunder.

Cygnet, under the captaincy of Charles Swan and with William Dampier as navigator, had in company a smaller, unnamed tender commanded by a Captain Teat and crewed by fifty men, 'besides slaves'. Swan, it would appear, was a reluctant captain of pirates. He had been forced into the role of privateer after his commercial endeavours with traders on the Spanish coast in Central America failed and he sold his cargo at a loss. While he knew what was expected of him, he struggled to relate to his repugnant and recalcitrant crew – so much so that a fractious atmosphere had developed not long after their departure from Mexico. This situation had worsened as the sea miles passed under the keel, especially after it was realised by the men – who were already on strict rations – that they might well run out of food before they reached Guam, their first port of call.

Concern had grown with the passing of each day, and eventually led the men to make serious suggestions that they would, if necessary, resort to cannibalism – and it was the officers who would be the food.

Thirty-seven year old navigator William Dampier was a man with two decades of seafaring adventure already behind him. He would later reflect on this disconcerting period in his much-used journal:

> It was well for Captain Swan that we got sight of it
> [Guam] before our provision was spent, of which we
> had but enough for three days more; for, as I was
> afterwards informed, the men had contrived first to kill
> Captain Swan and eat him when the victuals was gone,
> and after him all of us who were accessory in promoting
> the undertaking of this voyage. This made Captain
> Swan say to me after our arrival at Guam, 'Ah!
> Dampier, you would have made them but a poor meal;'
> for I was as lean as the captain was lusty and fleshy.

With food stocks replenished in Guam, *Cygnet* and the unnamed tender accompanying her sailed 1300 nautical miles to the west – threading their way through countless islands, stopping at some and bypassing others – until they reached Mindanao. The reason for choosing this destination was that it was not under Spanish control; the *Cygnet* crew knew they would not be welcomed in any Spanish port as the centuries-old Iberian distaste for the English had only been deepened by the humiliating defeat of the Spanish Armada in 1588. The fact that *Cygnet* was an English ship, and not owned by the detested Dutch – who had enslaved the residents of many nearby islands – meant that she and her men were well received by Mindanao's sultan and his brother Raja Laut, who probably hoped that the visitors would settle on this island and bring it greater wealth, as previous English visitors had suggested would happen one day. Swan rode the wave of welcome by befriending Raja Laut and spending much of his time ashore.

Many of the men were by then even less impressed by Swan's leadership. Their previous passage had been arduous, sailing in stifling, tropical weather and often in teeming rain, an environment that reignited the flames of tension between captain and crew. Onshore, Swan continued to be callous and cruel towards his men. Not surprisingly, then, it was agreed by the majority that they could not continue under his leadership: Captain Swan had to go.

A few of the crew didn't wait, but jumped ship, some running off into the hinterland so they could never be found, others purchasing a large canoe from the islanders, their intention being to sail it more than 300 nautical miles south-west to Borneo. Unfortunately for these men, Swan got word of their plan, intervened, and took possession of the canoe.

There was a growing concern that, under these circumstances, especially given the generous hospitality of Raja Laut, *Cygnet* might never leave Mindanao. This led the remaining crew to split into two opposing sides. Those with money moved ashore and were happy to stay there, while those without stayed on the ship and sank their sorrows by becoming increasingly drunk on a punch they had concocted.

'[Their] disorderly actions deterred me from going aboard', wrote Dampier, 'for I did ever abhor drunkenness, which now our men that were aboard abandoned themselves wholly to.'

It was at this point that the crew decided to initiate their mutiny: they demanded that the socialising Swan meet them aboard *Cygnet* to discuss where they were headed next, and when. Swan refused.

By now the tender, under the command of Captain Teat, had been rendered unseaworthy by the voracious appetite of the wood-eating teredo, or shipworm. The hull below the waterline was eaten through 'like honeycombs', according to Dampier. Teat, who had experienced his own falling out with Swan, took advantage of this situation by joining the other ship's disgruntled crew. Dampier's journal revealed what followed:

> Captain Teat … laid hold on this opportunity to be
> revenged for his injuries and aggravated the matter to
> the height; persuading the men to turn out Captain

Swan from being commander in hopes to have commanded the ship himself … [T]hey consented to what Teat proposed, and immediately all that were aboard bound themselves by oath to turn Captain Swan out and to conceal this design from those that were ashore until the ship was under sail; which would have been presently if the surgeon or his mate had been aboard; but they were both ashore, and they thought it no prudence to go to sea without a surgeon: therefore the next morning they sent ashore one John Cookworthy to hasten off either the surgeon or his mate by pretending that one of the men in the night broke his leg by falling into the hold …

If Captain Swan had yet come aboard he might have dashed all their designs; but he neither came himself, as a captain of any prudence and courage would have done … So we left Captain Swan and about 36 men ashore in the city, and six or eight that ran away; and about 16 we had buried there, the most of which died by poison. The natives are very expert at poisoning and do it upon small occasions …

The 14th day of January 1687 at three of the clock in the afternoon we sailed from the river of Mindanao, designing to cruise before Manila.

With *Cygnet* well gone, Swan and the other remnants of the ship's crew at first continued to enjoy their new life, but before long Swan was regretting his decision to stay, and his desire to return home increased. Sadly, it would prove to be a yearning with a fatal sting in its tail.

When a Dutch ship came to anchor off Mindanao, it was an opportunity too good for Swan to ignore. Carrying his few possessions – and some 5000 pounds of *Cygnet's* ill-gotten gains he had managed to purloin – Swan got to a beach, found a canoe, launched it and set out towards the Dutch ship.

However, he was spotted, pursued and caught by warriors loyal to Raja Laut. On reaching the canoe, they capsized it, and while Swan was helpless in the water, they speared him to death.

Meanwhile, *Cygnet*, with John Read as captain and Dampier still navigator, threaded her way through the many islands of the Philippines, towards her first intended port of call, Manila. Read had been elected captain by the remaining crew after he alerted them to the contents of Swan's journal, which he had managed to peruse surreptitiously. In it, Swan had noted his impressions of many of the crew, several of which were unfavourable. Swan's opinions had contributed to the crew's anger, leading to the mutiny.

This on-going passage would prove to be profitable for the pirates, as they were able to capture two Spanish ships and claim some booty about 8 leagues from their destination.

Not surprisingly, after sailing all the way from Mexico, *Cygnet* was the worse for wear; structural problems were evident, she needed to be re-rigged, and a general refit was also in order. After she left Manila, the decision was made to sail north in search of a place where the work could be carried out in relative safety and shelter.

Yet, as Dampier wrote, the passage north was not without incident. A mishap in mid-February had the potential to bring their voyage to an end:

> … we sailed hence with the wind at north. But going out we struck on a rock, where we lay two hours: it was very smooth water and the tide of flood, or else we should there have lost our ship. We struck off a great piece of our rudder, which was all the damage that we received, but we more narrowly missed losing our ship this time than in any other in the whole voyage. This is a very dangerous shoal because it does not break, unless probably it may appear in foul weather.

It was 16 March 1687 when a suitable site for *Cygnet* to be careened was found among a group of islands off the coast of Cambodia. Additionally, this landfall provided the timber needed to make a spare main-topmast and planks suitable to sheath the hull below the waterline. A new suit of sails was also made and fitted while *Cygnet* was there.

Once re-floated and ready to go, the chosen course for *Cygnet* was to the south. This would prove to be a torrid, storm-lashed and sail-busting passage of over 1500 nautical miles towards the island of Timor. For much of the time, the rain was torrential, the course often had to be changed to dodge violent waterspouts, and on one occasion, when caught in a calm, the crew had to use their oars as prodders to fend the ship off a sheer cliff:

> But we got out our oars and rowed, yet all in vain; for
> the tide set wholly on one of the small islands that we
> were forced with might and main strength to bear off
> the ship by thrusting with our oars against the shore,
> which was a steep bank, and by this means we presently
> drove away clear of danger …

The crew had no wish to stop at Timor, which at that time was a stronghold of both the Portuguese and the Dutch: they would head straight into the sea that bears that island's name.

As *Cygnet* sailed deeper into this region, Dampier's ever-active mind was extending way beyond his immediate experiences, back to the destinations he had visited, and the myriad of natural studies he had documented. He was also looking forward … to what the future might hold for him.

He was envisaging Mindanao as the pivotal location for English settlement in the East Indies — a port from which English trade and influence could be expanded throughout the entire Asian region:

> As the island Mindanao lies very convenient for trade,
> so, considering its distance, the way thither may not be

over-long and tiresome. The course that I would choose should be to set out of England about the latter end of August, and to pass round Tierra del Fuego, and so, stretching over towards New Holland, coast it along that shore till I came near to Mindanao ... returning you may probably touch somewhere on New Holland, and so make some profitable discovery in these places without going out of your way. And to speak my thoughts freely, I believe it is owing to the neglect of this easy way that all that vast tract of Terra Australis which bounds the South Sea is yet undiscovered ...

It is quite possible that this theory caused Dampier to encourage his captain and crew to sail *Cygnet* to the barely known northern coast of New Holland, just 250 nautical miles south of their current position.

His interest in this little-known land mass no doubt stemmed from the somewhat vague outlines of its coastline on navigation charts aboard *Cygnet*: charts he would have pored over for countless hours to plot the ship's course, but also to sate his curiosity and fire his unquenchable imagination.

The charts he was using would have been influenced by the work of VOC cartographers in Amsterdam, much of their detail being based on the exploratory endeavours of Dutch seafarers in the first half of the seventeenth century. The fact that Dutch exploration had all but dried up since the voyages of Abel Tasman four decades earlier could also have prompted

215

his decision to sail to New Holland on behalf of England, 'to see what that country would afford us'.

When Dampier was navigating and studying the maps aboard *Cygnet* it would have been obvious that there were still sizeable sections of this region that remained uncharted. In the south, nothing was known of the area between Frans Thijssen's 1627 discoveries and the portion of Van Diemen's Land navigated by Tasman; while in the east, everything from Van Diemen's Land to the southern coast of New Guinea – a distance of more than 2200 nautical miles – was missing from all current maps. The question remained: were the known stretches of coastline all part of a single land mass, or did they comprise a number of islands, large and small? Dampier's exceptional mind would have been full of wonder.

From this point in history, it would be easy to take a mental leap eighty-two years into the future … to the achievements of Captain James Cook, the great British seafarer, explorer and Royal Navy lieutenant. As we know, in 1770, sailing aboard His Britannic Majesty's Bark *Endeavour*, he delivered an almost complete answer to the mystery of what lay in the east, by discovering an extensive, north–south lying coast that stretched from Point Hicks – 340 nautical miles north from Tasman's last position on the coast of Van Diemen's Land – to the tip of what is now Cape York, where he turned to the west and finally confirmed the existence of Torres Strait.

Not surprisingly, Cook was hailed the world over for this outstanding discovery, one that would, just eighteen years later, lead to the colonisation of New South Wales by the British. However, had circumstances been only slightly different some seventy years before Cook's expedition, Dampier and not Cook would have been receiving that adulation. Dampier would return to this coastline three years later, and would twice have the opportunity to venture east – but he would first be beaten by bad timing and unfavourable weather, then forced to retreat when his ship literally began to fall apart around him.

*

Dampier was an intriguing and fastidious character who enjoyed adventure on land and sea while making meticulous scientific observations, then presenting them to the world in a most comprehensible manner.

He was a man of opposites: a well-educated, intelligent individual who exhibited consummate skill in the fields of navigation, exploration and hydrography – but one who initially chose a career as a swashbuckling pirate, raiding Spanish ships and villages in far-flung destinations.

His reason for becoming a pirate was 'more to indulge my curiosity than to get wealth'.

*

On 5 September 1651, a young couple, George and Anne Dampier, stood at the font in St Michael's Church atop a hill in East Coker, a tiny village a short distance from the southern coast of England. Anne cradled their baby in her arms, while George stood by, probably holding the hand of their elder son, also named George. A short time later, after a brief ceremony, the couple exited the 400 year old stone church, their newborn child having been christened William Dampier.

Baby William had been born just days earlier – no one is sure exactly when – at fourteenth-century Hymerford House, a thatch-roofed, two-level stone building set in a shallow valley, among the wide rolling meadows and farmed fields of East Coker. Though enveloped by some of the richest and most picturesque countryside in England, from his earliest years the boy had designs on a life under sail.

His father was one of the many tenant farmers in the region, and moderately well-to-do. For much of his schooling, William attended the century-old King's School, an extension of Bruton Abbey, which was located a 20-mile horse ride along the tree-lined lanes and winding roads that led north from his home. However, tragedy beset the family when George, William and their two younger siblings, Thomasina and Josias, were still quite young. Both parents died, and everything changed for the teenaged Dampier:

> My friends did not originally design me for the sea, but bred me at school till I came to years fit for a trade. But upon the death of my father and mother, they who had

the disposal of me, took other measures; and having removed me from the Latin school to learn writing and arithmetic, they soon after placed me with a master of a ship at Weymouth, complying with the inclinations I had very early of seeing the world …

Weymouth, on the south coast 20 miles from East Coker, was the nearest commercial port. Dampier's guardians arranged for the teenager to be indentured to a boat builder and ship's captain: an ideal first step that would soon see him finding his way to sea. His first two voyages were no doubt memorable for opposite reasons: the first for its brevity – a voyage across the English Channel to France and back that covered as few as 120 nautical miles – and the second for its length. It took him to the frigid waters of Newfoundland, a 4000 nautical mile trans-Atlantic experience:

[I] went to Newfoundland, being then about eighteen years of age. In this voyage I spent one summer; but so pinched with the rigour of that cold climate that upon my return I was absolutely against going to those parts of the world …

The waterfront at Weymouth could not deliver the exciting, long-term seafarer's life he was seeking, so in late 1670, William found himself in London, pacing the docks and seeking a position aboard the ship of his dreams.

He soon found it: the East Indiaman *John and Martha*, which would shortly be bound for Bantam, Java, sailing via the Cape of Good Hope. Young Dampier would later recall that:

> [T]he offer of a warm voyage and a long one, both which I always desired, soon carried me to sea again … I entered myself aboard, and was employed before the mast [as a deckhand], for which my two former voyages had some way qualified me.

Dampier signed on and was literally 'shown the ropes' – the techniques the crew applied to trim, reef and haul up the sails. Not long afterwards, the ship was riding the tide and heading downstream from London, her progress providing the ever-observant new recruit with a panorama of sights, the likes of which he'd never seen before.

About four days later – after sailing 350 or so nautical miles to the west and clearing the corner of the English Channel – *John and Martha* began surging south through the Atlantic, rolling rhythmically and leaving a wake of churning white water.

As the ship ploughed through the ocean, Dampier's mind was being recharged with the same fascination he had experienced on his two inaugural voyages: a life-changing fusion of intrigue and intellect. Once again he became immersed in the elements – the parts that the wind, waves, tide and weather played in the everyday life of a sailor – and the art of the navigator, whose role it was to best harness those conditions and safely pilot the ship to its destination under the guidance of the sun and the stars. Of particular interest to the budding navigator would have been the calculation of longitude as *John and Martha* progressed across the southern part of the Indian Ocean, the sector of the Brouwer Route where the course was towards the coast of New Holland before it swept to the north. Dampier would later note that he'd 'gained more experience in navigation' over those invigorating months at sea.

After two months in Bantam, the heavily laden ship made it back to England inside a year. Once on home shores, Dampier 'forbore going to sea that summer, retiring to my brother in Somersetshire'. But the salt in his blood was now flowing too strongly. The twenty-one year old heard the call of battle. He enlisted with the Royal Navy.

It was 1672, and English and French forces were at war with the Dutch in what became known historically as the Third Anglo–Dutch War. Dampier was posted to HBMS *Royal Prince*, a 167-foot long 100-gunner under the command of Sir Edward Spragge, with a complement of 780 men. A few months later the new recruit sampled the barbarous nature of maritime warfare in the Battles of Schooneveld, two intense encounters off the coast of the Netherlands:

We had three engagements that summer; I was in two of them, but falling very sick I was put aboard a hospital ship a day or two before the third engagement, seeing it at a distance only; and in this Sir Edward Spragge was killed.

In the course of that third engagement, the Battle of Texel, the tide of war turned in favour of the Dutch and what was left of the Anglo-French fleet retreated: the Dutch had saved their country from invasion.

The nature of Dampier's illness is unknown, but it was sufficiently severe for him to be transferred ashore from the hospital ship: 'I was sent to Harwich, with the rest of the sick and wounded, and having languished a great while, I went home to my brother to recover my health.'

Within a year he was well enough to turn his thoughts towards the next stage of his life:

I recovered my old inclination for the sea. A
neighbouring gentleman, Colonel Hellier of East Coker
in Somersetshire, my native parish, made me a
seasonable offer to go and manage a plantation of his in
Jamaica, under one Mr Whalley: for which place I set
out with Capt. Kent in the *Content* of London.

Hellier is believed to have been William's father's landlord in East Coker – the lord of the manor. If so, he would no doubt have been impressed by William during the latter's childhood. Even at a very young age, the boy was displaying a propensity to understand crops, part of an instinctive appreciation of all things natural that must surely have influenced the landlord's decision:

> I came acquainted with them all [the crops], and knew
> what each sort would produce, (*viz.*) wheat, barley,
> maslin, rice, beans, peas, oats, fetches, flax, or hemp: in
> all which I had a more than usual knowledge for one so
> young; taking a particular delight in observing it ...

Fate was now dealing a new hand in Dampier's life: his decision to go to Jamaica would prove to be his first step towards becoming a pirate, and subsequently an explorer and author of the highest level.

When Captain Kent declared *Content* ready for sea, the anchor was weighed. Dampier would recall, 'We sailed out of the River Thames in the beginning of the Year 1674, and meeting with favourable winds, in a short time got into the trade-wind, and went merrily along.' Dampier paid for his passage by working as a member of the crew during the Atlantic crossing to the Caribbean.

The day after arriving in the Jamaican port of Kingston, he met with his employer, Mr Whalley, and travelled to the plantation, which was located on Sixteen Mile Walk, inland and about 12 miles to the north-west of the town. The relationship between the two men soon became strained, because while Dampier had been led to believe he was there to manage the estate, Whalley would have no part of it. This conflict of opinion soon escalated to the point where the two men came to blows.

After six months in that hostile environment, Dampier decided he had had enough. He quit and moved on to another plantation. That, too, would be a short engagement:

[I] entered myself into the service of one Captain Heming, to manage his plantation at St. Anns, on the north side of the island … I was clearly out of my element there, and therefore as soon as Captain Heming came thither I disengaged myself from him, and took my passage on board a sloop to Port Royal, with one Mr Statham, who used to trade round the island, and touched there at that time.

Having joined Statham, Dampier resumed his harmonious relationship with the sea. Mr Statham's vessel traded right around the Jamaican coast: a satisfying experience that saw Dampier become acquainted with 'all the ports and bays about Jamaica'.

Then, eighteen months after leaving London, Dampier's first opportunity of any real significance arrived: 'I left that employ also, and shipped myself aboard one Capt. Hudscl, who was bound to the Bay of Campeachy [Campeche] to load logwood.'

Logwood timber was fetching around 110 pounds per ton in London, because the extract obtained from the dark heartwood of the logwood trees provided a purplish-red dye that was much sought after in Europe. The tree was native to northern Central America and southern Mexico, where the Bay of Campeche is located.

Hudsel's vessel was not large, and the crew comprised only six men and a boy. It took them two weeks to reach the Bay of Campeche on a non-stop passage. As they rounded Cabo (Cape) Catoche on the bay's eastern edge and commenced the long sail into the huge bay, it was again obvious that Dampier was much more than a sailor. His ever-alert eyes could not rest:

> The Cape is very low land by the sea ... It is all over-
> grown with trees of diverse sorts, especially logwood;
> and therefore was formerly much frequented by the
> Jamaica men, who came thither in sloops to load with
> it, till all the logwood trees near the sea were cut down;
> but now 'tis wholly abandoned, because the carriage of
> it to the shore requires more labour than the cutting,
> logging and chipping. Besides they find better wood
> now in the Bays of Campeachy and Honduras, and have
> but a little way to carry it [to the shore].

Then there was his first mention of the word 'barbecue', during his description of nearby Río Lagartos (Alligator River): 'A little to the east of this river is a fish-range ... where the Indian fishers who are subject to the Spaniards lie in the fishing seasons ... Here are poles to hang their nets on, and barbecues to dry their fish'.

The destination of Dampier's ship was a small inlet on the coast named One-Bush-Key. Here they purchased their cargo of logwood in exchange for rum, 'a very good commodity for the logwood cutters, who were then about 250 men, most English'.

With the vessel soon laden to the gunwales with timber, it was time for the return voyage to Jamaica, where the cargo would be put aboard commercial ships and sent to England. The first stage of the passage away from the coast was not without incident. Dampier would experience his first encounter with Spanish pirates:

In the morning, near 12 or 14 leagues W.S.W. from Campeachy, we saw two sail about 3 leagues to windward coming directly towards us ... Upon this we edged off more to sea, and they also altered their course steering away still directly with us; so that we were now assured they were Spaniards; and therefore we put away [increased speed under sail] ... though they still fetched on us apace ... [One of the vessels] being a good sailer came within gunshot of us; when, as it pleased God, the landwind died away all of a sudden, and the sea breeze did not yet spring up.

While the wind lasted we thought our selves but a degree from prisoners; neither had we yet great hopes of escaping; for our ketch, even when light, was but a dull sailer ... At last the wind freshening on by the coming

226

of a tornado, we gained considerably of them; so they
fired a gun and left their chase, but we kept *crowding* [on
sail] till night; and then clapped on a wind again and
saw no more of them.

The return passage to Jamaica proved to be punishing in every
sense. Apart from barely escaping the pirates, the heavily laden
vessel could barely make forward progress in the headwinds
that seemed to be incessant. Dampier wrote that the voyage
'proved very tedious and hazardous to us by reason of our
ship's being so sluggish a sailer that she would not ply to
windward, whereby we were necessarily driven upon several
shoals that otherwise we might have avoided, and forced to
spend thirteen weeks in our passage, which is usually
accomplished in half that time'.

At one stage, they went close to losing their ship when it
struck a rock, an event that justified Dampier's concerns
regarding the navigational ability of the vessel's captain, who
at the time was asleep on deck. Fortunately, the surge of the
following waves was enough to lift the ship off the rocks and
move her into deep water. 'Otherwise,' Dampier would write,
'we must certainly have been lost.'

Dampier, impressed by the lifestyle of a logger, and the
money he had earned, went back to the Bay of Campeche as
soon as he could. It was during his time as a logger that he
first began to refine his unique ability to describe the features,
and forces, of nature. He would prove to be as interested in

ornithology as he was in zoology, in weather as in water. Here is one of his earliest descriptions, among the thousands he would complete during his lifetime:

> The armadillo (so called from its suit of armour) is as big as a small sucking pig: the body of it pretty long. This creature is enclosed in a thick shell, which guards all its back, and comes down on both sides, and meets under the belly, leaving room for the four legs; the head is small, with a nose like a pig, a pretty long neck, and can put out its head before its body when it walks; but on any danger she puts it in under the shell; and drawing in her feet, she lies stock still like a land-turtle: And though you toss her about she will not move herself. The shell is jointed in the middle of the back, so that she can turn the fore-part of her body about which way she pleases … The flesh is very sweet, and tastes much like a land-turtle.

Yet this fruitful period of observation could not last. It was late 1676 when, after a year of effort, Dampier had to accept that his endeavours to make a fortune as a logwooder had failed to the point where he, like many others, did not have the money to purchase the provisions he needed to survive. He and other English logwooders were the victims of a dispute between England and Spain over control of the log-wooding industry and the ambiguously worded Treaty of

Madrid, which included guidelines for the government of the industry. It was drafted in 1670 and subsequently led to the demise of the industry.

He soon realised his only alternative lay not on the land, but in the bay before him: 'I ... was forced to range about to seek a subsistence in company of some privateers then in the bay.'

But in reality the ship was not a privateer – authorised by the government to attack enemy ports and shipping, in exchange for any booty they could pillage and plunder. Instead, these were buccaneers – pirates.

CHAPTER THIRTEEN

A Life of 'Crime': Buccaneers and the Bachelor's Delight

July 1687

At this time, there was little distinction between the activities of buccaneers and pirates. At best, a buccaneer was a pirate with some degree of respectability. The difference was nothing more than a piece of paper: a letter of marque under which a government gave authority for an armed vessel to capture enemy merchant shipping and commit acts which would otherwise be recognised as piracy.

In the West Indies, buccaneers were supposed to share their spoils with the authorities who issued their letter of marque; for pirates, it was simply winner takes all.

Buccaneering became a part of life in the West Indies soon after the English captured Jamaica from the Spanish in 1655.

With that stronghold in the Caribbean secured, the English then saw this version of piracy as a low-cost way to continue waging an undeclared war against their arch enemy, Spain, and to control its activities in the region.

Just as the Dutch controlled the spice trade in the East Indies and the English dominated trade with India, the Spanish were sailing on what could be termed a sea of silver. They had focussed their attention on the vast wealth that came from the silver mines in Mexico and Bolivia, a fortune that they were transporting back across the Atlantic to Spain. The capture of Jamaica signalled that the English wanted a share of that wealth and any other trade opportunities in the Caribbean. Holding Jamaica meant that the English had a base from where they could challenge the Spanish both on sea and land, and the simplest way to achieve this was with a fleet of ships based in Jamaica and manned by buccaneers-cum-pirates.

While their activities were considered lawless, the captains and officers of these ships generally conducted themselves within the bounds of the existing rules of war, by which they treated the Spanish with a degree of respect. However, the crew members often saw it differently. Their conduct was comparable with those who manned legitimate ships of war and merchantmen: some were of good behaviour, but the majority were uneducated and lived lives of lawlessness and drunkenness. They were nothing more than sailors of fortune.

That buccaneers could hold high status in English society is no better reflected than in the story of Sir Henry Morgan, the most notorious buccaneer-cum-pirate of them all. After being prosecuted for committing ruthless acts of piracy, he received a knighthood and was appointed Lieutenant-Governor of Jamaica in 1675.

Having accepted their new shipmate into the fold, the pirate crew took Dampier on hunting expeditions into the countryside, and on visits to villages in search of sought-after food items. But pirates they were, and a raid on a Mexican waterfront town soon followed:

Alvarado was the westermost place I was at. Thither we went in two barks with 30 men in each, and had 10 or 11 killed and desperately wounded in taking the fort; being four or five hours engaged in that service, in which time the inhabitants having plenty of boats and canoes, carried all their riches and best moveables away. It was after sunset before the fort yielded; and growing dark, we could not pursue them, but rested quietly that night; the next day we killed, salted and sent aboard 20 or 30 beefs, and a good quantity of salt-fish, and Indian corn, as much as we could stow away. Here were but few hogs, and those eat very fishy; therefore we did not much esteem them: but of cocks, hens and ducks were sent aboard in abundance.

Then, as if taking his first pirate raid in his stride, Dampier added:

> The tame parrots we found here were the largest and
> fairest birds of their kind that I ever saw in the West
> Indies. Their colour was yellow and red, very coarsely
> mixed; and they would prate very prettily; and there
> was scarce a man but what sent aboard one or two of
> them. So that with provision, chests, hen coops and
> parrot cages, our ships were full of lumber, with which
> we intended to sail ...

Everything was in readiness for the two ships to put to sea and commence the passage back to Jamaica ... until one of the crew looked out to sea and saw seven large vessels under full sail heading their way. It was a Spanish fleet, and it was the fleet's intention to blast the pirates and their ships into extinction.

Dampier and his cohorts had no option but to try to escape their anchorage in the river mouth and get to the safety of the open sea before their attackers reached them. However, the tide was too low for their ships to clear the sand bar across the river entrance. They had to lighten ship, and they did this by clearing the decks – heaving overboard all the valuable logwood they were carrying, along with any other heavy item they could dispense with.

It was a successful move, though once clear of the river, the pirates were forced to engage the Spanish in a close-quarter battle, gain the upper hand then make good their getaway, virtually unscathed.

Once back in Jamaica, Dampier took time to assess his situation: did he want to continue as a pirate, or go back to England, then perhaps return to the Caribbean and, for reasons unknown, try the logwood trade once more?

He chose the latter ... but destiny had other plans for him.

*

After another relatively comfortable trans-Atlantic voyage of nearly 4500 nautical miles, Dampier arrived back in London in August 1678 ... for what would be a short stay: just six months, enough time to get married.

Little is known of that happy event, except that his wife's name was Judith, and she came from the household of the recently appointed Duke of Grafton. This title had been created only three years earlier by King Charles II for Henry FitzRoy, his second illegitimate son by the Duchess of Cleveland.

Apart from Judith's employment in the Duke's household, and the fact that she and William did not have any children, nothing is known of her. Dampier's travels meant he did not see her for twelve years after he left London in about February 1679, bound once again for Jamaica. This unexpected separation came about because, as he later explained, what was to be another logging expedition to Campeche 'proved to be a voyage round the world'.

Soon after reaching the West Indies again and coming to anchor off Kingston, Dampier joined a ship captained by a Mr Hobby with the intention of sailing to the Bay of Campeche and resuming logging. This plan was abandoned after Mr Hobby's ship sailed to the western end of the island and anchored in Negril Bay [now Long Bay] alongside a small squadron of square-riggers manned by buccaneers.

Among the numerous captains in the squadron was Bartholomew Sharp, whose career as a pirate, while short-lived, was highly successful. In ranging along the coast of South America and through the Caribbean, he would be responsible for claiming twenty-five treasure-laden Spanish ships, and plundering numerous Spanish towns. He would also be recognised for being the first Englishman to sail eastwards around the world's most feared promontory, Cape Horn.

When Hobby's crew made contact with the pirates, they learned that they were planning exciting forays into foreign territory that promised rich rewards, and there was ample opportunity for new men to join them. Not surprisingly, all except Dampier immediately quit Mr Hobby and joined the rogue ships. A few days later, Dampier too surrendered to the temptation.

It appears that in part Dampier was in good company, and he adapted himself to the ways of the crew while the leaders of the fleet – two of them French – plotted a major assault on Portobello (now Portobelo) on the shore of a picturesque bay on the eastern side of Panama. It was Christopher Columbus who had given the location its name on his fourth voyage to the New World in 1502.

Dampier joined Captain Sharp's ship for the attack on Portobello – then a fortified town of considerable wealth, since it was a port from which the Spanish shipped home gold and silver that had been mined from the highlands not far inland. This would not be the first time it had been plundered: Sir Henry Morgan had sacked the town eleven years earlier.

This mission, in April 1680, proved to be highly lucrative, and each of the 477 men involved received a reward of 40 pounds (in the region of 10,000 pounds today). After leaving their ships at anchor, the pirates next decided to march more than 60 miles across rugged terrain to the opposite side of the Panamanian isthmus and the city of Santa Maria, where Panama City is located today. Dampier noted that this involved a force of 331 men – the two French crews having withdrawn by this stage – and that 'all or most of them were armed with a fusee flintlock pistol and hanger'.

The men were divided into seven companies before they headed inland behind many colourful and fluttering flags. After a march that took ten days to complete, Santa Maria was taken with minimal resistance, and little gain, but the venture did provide Dampier with his first view of the mighty and massive Pacific Ocean, which would play a significant role in his life.

Good fortune came soon afterwards, when some of the English pirates, manning canoes provided by local Indians, led a successful attack on the Spanish fleet anchored off the island of Perico (part of the Causeway Islands), claiming 'five great ships and three pretty big barks'. It was a desperate battle over many hours, in which eighteen of the sixty-eight English buccaneers were killed and twenty-two were wounded. On the opposing side, the Spanish admiral was slain, along with sixty-eight of his eighty-six men. The great reward that came for the English pirates through this victory was that as well as having their ships still at anchor off Portobello, they now had a fleet of vessels on the Pacific side of the isthmus, which would enable them to execute raids along the Pacific coast, all the way south to Peru and Chile.

That they did, over a distance of more than 2000 nautical miles, all the way to Arica in the north of Chile, where, despite their best endeavours, they were repelled by the Spanish.

By this time, Dampier and others had had enough of this part of the world, so they joined one of the ships that was returning north to the region near Santa Maria. Once there, they recrossed the isthmus to Portobello, an exhausting journey, which, due to incompetent guides who led them over physically demanding terrain, took twenty-three days to complete – more than twice the time it had taken them to cross from east to west.

When they eventually reached Portobello, they had been away thirteen months but had virtually nothing to show for it. Their numerous raids had provided little loot – such an insignificant amount, in fact, that Dampier was worth virtually no more than when he left London two and a half years earlier. But he did have in his possession an asset that would prove to be of far more lasting value: his highly detailed and prized journal, which he had preserved in a 'large joint of bamboo, which I stopped at both ends, closing it with wax, so as to keep out any water. In this I preserved my journal and other writings from being wet, though I was often forced to swim [across rivers]'.

A French privateer under the command of Captain Tristian was lying calmly at anchor in the bay when Dampier and others reached the coast, and, as would have been expected, they were invited aboard.

This heralded the start of the next stage of Dampier's life: more pirating in the Caribbean. But after this experience, and a stint aboard one other French ship, he wrote that he 'grew weary of living with the French', because 'the seamen were the saddest creatures that ever I was among; for though we had bad weather that required many hands aloft, yet the biggest part of them never stirred out of their hammocks but to eat or ease themselves'.

The chance for Dampier to move on again came in August 1683, after the second French vessel had sailed north along the east coast of North America, benefiting from the then unidentified Gulf Stream, which carried her all the way to England's first outpost in the Americas: Virginia. Once there, Dampier accepted an invitation to join another buccaneer ship, the eighteen-gun *Revenge*.

By this time, he had designs on sailing around the world, and the course planned for *Revenge* suited his plans: she would cross the Atlantic to the Cape Verde Islands off the west coast of Africa, then sail to the south-west and around Cape Horn before turning north for a cruise along the western coast of South America.

His record of that memorable day of departure read:

> August 23 1683 we sailed from Achamack in Virginia
> under the command of Capt. Cook [John Cook] bound
> for the South Seas. I shall not trouble the reader with an
> account of every day's run, but hasten to the less known
> parts of the world, to give a description of them ...

Dampier remained true to his word by not burdening his journal with irrelevant writings, but as the journey progressed he excelled in detailing his observations, particularly of flora and fauna. His attention to detail, and ability to explain eloquently what he was seeing, surfaced in spectacular fashion during *Revenge*'s first stop at the Cape Verde Islands:

> THE FLAMINGO, AND ITS REMARKABLE NEST.
> I saw a few flamingos, which is a sort of large fowl,
> much like a heron in shape, but bigger, and of a reddish
> colour. They delight to keep together in great
> companies, and feed in mud or ponds, or in such places
> where there is not much water: they are very shy,

therefore it is hard to shoot them … They build their nests in shallow ponds, where there is much mud, which they scrape together, making little hillocks, like small islands appearing out of the water a foot and a half high from the bottom. They make the foundation of these hillocks broad, bringing them up tapering to the top, where they leave a small hollow pit to lay their eggs in; and when they either lay their eggs or hatch them, they stand all the while, not on the hillock but close by it with their legs on the ground and in the water, resting themselves against the hillock, and covering the hollow nest upon it with their rumps: For their legs are very long; and building thus, as they do, upon the ground, they could neither draw their legs conveniently into their nests, nor sit down upon them otherwise than by resting their whole bodies there, to the prejudice of their eggs or their young, were it not for this admirable contrivance, which they have by natural instinct. They never lay more than two eggs, and seldom fewer. The young ones cannot fly till they are almost full-grown; but will run prodigiously fast; yet we have taken many of them. The flesh of both young and old is lean and black, yet very good meat, tasting neither fishy, nor any way unsavoury. Their tongues are large, having a large knob of fat at the root, which is an excellent bit: a dish of flamingo's tongues being fit for a prince's table.

Off the coast of Sierra Leone, while *Revenge* continued to sail south, an incident occurred that, it would appear, concerned Dampier to the degree where he never wrote of it, possibly because he was so ashamed. It was here that *Revenge* intercepted a thirty-six gun Danish vessel, the captain of which would no doubt not have expected any aggression, as England and Denmark were allies. But the crew of *Revenge* treated the ship as a pirate's prize and went aboard to claim it. Apart from being well laden with high-quality brandy and a considerable quantity of provisions, she was found to be carrying sixty female African slaves.

What happened to these women after the pirates took possession of the ship is unknown, but they did, from there on, refer to her as *Bachelor's Delight*. This ship proved to be a considerably superior vessel to *Revenge*, so Cook decided to transfer his men and equipment to their new prize and dispose of *Revenge* by burning her to the waterline.

By the middle of November 1683, *Bachelor's Delight* was on a south-westerly course towards the Straits of Magellan, Cook having decided to take that 350 nautical mile short-cut into the south seas. This was a course that Dampier had strongly recommended against:

> I urged to hinder their designs of going through the
> Straits of Magellan, which I knew would prove very
> dangerous to us; the rather because our men ... would
> not be so ready to give a watchful attendance in a

passage so little known. For, although these men were more under command than I had ever seen any privateers, yet I could not expect to find them at a minute's call in coming to an anchor or weighing anchor: beside, if ever we should have occasion to moor or cast out two anchors, we had not a boat to carry out or weigh an anchor.

But Cook would have no part of Dampier's suggestion or concerns, and continued on until 6 February 1684, when the two ships 'fell in with the Straits Le Maire'. Within a very short time the captain and crew realised why Dampier had strongly urged against venturing there:

[S]eeing the opening of the straits, we ran in with it, till within four mile of the mouth, and then it fell calm, and we found a strong tide setting out of the straits to the northward, and likely to founder our ship … [I]t made such a short cockling sea as if it had been in a race, or place where two tides meet; for it ran every way, sometimes breaking in over our waist, sometimes over our poop, sometimes over our bow, and the ship tossed like an eggshell, so that I never felt such uncertain jerks in a ship …

At eight o'clock that night, Cook was forced to acknowledge that Dampier's concerns had been justified; *Bachelor's Delight* was then set on a reciprocal course that took her back into the South Atlantic. Once clear, she would sail south and round Cape Horn.

To achieve this doubling of the cape against the prevailing headwinds, *Bachelor's Delight* had to sail a long way south. Dampier recorded that they were 'in latitude 60 by reckoning, which was the farthest south latitude that ever I was in'. This position was about 250 nautical miles south of the Horn.

By 3 March, Dampier's sun sights (observations of the altitude of the sun made for navigational purposes using a mariner's astrolabe) confirmed they were safely around Cape Horn. They could then tack and head north on a course that would give them a safe gauge to leeward, off the west coast of South America. The call came for the ship to be tacked and with that done, they 'stood into the South Seas'.

Nearly three weeks later, on 22 March 1684, the island of Juan Fernández, 450 nautical miles to the west of the Chilean coast, was sighted off *Bachelor's Delight*'s bow. The course was then changed so she was heading directly towards it, because, as Dampier explained, they had resolved some time earlier to stop there:

> We presently got out our canoe, and went ashore to see
> for a Moskito Indian [native to Central America] whom
> we left here when we were chased hence by three
> Spanish ships in the year 1681, a little before we went to
> Arica …

Dampier would also write of a similar situation that occurred two years later: his involvement in the recovery of Scottish castaway Alexander Selkirk from the very same island, where Selkirk had been marooned for more than four years. Many disciples of Dampier's writings believe that the rescue of Selkirk formed the foundation of Daniel Defoe's classic novel *Robinson Crusoe*. There is also ample evidence – including the name of one of the individuals involved – that this first recovery mission could well have inspired the portrayal of Crusoe's companion Friday. Dampier's description of the encounter with the Indian reads in part:

> This Indian lived here alone above three years and, although he was several times sought after by the Spaniards, who knew he was left on the island, yet they could never find him ...
>
> He saw our ship the day before we came to an anchor, and did believe we were English, and therefore killed three goats in the morning before we came to an anchor, and dressed them with cabbage, to treat us when we came ashore. He came then to the seaside to congratulate our safe arrival. And when we landed a Moskito Indian named Robin [who was with us] first leapt ashore and, running to his brother Moskito man, threw himself flat on his face at his feet, who helping him up, and embracing him, fell flat with his face on the ground at Robin's feet, and was by him

taken up also. We stood with pleasure to behold the
surprise and tenderness and solemnity of this
interview, which was exceedingly affectionate on both
sides; and when their ceremonies of civility were over
we also that stood gazing at them drew near, each of
us embracing him we had found here, who was
overjoyed to see so many of his old friends come
hither, as he thought purposely to fetch him. He was
named Will, as the other was Robin. These were
names given them by the English, for they had no
names among themselves ...

Dampier described how 'Will' had survived his solitary life,
making tools to build 'a little house or hut half a mile from
the sea, which was lined with goat's skin', and weapons he
could use to hunt goats for food:

He had with him his gun and a knife, with a small horn
of powder and a few shot; which being spent, he
contrived a way by notching his knife to saw the barrel
of his gun into small pieces wherewith he made
harpoons, lances, hooks, and a long knife.

In the beginning he was 'forced to eat seal, which is very
ordinary meat, before he had made hooks: but afterwards he
never killed any seals but to make lines, cutting their skins
into thongs ... He had no clothes left, having worn out those

he brought from [the ship that had abandoned him there], but only a skin about his waist.'

After departing the island with Will as a guest, the crew returned to the ways of buccaneers, and it was at this point that Dampier finally met with success. By May, *Bachelor's Delight* was escorting three more prize ships, one of which had been carrying 800,000 pieces-of-eight from Lima to Panama.

Their desire to sail north along the coast of South America was thwarted by adverse weather. This led to a change of plans: it was decided to head offshore to another destination – the Galapagos Islands.

For Dampier the naturalist, this was like visiting a living museum:

> The iguanas here are as fat and large as any that I ever
> saw; they are so tame that a man may knock down
> twenty in an hour's time with a club. The land-turtle
> are here so numerous that 5 or 600 men might subsist
> on them alone for several months without any other sort
> of provision: they are extraordinary large and fat; and so
> sweet that no pullet eats more pleasantly. One of the
> largest of these creatures will weigh 150 or 200 weight,
> and some of them are 2 foot, or 2 foot 6 inches over the
> challapee or belly.

His attention to detail on this visit went well beyond the wildlife: he also wrote at considerable length of 'The air and weather at the Galapagos', and 'Some of the islands described, their soil, etc'.

After weighing anchor and departing the Galapagos Islands, *Bachelor's Delight* sailed north-east towards the mainland, and in July reached Cape Blanco 'on the Main of Mexico'. It was here that Dampier recorded the death of his captain:

> Captain Cook, who was taken sick at Juan Fernandez, continued so till we came within 2 or 3 leagues of Cape Blanco, and then died of a sudden, though he seemed that morning to be as likely to live as he had been some weeks before; but it is usual with sick men coming from the sea, where they have nothing but the sea air, to die off as soon as ever they come within the view of the land.

For the next twelve months the pirates continued with their marauding ways – sometimes successfully, other times not – along the coast of Central America, until August 1685, when they and their Spanish quarry essentially reached a stalemate. By then they were battling on the waters of Panama Bay, and there was no longer much to be gained by either side: the anticipated rewards on sea and land were not there for the taking.

Dampier realised it was time for him to move on; plying back and forth along coastal waters in a too often vain search of treasure ships was becoming monotonous and sapping him of his spirit of adventure. Instead of looking towards his wife, Judith, and the fields of East Coker – neither of which he had seen for six years – in March 1686 he decided to join Captain Swan aboard *Cygnet* and sail to the west across the Pacific – towards unimaginable destinations and subjects to write about.

CHAPTER FOURTEEN

From Buccaneer to Bestseller

January 1688

Almost two years after she departed the coast of Mexico with William Dampier as navigator, *Cygnet* lay aground on the northern coast of New Holland. It was here that Dampier – no doubt after much consideration – decided he was tiring of the lifestyle of a pirate and rover on the high seas. It was time for him to move on, do different things ... maybe even head home.

The current plan was for *Cygnet* to sail to Cape Comorin, on the southern tip of India, but that voyage no longer held any appeal for him. He felt they should make for the East Indies – but he wasn't expecting the response that came from his shipmates when he dared mention this idea:

> While we lay here I did endeavour to persuade our men
> to go to some English factory [trading post]; but was
> threatened to be turned ashore and left here for it. This

made me desist and patiently wait for some more convenient place and opportunity to leave them than here: which I did hope I should accomplish in a short time …

On 12 March 1688, after a two-month stay on the shores of New Holland, her crew guided *Cygnet* cautiously out of King Sound while her navigator checked his charts. He reluctantly plotted her course towards a speck located 1500 nautical miles to the north-west, and 600 nautical miles from the coast of Java. This speck was the Cocos Islands (today the Australian Territory of the Cocos (Keeling) Islands), two atolls and twenty-seven coral islands that would be the next staging point en route to India.

Two weeks later, the islands were in sight, proof that Dampier's navigation had been spot-on. More importantly they represented 'hopes to make my escape from them to Sumatra or some other place'. That opportunity did not eventuate, but the desire to abandon his ship and its unruly bunch of marauders continued to intensify.

Sighting the coast of Sumatra not long after departing the Cocos Islands caused added frustration: Sumatra would be the ideal destination for the would-be absconder, but *Cygnet* was not going anywhere near that island, for the time being at least.

On 29 April – four days after crossing the Equator – Dampier realised that Captain Read was more determined than ever to keep him on board:

The 29th we saw a sail to the north of us which we chased … Captain Read went into a canoe and took her and brought her aboard. She was a proa with four men in her … She came from one of these coconut islands that we passed by and was laden with coconuts and coconut-oil. Captain Read ordered his men to take aboard all the nuts and as much of the oil as he thought convenient, and then cut a hole in the bottom of the proa and turned her loose, keeping the men prisoners.

It was not for the lucre of the cargo that Captain Read took this boat, but to hinder me and some others from going ashore; for he knew that we were ready to make our escapes if an opportunity presented itself; and he thought that by abusing and robbing the natives we should be afraid to trust ourselves among them.

On 1 May, *Cygnet* was coasting north, about 8 leagues off the western shore of Sumatra. As she went, Dampier befriended the prisoners … and a valuable friendship it became, as they explained to him the finer details of the islands the ship was passing, and, most importantly, revealed the existence of a much-desired English factory in the province of Achin (Aceh), at the northern end of Sumatra.

'I wished myself there', he wrote, 'but was forced to wait with patience till my time was come.'

He did not need to be patient for long. Captain Read decided to visit one of the islands so *Cygnet* could be careened, the caulking checked and her bottom scraped free of the speed-sapping crustaceans and weed that had become attached to the hull.

It was only a brief stop, the duration of one tide, but that gave Dampier enough time to quit the ship – not by stealth, as he had expected, but with the consent of the captain:

> I had till this time made no open show of going ashore here: but now, the water being filled and the ship in a readiness to sail, I desired Captain Read to set me ashore on this island. He, supposing that I could not go ashore in a place less frequented by ships than this, gave me leave: which probably he would have refused to have done if he thought I should have gotten from hence in any short time; for fear of my giving an account of him to the English or Dutch. I soon got up my chest and bedding and immediately got some to row me ashore, for fear lest his mind should change again.

Dampier was rowed ashore into a small, sandy bay, and was immediately made most unwelcome by the occupier of one of two small houses located there. Using sign language, the man gestured to the ship's boat to turn around, then pointed to his own small craft on the beach and indicated that the interloper should depart without delay. The stalemate soon eased, however, and Dampier was made welcome.

To Dampier's surprise, the boat that had brought him ashore from *Cygnet* soon returned to the cove containing armed men, who ordered Dampier back aboard:

> They need not have sent an armed posse for me; for had
> they but sent the cabin-boy ashore for me I would not
> have denied going aboard. For though I could have hid
> myself in the woods, yet then they would have abused
> or have killed some of the natives, purposely to incense
> them against me. I told them therefore that I was ready
> to go with them and went aboard with all my things.

When Dampier stepped onto the deck, the ship was in uproar: three more men wanted to follow his lead to abandon *Cygnet*, including the surgeon. Two of them, by the names of Robert Hall and Ambrose (surname unknown), were allowed to join Dampier, but the all-important surgeon was dragged back on board after boldly leaping into the boat with them.

Soon after the three men who had deserted the ship gathered on the beach, the ship's boat returned with five more men to join them: the Malayan prisoners and a Portuguese crewman who had joined *Cygnet* when she was off the coast of Cambodia.

That evening, Dampier noted:

> It was a fine clear moonlight night in which we were
> left ashore. Therefore we walked on the sandy bay to

watch when the ship would weigh and be gone, not thinking ourselves secure in our new-gotten liberty till then. About eleven or twelve o'clock we saw her under sail and then we returned to our chamber and so to sleep. This was the 6th of May.

They were free, but far from safe.

There was no future for them on this island, as it was highly unlikely that another ship would visit there in the foreseeable future, so they would have to get to Sumatra – more specifically Achin – through their own endeavours:

I was very well satisfied, and the rather because we were now men enough to row ourselves over to the island Sumatra; and accordingly we presently consulted how to purchase a canoe of the natives.

A native boat, a proa fitted with outriggers (floats) on each side, would be ideal for the task, so they purchased one in exchange for an axe one of *Cygnet*'s crewmen had given them. She was about 22 feet long, the main hull being shaped like a canoe, and completely open. She was 'so thin and light that when empty four men could launch her or haul her ashore on a sandy bay'.

The proa was unlike anything these able seafarers had been aboard, and they soon realised it demanded completely different sailing skills from those they held:

When our things were stowed away we … entered with
joy into our new frigate and launched off from the
shore. We were no sooner off but our canoe overset,
bottom upwards. We preserved our lives well enough
by swimming and dragged also our chests and clothes
ashore; but all our things were wet. I had nothing of
value but my journal and some draughts [drawings] of
land of my own taking which I much prized, and which
I had hitherto carefully preserved …

Back on the beach, the men toiled for days refitting the boat:
some reattached the outriggers using stronger poles and
lashings, while others 'cut a good mast for her and made a
substantial sail with mats'. With all jobs complete, and with
their clothes and books now dry, they relaunched the proa and
set out once more – this time with success.

After some further troubles with the inhabitants of the
islands, they reached the southern tip of one of the Nicobar
Islands and went ashore to replenish supplies, particularly
water. They then sailed for Achin, 'about 40 leagues, bearing
south south-east'. Dampier logged their departure:

It was the 15th day of May 1688 about four o'clock in
the afternoon when we left Nicobar Island, directing
our course towards Achin, being eight men of us in
company, *viz.*, three English, four Malayans, who were
born at Achin, and the mongrel Portuguese …

While waiting for the opportunity to escape *Cygnet* – by either consent or cunning – Dampier had prepared himself well for the anticipated navigational challenge of trying to reach a safe destination on any of the coasts of Malacca, Sumatra or Siam. He had checked charts and made notes regarding the distance to and bearings of those destinations, and had managed to hide a pocket-compass among his possessions.

In order to set sail from the Nicobar Islands on the proa, they had to escape the lee of the island, so Dampier had four men man the paddles while he and Hall took it in turns to steer. When the breeze arrived and allowed them to begin sailing, they made reasonable progress towards Achin.

Two days later, Dampier calculated they had covered half of the 40-league passage between their point of departure and Achin. They were starting to feel confident that they would make it – but later that day an ominous-looking halo appeared around the sun, a certain sign that foul weather was approaching.

Before long, their worst fears were fact: they were being hammered by howling winds and tumultuous seas. Dampier knew their only hope for survival in their fragile open boat was to forget about their destination and run with the weather. Sail was reduced to little more than a rag so they could maintain steerage, but that was soon proving to be too much:

> [T]he poles of the outlayers [outriggers] going from the
> sides of the vessel bent as if they would break; and

should they have broken our overturning and perishing had been inevitable ... But the wind still increasing ... we put away right before wind and sea, continuing to run thus all the afternoon and part of the night ensuing. The wind continued increasing all the afternoon, and the sea still swelled higher and often broke, but did us no damage; for the ends of the vessel being very narrow he that steered received and broke the sea on his back, and so kept it from coming in so much as to endanger the vessel: though much water would come in which we were forced to keep heaving out continually. And by this time we saw it was well that we had altered our course, every wave would else have filled and sunk us ...

The sea was already roaring in a white foam about us; a dark night coming on and no land in sight to shelter us, and our little ark in danger to be swallowed by every wave; and, what was worst of all, none of us thought ourselves prepared for another world ... I had been in many eminent dangers before now, some of which I have already related, but the worst of them all was but a play-game in comparison with this.

Dampier resigned himself to the fact that they were probably going to perish, and in doing so became remarkably remorseful. He wrote of how his courage had suddenly abandoned him, and was full of 'sad reflections' on his former life, adding that he 'looked back with horror and detestation on actions which before I disliked but now I trembled at the remembrance of'.

> Submitting ourselves therefore to God's good
> providence and taking all the care we could to preserve
> our lives, Mr Hall and I took turns to steer, and the rest
> took turns to heave out the water, and thus we provided
> to spend the most doleful night I ever was in.

The night soon became even more hellish. At about 10 o'clock, the skies opened and delivered a frightening meteorological mêlée: dazzling lightning fractured the jet-black sky, each bolt followed by a thundering rumble that sounded like a blast from a carronade. Throughout this onslaught, teeming rain peppered every man's barely clad body.

However, by dawn, Dampier's greatest fears had not been realised. The worst of the storm was behind them, and the exhausted crew was able to resume the desired course to the south-east.

At about eight o'clock there was sudden alarm when one of the Malayans shouted in an excited high-pitched voice what Dampier and Hall thought was 'pull away', which, for English seafarers, means 'row harder'. Instead, he was shouting 'Pulo Way': in the distance ahead he could see the grey outline of Pulau Weh (Weh Island), close to the north-west coast of Sumatra.

When they changed course to head directly towards the island, the still-strong wind was coming from a favourable angle, so all they needed to do was re-trim the 'small sail no bigger than an apron', and make good speed in the right direction, with no paddling required.

Five arduous days after they had set off from Nicobar Island, the bow of the proa finally nudged onto the edge of a sandy river bank, adjacent to a small fishing village to which the Malayans had directed them.

Despite having beaten the odds, the survivors were quick to realise they were spent; they did not have the energy to show any form of elation. The adrenalin that had kept them going now suddenly dissipated. They were exhausted physically and mentally, famished and ailing to the degree where not one of them had the strength to raise himself out of the cramped confines of the narrow-hulled boat and stand on dry land.

Local fishermen carried the sailors to their village, where, as Dampier recorded, they 'provided a large house for us to live in till we should be recovered of our sickness, ordering the townspeople to let us want for nothing'.

None of the men was fully recovered even after two weeks of rehabilitation, but Dampier remained keen to get to the English factory in Achin. He advised the local fishermen of this wish and they agreed to assist. They arranged for one of their large proas to take them there almost immediately.

After a mercifully easy three-day voyage, they arrived in Achin early in June 1688. Within a few days the four Malayans from their party disappeared, and the Portuguese sailor died from the effects of a severe fever, the same virus that was plaguing Hall, Ambrose and Dampier. Fortunately, they were assisted by a local resident, an Irishman, Dennis Driscal, who worked at the English 'factory'.

On seeing the men's declining condition, Driscal suggested a possible remedy to Dampier:

> Therefore Mr Driscal and some other Englishmen persuaded me to take some purging physic of a Malayan doctor. I took their advice, being willing to get ease. But after three doses, each a large calabash of nasty stuff, finding no amendment, I thought to desist from more physic, but was persuaded to take one dose more; which I did, and it wrought so violently that I thought it would have ended my days … [M]y strength being almost spent, I even threw myself down once for all … I thought my Malayan doctor, whom they so much commended, would have killed me outright. I continued extraordinary weak for some days after his drenching me thus, but my fever left me for above a week: after which it returned upon me again for a twelvemonth and a flux with it.

Dampier's recovery was slow, but despite remaining very weak he hankered for a return to sea, most particularly so he could complete a circumnavigation of the globe; but at this stage he knew not when or how he would be able to leave the island.

In the end he stayed in Achin for more than a year, until September 1689, when he sailed with a Captain Welden on a series of long and short voyages in the region aboard the trading ship *Curtana*. One of those trading missions took him to Malacca, a port that provided him with a banquet of subjects to note in his journal, the majority relating to the widely varying environments he saw, and others of a cultural or historic nature. For instance, a reflection on the Portuguese:

> The Portuguese were the first discoverers by sea of the East Indies, and had thereby the advantage of trade with these rich Eastern People, [and] also an opportunity, through their weakness, to settle themselves where they pleased. Therefore they made settlements and forts among them ... and presuming upon the strength of their forts, they insulted over the natives; and being grown rich with trade they fell to all manner of looseness and debauchery; the usual concomitant of wealth, and as commonly the fore-runner of ruin. The Portuguese at this place, by report, made use of the native women at their pleasure, whether virgins or married women; such as they liked they took without control ...

By early January 1690, Dampier found himself on his way from Achin to Fort St George on the east coast of India, 1000 nautical miles away to the north-west. Before *Curtana* set sail, he was able to learn of the fate of *Cygnet* when, by chance, he met a fellow crewman from his days aboard that ship.

The shipmate reported that after *Cygnet* departed the island where Dampier and his companions had been marooned, half the crew had quit the ship on the Coromandel coast. The remaining crew captured and plundered a richly laden Portuguese ship, but at Madagascar, soon after they claimed that rich reward, Captain Read and five or six joined a slave trader bound for New York.

Cygnet – with Captain Teat, leader of the mutiny at Mindanao, having finally gained command – set sail for England. However, the ship's lack of maintenance at last caught up with her: her hull planks began opening up and she became very leaky. By the time she reached Saint Augustin, on the west coast of Madagascar, she was beyond help, and there she sank.

The next intriguing episode in Dampier's already remarkable life occurred in April 1690, soon after *Curtana* sailed into Fort St George. A merchant ship, *Mindanao*, arrived in port. As was often the case, the two crews met, and this led Dampier to befriend *Mindanao*'s supercargo, Mr Moody: 'This gentleman bought at Mindanao the painted prince Jeoly and his mother'. Applying his usual eye for detail, Dampier described the prince as follows:

He was painted all down his breast, between his
shoulders behind; on his thighs (mostly) before; and in

the form of several broad rings or bracelets round his arms and legs. I cannot liken the drawings to any figure of animals or the like; but they were very curious, full of great variety of lines, flourishes, chequered work, etc, keeping a very graceful proportion and appearing very artificial, even to wonder, especially that upon and between his shoulder-blades.

He and his similarly tattooed mother 'were much admired by all that saw them' in Fort St George.

The always inquisitive Dampier was told that Prince Jeoly had been 'painted' by one of his five wives, before he and his mother were taken as slaves from their home on 'a small island called Meangis', between the Celebes and Mindanao. They had been tattooed using a technique in which, after their skin was pricked, a dark, powder-like pigment made from the sap of a tree was rubbed into the lesions. This fact didn't really matter for Dampier; all he knew was that no people like this had ever been seen in Europe, and there he foresaw a business opportunity.

He subsequently came to an arrangement with Moody where they would each take a half-share in the prince and his mother, whom Moody had bought together as slaves for sixty dollars in Mindanao. The plan that eventuated was for Dampier to take Prince Jeoly and his mother back to England, put them on public display and reap considerable profits, which he would split fifty–fifty with Moody.

Until Jeoly and his mother became part of Dampier's life, Dampier had given little thought to when he might actually head home to England, but now there was a good reason to consider. Also, he was becoming increasingly tired of the buccaneer lifestyle: he wrote that he 'began to long after my native country after so tedious a ramble from it'. Even so, the time of his departure for home was still some way off.

Dampier and Moody left Fort St George with Prince Jeoly and his mother, and sailed south again, to another English factory on the west coast of Sumatra: 'Bencoolen' (Bengkulu), 700 nautical miles from Achin. Once there, Dampier gained employment as a military gunner, but Moody soon moved on, plying the coast of Sumatra and other islands while continuing to be employed as a supercargo. As agreed, though, he left Prince Jeoly and his mother with Dampier.

But sadness would soon follow: mother and son were struck down by a debilitating illness. The mother died, and Jeoly took three months to recover.

By January 1691, Dampier had tired of the tyrannical behaviour of the local governor (an employee of the English East India Company (EIC)). He knew the time to return to England had arrived, and he found the ideal opportunity when *Defence*, a ship en route to England, came to anchor off Bencoolen. As he explained, '[The crew] had been at Indrapore [an English factory on the west coast of Sumatra] where Mr Moody then was, and he had made over his share in Prince Jeoly to Mr Goddard, chief mate of the ship.' Dampier delivered Jeoly into Goddard's hands on board *Defence*, intending to follow as soon as he could.

The governor and council had previously consented to Dampier's departure – but to Dampier's dismay, when *Defence* arrived in port that consent was withdrawn. Now the only way he could leave was to desert his position as a military gunner and escape: a risk-ridden exercise. If he were caught, he would suffer severe consequences from his superiors – imprisonment, if not worse.

The captain had agreed to have Dampier aboard, so Goddard promised to hide him until after they set sail. Within days, Dampier had implemented a plan:

> I slipped away at midnight (understanding the ship was to sail away the next morning and that they had taken leave of the fort) and, creeping through one of the portholes of the fort, I got to the shore where the ship's boat waited for me and carried me on board. I brought with me my journal and most of my written papers; but some papers and books of value I left in haste and all my furniture; being glad I was myself at liberty, and had hopes of seeing England again.

It was an arduous and often rough eight-month voyage of more than 11,000 nautical miles back to England via the Cape of Good Hope, a voyage in which nearly half the crew were incapacitated through disease, and many died. During a stopover at the EIC colony of St Helena, Dampier and Goddard parted company, and Jeoly was made over entirely into Dampier's hands.

Eventually, the coast of England hove into view. *Defence* headed for the entrance to the Thames River – with Jeoly no doubt standing on deck, looking in awe at the unfamiliar landscape, and thirty-nine year old Dampier alongside him, feeling a twinge of excitement on seeing home shores for the first time in nearly thirteen years. The ship 'luffed in for the Downs where we anchored September the 16th 1691'.

During his long absence, Dampier had been a pirate, pioneer, adventurer and explorer. Yet, apart from the value of his countless extraordinary experiences on a circumnavigation of the globe covering some 60,000 nautical miles, he was returning home poorer than when he had left.

In reality, he had just one asset to show for all that time away: the painted Prince Jeoly.

*

It is likely that, once the wind and a flood tide cooperated, *Defence* cruised up the Thames River all the way to the crowded docks in London. Soon afterwards, Dampier would have been treading on English soil for the first time in more than a decade. Prince Jeoly would, no doubt, have already been commanding the attention that Dampier had expected.

However, from this moment, Dampier had a major problem: he was struggling for sufficient cash to support both himself and Jeoly. His only solution was to sell his one remaining asset.

That opportunity presented itself when he met some showmen who were interested in Jeoly. A deal was struck, but in no time Dampier was referring to them as 'rooks' – swindlers. Almost immediately, these shady characters cut Dampier out of the deal and were exhibiting Jeoly in 'freak shows' around London.

Sadly, in less than a year, Jeoly's demeaning existence came to an end. He contracted smallpox while in Oxford and died there.

*

The vast majority of the next seven years of Dampier's life is as clouded as the dense, grey ocean fogs he encountered during his twelve years at sea. Little is known of where he went, where he resided, nor what he did in the way of work.

It is widely believed that in 1694 he signed up as second mate aboard *Dove*, part of a fleet of four English warships under the flag of the King of Spain, to plunder French possessions and recover treasure from wrecked galleons in the West Indies. After many delays during which the crews were not paid, the first mate of the ship *Charles II*, Jack Avery (also known as Henry Every, possibly a friend of Dampier's), led a successful mutiny at the Spanish port of Corunna. *Charles II* was renamed *Fancy*, and over the next two years she and her crew committed dazzling acts of piracy off the coast of Africa, including an attack on the Grand Mogul of India that is thought to be the most profitable pirate raid of all time. The Spanish expedition, meanwhile, never proceeded, and Dampier returned to England, where his legal attempts to retrieve the pay he was owed were unsuccessful.

*

At no stage in his books does Dampier mention his wife, nor does he ever refer to having written to her during his decade-plus absence. To his readers she simply became 'Judith', a woman whose surname prior to marriage was never stated.

It's quite possible that for the duration of her husband's long absence, 'Mrs Dampier' didn't know if he was dead or alive – until he suddenly arrived back in England. Under the circumstances, it can only be assumed that there was some sort of reunion, either short- or long-term, because when he left England in 1698 on his next adventure, he is said to have arranged for Judith to be the recipient of his salary.

With his small estate in Dorset, or thereabouts, unlikely to have been able to provide Dampier with a decent standard of living, it's safe to assume he spent a considerable amount of time in London, especially during the years when he was writing the story of his unmatched voyage around the world.

The journals of his travels and his personal diaries, which he brought back to England, were his only asset now besides his small land holding. Somehow, though, he and Judith managed to exist, probably in a meagre manner, until the book was ready for release in 1697.

At this time, life in London was literally 'full steam ahead'. Newly rebuilt after the Great Fire of 1666, the city boasted a population of nearly half a million during the twilight decades of the seventeenth century. The hub of social and business activity were the myriad coffee houses sprouting up everywhere. These dimly lit establishments were filled with individuals from all walks of life – elitists, populists, academics, capitalists and the bourgeoisie – propounding their theories about whatever took their fancy. No doubt, as Dampier's life as an author progressed, he was found among them.

The one scrap of certainty is that he eventually impressed everyone – including the Admiralty, the erudite patrons of the Royal Socicty, the London establishment and the public in general – not through his deeds but through the power of his quill. *A New Voyage Round the World*, an amazing dissertation that (including subsequent editions) exceeded 180,000 words, was published in 1697 and became an instant bestseller.

It detailed in the most elaborate, eloquent and lively manner almost every significant experience he had enjoyed – and not enjoyed – during his circumnavigation. Its level of detail was so impressive that the Admiralty adopted it as a template for future voyages of exploration. Today it is recognised for its part in paving the way for Charles Darwin in the creation of his theories, and it influenced English poet, literary critic and philosopher, Samuel Taylor Coleridge when he wrote the classic poem, 'The Rime of the Ancient Mariner'. Coleridge referred to Dampier as a 'man of exquisite mind'. Dampier's writings also influenced Jonathan Swift when he penned *Gulliver's Travels* (1727).

Dampier's achievements have had a remarkable impact on everyday life. He is recognised for contributing more than 1000 words to the English lexicon, many of which we now take for granted, like 'avocado', 'breadfruit', 'cashew', 'chopsticks', 'posse', 'serrated', 'tortilla' and the reference to a row of buildings as a 'parade'.

The book also precipitated the next major stage in Dampier's life: as the leader of an Admiralty-authorised voyage of exploration to New Holland. His life changed dramatically from the moment *A New Voyage Round the World* was published. It was a literary sensation that instantly propelled him to celebrity status, a popularity that continued to climb in proportion to the unparalleled sales achieved. To meet the market, three reprints were required in the first nine months of release, a success not previously seen in publishing in England. Within twelve months of release, the book had been translated into French and Dutch and three years later into German. His impact on English society was such that on two occasions he was summoned to appear before the Honourable Council of Lords of Trade and Plantations so he could advise them of his thoughts on matters of importance to the national interest.

His writing created an unprecedented wave of interest in travel and adventure among the population, and tantalised the academic minds of members of the Royal Society. He presented fine detail, facts and theories on the broadest imaginable range of humanity, nature and climate like no one before, and every word was worthy of consideration. There was no denying that this single publication made Dampier worthy of consideration as one of England's 'greats'. And there was no stopping him.

In 1699, he published an addendum to his initial work: *A Discourse of Trade-winds, Breezes, Storms, Seasons of the Year, Tides and Currents of the Torrid Zone Throughout the World Detailing Oceanographic and Other Phenomena*. It would become a long-lasting reference work for seafarers in which he presented the conclusions he reached during his twelve years of sailing around the world. In it he detailed the ebb and flow of tides twice daily, and how their influence is strongest closest to coastlines; how offshore islands generally experience a smaller tide range than those close to a mainland. He also explained how his experiences had led to him to distinguish between tidal flows and actual currents. He went on to observe that 'in all places where the trade [wind] blows, we find a current setting with the wind'. His research, findings and discourse were subsequently described by learned people as being remarkable for a man of limited education.

He soon found himself being courted in London's social whirl. Famous English naval administrator, parliamentarian and diarist, Samuel Pepys, was so impressed and fascinated by Dampier's experiences that he invited him to his home for a private dinner with friends. One of the guests was highly regarded diarist and author, John Evelyn, who made reference to the dinner in his diary entry for 10 August 1698:

> I dined with Mr Pepys, where was Captain Dampier, who had been a famous buccaneer … He brought a map, of his observations of the Course of the winds in the South-Sea, & assured us that the maps hitherto extant, were all false as to the Pacific-sea … He is now going abroad again by the King's encouragement, who furnished a ship of 290 tons

It was the reference that Dampier was *going abroad again by the King's encouragement* that confirmed the level of regard he had achieved. More importantly though, it indicated he was about to lead another great maritime expedition: he was going in search of the unknown eastern outline of New Holland.

CHAPTER FIFTEEN

Return to New Holland

1698

It was inevitable that Dampier would come to the attention of the Admiralty, both through the success of his publications and through his contact with influential individuals such as Pepys. The reformed pirate must have enthralled his listeners with stories of his adventures on land and sea, especially his visit to the coast of New Holland. His theories about the eastern side of that land must have intrigued them.

Because of this, the government decided that there were few, if any, better qualified to lead England's first ever expedition into the southern seas dedicated to scientific research and exploration, an endeavour designed, in particular, to unlock the remaining secrets of the Great South Land.

The inspired First Lord of the Admiralty, Lord Orford, initiated moves for such an expedition. He invited Dampier to submit a proposal for such a voyage, which he did in late 1698.

His submission, which suggested a search for the Great South Land, read in part:

> Your Lordship has been pleased to order me to make a proposal of some voyage wherein I might be serviceable to my nation. I know there are several places which might probably be visited with good advantage: but as there is no larger tract of land hitherto undiscovered than the Terra Australis (if that vast space surrounding the South Pole, and extend so far into the warmer climate be a continued land, as a great deal of it is known to be) so 'tis reasonable to conceive that so great a part of the world is not without very valuable commodities to encourage discovery.

The proposal was deemed appropriate, so almost immediately, he was appointed as the expedition's commander. It was an appointment that some observers might have questioned because of his swashbuckling past, but any opposition faded when it was realised his commission came with a royal nod: King William III himself signed off on the voyage. Despite the tens of thousands of nautical miles that forty-seven year old Dampier had logged, this would be the first time he had actually commanded a ship.

Unfortunately, there was no gentle start to it, no time for him to ease himself comfortably into the role of commander.

The mission was trouble-plagued even before the first sail had been hoisted.

Initially, the navy presented Dampier with a vessel named *Jolly Prize*, but he rejected her almost the moment he stepped aboard because she was in such a run-down condition. The next offer, which he accepted, was His Majesty's Britannic Ship *Roebuck*, which had been launched at Wapping, on the Thames, in April 1690.

Measuring 96 feet overall and having a burthen of 292 tons, she was designed to be a navy fireship. She saw action the year of her launch when she took part in the Battle of Beachy – a confrontation with the French on the waters of the English Channel that the English lost. *Roebuck* survived the battle, and about five years later she was upgraded to a 26-gun, fifth-rate fighting ship. However, while initial indications were that she was a well-built vessel capable of undertaking the cruise Dampier was planning, time would reveal she was in not much better condition than *Jolly Prize*: her hull and rig hid a myriad of faults.

What would make matters even worse for the commander was the crew selection process. It was based on a formula that immediately established a 'them and us' mentality. The 'them' side were the nominees from the Royal Navy, while the 'us' were men selected by Dampier himself.

It was the navy's nomination of Lieutenant George Fisher for the position of second-in-command that would create the greatest angst for Dampier.

Dampier was derisive of Fisher, seeing him as a recalcitrant old salt. Fisher held even less respect for his commander, expressing a concern to supportive shipmates that Dampier might resume buccaneering activities with *Roebuck*. Fisher's disdain is said to have led him to refer to Dampier as an 'old dissembling cheating rogue', adding that he 'did not care a fart' for Dampier, and that Dampier 'did not understand the affairs of the navy'.

But there was nothing Damper could do about the appointment; he certainly could not overrule his superiors.

Fisher was one of fifty men and boys making up the crew. Dampier had requested 100 – a figure that took into consideration the likely loss of life due to illness or accident – but the financially strapped navy would have no part of it. The ship was also provided with victuals designed to last just twenty months of what was expected to be a three-year voyage, the theory being that the crew would be able to restock their supplies at numerous ports of call.

There was an even more serious problem. *Roebuck* was being prepared at Deptford Dockyard on the Thames. The sluggish, careless work of naval shipwrights and riggers at this facility would, in years to come, make the dockyard infamous for frustrating efforts to get projects completed. On this occasion, the workers' lethargy and tardiness meant that Dampier's intention to sail from England in late autumn 1698 proved far too optimistic. Before he knew it, he had gone beyond his planned departure date.

With each week lost, his desire to enter the southern seas via the Magellan Straits, north of Cape Horn, became less practicable. While sailing through the strait would be less threatening than rounding the cape, no seafarer worth his salt would dare venture into those waters in the depth of winter.

Dampier's reason for wanting to take that course was understandable: it was the fastest route towards his desired 'discoveries upon the eastern and least known side of the Terra Australis'. By sailing to the west from where the Magellan Straits met with the Pacific Ocean, then directing a course for the known latitudes and longitudes as plotted by Abel Tasman on his 1642 voyage, Dampier would have the best possible chance of discovering the entire coast, or whatever else might be there, thus solving the mystery.

However, like Dampier, the Lords of the Admiralty recognised that it was too late for *Roebuck* to sail through the Magellan Straits, so directed that the ship should sail via the Cape of Good Hope, then 'stretch away towards New Holland'. This course would see *Roebuck* follow the same route sailed by the Dutch East Indies trading ships, one that took them towards the *west* coast of New Holland.

Once Dampier had reached that coast, he was to explore as much of it as he could, loop across the northern coast of New Guinea (since the English still had no knowledge of Torres Strait), then, when able to turn south, head towards the assumed position of the eastern shores of the Great South Land.

It was a bitingly cold January day when Dampier ordered the sailing master and Lieutenant Fisher to prepare *Roebuck* for sea. The commander had received final orders from the Admiralty in late November, so there was no reason to delay the departure any longer, especially when there was an ideal offshore wind blowing across the Downs where *Roebuck* was at anchor.

Just minutes after the call came from the captain to set sail, the windlass was clacking away, the bower was being raised, pulley blocks were screeching under the load of halyards, sheets and braces, and sails were being progressively hauled down. At the same time, the scruffy-looking deckhands – most wearing dreary garb as grey as that miserable winter day – were either hauling away on the lines or working precariously across the yards and in the rig.

Soon the Royal Navy's historic mission to regions unknown was under way. Dampier later recorded:

> I sailed from the Downs early on Saturday, January 14, 1699, with a fair wind, in His Majesty's Ship the *Roebuck*; carrying but 12 guns in this voyage … We had several of the King's ships in company, bound for Spithead and Plymouth, and by noon we were off Dungeness.

In little more than a week, *Roebuck* was beyond the entrance to the English Channel, rolling and surging her way south towards Tenerife, which was more than 1600 nautical miles from the Downs. Tension between the two factions in the crew had already surfaced, influenced no doubt by the obviously growing disrespect between Dampier and his second-in-charge. The pair continually exchanged terse and derogatory words, before eventually agreeing that it was not in the best interests of the voyage for them to continue in such a manner. But the peace between them was short-lived.

After a brief stay in Tenerife, *Roebuck* headed back out to sea. Dampier had decided before leaving England that he would not stop at Cape Town unless it was absolutely necessary. Instead, he would sail from Tenerife to Bahia, 'the most considerable town in Brazil', 700 nautical miles north-east of Rio de Janeiro, and some 3000 nautical miles away to the south-west of Tenerife.

He explained the main reason for this decision: 'there I might refresh my men and prepare them for a long run to New Holland'. Dampier realised that this port of call might provide a second, equally important, benefit. The acrimony between himself and Fisher was worse than ever; if it continued, this landfall would provide him with the perfect opportunity to rid the ship of his unwanted deputy.

But long before Bahia was in sight, the relationship was becoming untenable. At one stage Dampier had Fisher caned for his rebellious attitude, an action he hoped would bring his first lieutenant to his senses. Instead, all it did was widen the gulf between 'them and us', a circumstance that made Dampier fear that Fisher might soon lead a mutiny against him. There was only one way to prevent this: Fisher was clapped into irons and confined to his quarters.

Each day, as *Roebuck* crossed the Equator and rode the tradewinds towards Bahia, the toxic relationship between the two men further aggravated the already existing air of distrust between the two factions in the crew. The situation was so tense that Dampier is said to have spent much of his time sleeping on deck well-armed, with his loyal men around him.

Not even when *Roebuck* rounded the headland where Brazil's then capital, Salvador, was located and sailed into Bahia's port, did he feel he could relax. He hastened to get permission from local authorities to anchor *Roebuck* some distance inside the harbour because of 'the fear I had lest my people should run away with the ship'. His next priority was to arrange for Fisher to be taken ashore and imprisoned, which, much to his delight, was achieved successfully: the lieutenant was handed over to the Portuguese governor in the colony and put in jail. The plan was for Fisher to be detained there until a ship arrived that could ferry him back to England. Once there, Dampier hoped he would be charged with misconduct under Royal Navy regulations.

On 22 April 1699, while in Bahia, Dampier drafted a letter to the Admiralty which explained his reasons for putting Fisher ashore and sending him home. He documented the events that led to Fisher being caned, and insisted he had only struck Fisher in self-defence. Dampier also told of a series of disputes, including one relating to the quality of the bread on the ship, and how Fisher had reacted angrily after he was not permitted to have 'two little boys' on board as his servants. On this point he suggested sodomy might have been the actual real reason for the boys being aboard.

It was good riddance as far as Dampier was concerned: he could now get on with his real task. Before setting sail again, he took time to note as much information as he could in his journal relating to the town, its people, their lifestyle, commerce, community and climate – all written with his usual keen eye for detail. While conducting this research – which was a requirement in his orders from the Admiralty – he had his men carefully examine the rigging and sails, and place an additional 10 tons of rock ballast in the bilge. These measures would ensure that *Roebuck* was more stable, and thus better prepared for the rigours that would come should wild winds and rough seas bedevil them in the latitudes of the Roaring Forties.

After spending a month in Bahia, Dampier and his ship were finally ready for sea:

[H]aving a fine land-breeze on the 23rd [April] in the morning, I went away from the anchoring place before it was light; and then lay by till daylight that we might see the better how to go out of the harbour. I had a pilot … who went out with me, to whom I gave 3 dollars; but I found I could as well have gone out myself by the soundings I made at coming in. The wind was east by north and fair weather. By 10 o'clock I was got past all danger and then sent away my pilot.

Six weeks later, after skirting the near-windless high-pressure weather system in the South Atlantic, *Roebuck* was closing on the Cape of Good Hope. It was early in the day, and all eyes were eagerly scanning the horizon to the east and south-east in the hope of seeing land. Instead, a sail was sighted off to leeward: a ship flying English colours. Dampier ordered the helmsman to change course towards the ship so he could 'speak with her'. She was *Antelope*, of London, and carrying English migrants to the Bay of Bengal.

Having been rowed across to *Antelope* and invited aboard by her captain, Dampier took time to compare notes with that ship's navigator, and confirmed they were about 60 nautical miles west of the Cape. Ironically, the ship's commander, Captain Hammond, told Dampier that he had feared *Roebuck* might be a pirate ship. He was no doubt relieved to learn that *Roebuck*'s captain had retired from the trade.

This was also a most hospitable encounter for *Roebuck*'s crew, as Dampier revealed:

When I took leave I was presented with half a mutton, 12 cabbages, 12 pumpkins, 6 pound of butter, 6 couple of stock-fish, and a quantity of parsnips; sending them some oatmeal which they wanted.

As both ships were planning to double the cape, they sailed on in company, and by mid-afternoon the jagged profile of the peninsula, about 30 nautical miles away, could be seen by the lookouts stationed at the masthead.

By four o'clock the following afternoon they were well round the cape, and there the two ships parted company. *Antelope* of London turned to the north-east and headed to her destination, while *Roebuck* was pressed deeper to the south, towards the Roaring Forties.

On the evening of 6 June, the men on deck were treated to a superbly colourful sunset. But for Dampier the well-seasoned sailor, spectacular as this sight was, it was also an omen:

> [T]he clouds were gilded very prettily to the eye,
> though at the same time my mind dreaded the
> consequences of it ... I took the more particular notice
> of all this because I have generally observed such
> coloured clouds to appear before an approaching storm:
> and, this being winter here and the time for bad
> weather, I expected and provided for a violent blast of
> wind by reefing our topsails, and giving a strict charge
> to my officers to hand them or take them in if the wind
> should grow stronger.

Dampier's concern was justified. *Roebuck* was soon feeling the full ferocity of a blisteringly cold winter storm in the Southern Ocean:

Before 2 in the morning it came on very fierce, and we kept right before wind and sea, the wind still increasing: but the ship was very governable, and steered incomparably well. At 8 in the morning we settled our foreyard, lowering it 4 or 5 foot, and we ran very swiftly; especially when the squalls of rain or hail from a black cloud came overhead, for then it blew excessive hard. These, though they did not last long, yet came very thick and fast one after another. The sea also ran very high; but we running so violently before wind and sea we shipped little or no water; though a little washed into our upper deck ports; and with it a … cuttlefish was cast up on the carriage of a gun.

It was an incredible tempest, during which the wind blew extraordinarily hard for two days, then remained a westerly gale for the next eight days. While there were mounting concerns about *Roebuck*'s structural integrity, she came through it remarkably well. By 19 June, when conditions began to abate, the ship had covered about 600 leagues – 1800 nautical miles, an impressive run in those days.

Dampier had little wildlife to observe and report on during this part of the voyage, except for the occasional sighting of a whale. But by the time he calculated they were about 180 nautical miles to the west of the coast of New Holland, there was an increasing number of objects – some known and others unknown – to be seen every day. On one occasion he saw 'a large garfish leap 4 times by us, which seemed to be as big as a porpoise'.

He had also noted with interest 'how backward and refractory the seamen are apt to be in long voyages when they know not whither they are going, how ignorant they are of the nature of the winds and the shifting seasons of the monsoons, and how little even the officers themselves generally are skilled in the variation of the needle and the use of the azimuth compass'. His own love of navigation saw him fascinated by the variation he observed in the compass needle as *Roebuck* sailed through these waters. He logged these changes almost daily, so as to satisfy the requirements of the Royal Navy.

Late July proved to be a taxing time for Dampier. The sighting of weed and other features of nature floating on the sea surface confirmed that *Roebuck* was close to land. But while this delivered a level of anticipation and excitement to those on board, it also meant the highest degree of caution was called for. While many ships had sighted this coast and logged its dominant features, the charts from which the commander was working could be highly inaccurate – and that proved to be the case.

Based on the information at hand, Dampier believed *Roebuck* was closing on the coast of New Holland to the south of the treacherous Abrolhos Islands. Then, through his own careful analysis of soundings and plots, he deduced that 'we had fallen into the north of the shoal, and that it was laid down wrong in my sea-chart'. His considerable ability as a navigator led him to quickly discover the reason why his charts were wrong – why they showed land and shoals that did not exist at those locations: 'the latitudes marked in the draughts, or sights here given, are not the latitude of the land, but of the ship when the sight was taken.'

This error meant *Roebuck* was sailing blind: nothing on the chart could be relied upon. So it was only through greater vigilance from the lookouts, with the leadsman constantly sounding the bottom, and with the crew operating on high alert, that they could proceed with any degree of comfort. Regardless, only the smallest of sails were set during the night, enough to have *Roebuck* barely making headway, and only enough so that she would respond when the helmsman turned the rudder.

Relief came around nine o'clock the following morning. It was 1 August 1699 and they were finally in sight of the coast of New Holland:

> [W]e saw it from our topmast-head, and were distant
> from it about 10 leagues; having then 40 fathom water,
> and clean sand. About 3 hours after we saw it on our
> quarter-deck, being by judgment about 6 leagues off,
> and we had then 40 fathom [water], [and] clean sand.

Dampier's most pressing need was to find a safe anchorage, preferably a harbour, 'to refresh us after our tedious voyage' –

a non-stop passage from Brazil that had covered some 10,000 nautical miles and taken more than three months to complete. *Roebuck*'s average speed for the distance had been around 4.5 knots, which was about normal for a ship of this type.

The search for a safe haven was not easy. Each time *Roebuck* was guided closer to the coast, the lookout stationed at the masthead would shout warnings of rocks and shoals ahead. These constant alerts, and Dampier's weather eye, dictated the next plan of action:

> I stood off to sea again, in the evening of the second of
> August, fearing a storm on a lee shore, in a place where
> there was no shelter, and desiring at least to have sea-
> room … By nine o'clock at night we had got a pretty
> good offing; but, the wind [was] still increasing …
> At two in the morning August 3 it blew very hard,
> and the sea was much raised; so that I furled all my
> sails but my mainsail.

For the next three days Dampier and his crew fought hard to hold their ship well clear of the coast in conditions where the wind 'would blow very fierce while the squalls of rain were over our heads'.

By 6 August the wind had eased and the sea-state had dropped, so Dampier resumed his search for a harbour. Land soon came into view, and not long afterwards they saw 'an opening' in the long stretch of low-profile, ochre-coloured cliffs. Dampier ordered one of the ship's boats to be launched over the side then sent ahead of *Roebuck*, so any dangers in the form of reefs or shallows could be identified and avoided. As land was approached, Dampier was able to confirm that the southern end of this 13 nautical mile wide entrance was the northern tip of Dirk Hartog Island.

The following day, the commander and his men were more than pleased when *Roebuck*, under the minimum amount of sail, glided into what was an exceptionally large sound, which Dampier almost immediately named Shark's (now Shark) Bay, because of the 'abundance' of sharks they sighted. More than two centuries later, the surface area of this sound would be calculated as 13,000 square kilometres.

Roebuck having been at sea for so long, the priority was to replenish the ship's water supply. As soon as the bower was set and *Roebuck* declared to be safely at anchor, the order was for a boat to go ashore 'to seek for fresh water'.

This exercise would do little more than make the crew brutally aware of the arid nature of the coast. The men returned to the ship with empty water casks, which made Dampier decide to lead a new search for water the following day:

> The next morning I went ashore myself, carrying
> pickaxes and shovels with me, to dig for water: and axes
> to cut wood. We tried in several places for water but,
> finding none after several trials, nor in several miles
> compass, we left any farther search for it and, spending

the rest of the day in cutting wood, we went aboard at
night.

His time onshore did, however, allow him to detail in his
journal, in his usual eloquent manner, the flora and fauna he
observed. The description in his 1703 publication *A Voyage to
New Holland* (which became Volume III of *A New Voyage
Round the World*) reads in part:

> [I]n this bay or sound we were now in the land is low
> by the seaside, rising gradually in within the land. The
> mould is sand by the seaside, producing a large sort of
> samphire, which bears a white flower ... The grass
> grows in great tufts as big as a bushel, here and there a
> tuft; being intermixed with much heath, much of the
> kind we have growing on our commons in England ...
> [W]e saw none but eagles of the larger sorts of birds;
> but 5 or 6 sorts of small birds. The biggest sort of these
> were not bigger than larks; some no bigger than wrens,
> all singing with great variety of fine shrill notes ... The
> land animals that we saw here were only a sort of
> raccoon ... [T]hese have very short forelegs; but go
> jumping upon them as the others do (and like them are
> very good meat) and a sort of iguana ... There are also
> some green-turtle weighing about 200 pounds. Of
> these we caught 2 ... These served all my company 2
> days; and they were indifferent sweet meat. Of the

sharks we caught a great many which our men eat very savourily.

History would recognise these words as being the first proper detailing of Australian flora and fauna. As a consequence, Dampier would later be acclaimed as Australia's first naturalist. The botanical drawings that accompanied the notes were, it is believed, created by Dampier's clerk, James Brand.

Roebuck was anchored in three different locations on the western side of the sound during her visit to Shark's Bay. Fortunately, while the crew were unable to locate water, even when they dug wells, Dampier recorded that 'my company were all here very well refreshed with raccoons, turtle, shark, and other fish, and some fowls; so that we were now all much brisker than when we came in hither'.

Having explored as much of Shark's Bay as possible over a week, and with the need to find water becoming increasingly urgent, on 14 August Dampier weighed anchor and sailed *Roebuck* back to the open sea via a challenging course, then turned north. While he had gathered a considerable amount of detail relating to the land, flora and fauna, he made no record of having sighted any of the Indigenous population, probably because of the lack of water in the region. It was becoming increasingly unlikely that he would be able to meet one of the directions contained in his orders from the Admiralty: to return home with any inhabitants of New Holland, or other destinations he might visit, who were 'willing' to join him.

Soon *Roebuck* was riding a strong south-easterly wind up the coast and making good speed, but the continual sightings of shoals and reefs kept Dampier cautious. By day, they would close on the coast so they could get an appreciation of what was there; by night, sail was reduced to the minimum so *Roebuck* could amble offshore and remain in deep water. Alternatively, if the water off the coast was shallow enough, the ship would be anchored for the night.

Around 20 August, they were off what is now known as Exmouth Gulf and soon after the commander, having closely monitored the direction and strength of the tides, wondered if there might be a passage 'to the south of New Holland and New Guinea *into the Great South Sea eastward*'.

Later, when he related the story of this voyage in *A Voyage to New Holland*, he wrote, '[I] told my officers so: but I would not attempt [to look for] it at this time because we wanted water and could not depend upon finding it there.' Excellent navigator that he was, Dampier partly based his theory on the discrepancies he found between water depths he had recorded and those of Tasman, which he was finding to be inaccurate.

As *Roebuck* sailed further north, an ever-increasing number of islands, large and small, began appearing over the horizon. Dampier eventually decided to anchor off one of the larger islands, about 12 miles offshore:

We rode a league from the island and I presently went ashore, and carried shovels to dig for water, but found none. There grow here 2 or three sorts of shrubs, one just like rosemary; and therefore I called this Rosemary Island.

This island has the same name on modern charts. It is located directly north of the West Australian town that now bears the explorer's name, and 10 nautical miles west of an archipelago that has also been given his name. Today, the town of Dampier is a major industrial port servicing the petrochemical, iron ore and natural gas export industries. Prophetically, on observing the latitude and his surrounds while at anchor off Rosemary Island, Dampier speculated that 'among so many islands we might have found some sort of rich mineral'.

At 5 a.m. on 23 August, as a dusty orange sunrise was breaking in the east, Dampier decided to weigh anchor and continue on what he hoped would be a casual cruise. It was far from that:

[B]efore 9 the sea breeze came on us very strong, and increasing, we took in our topsails and stood off under 2 courses and a mizzen, this being as much sail as we could carry. The sky was clear, there being not one cloud to be seen … The wind continued very strong til 12, then it began to abate: I have seldom met with a stronger breeze.

It was not until 31 August that *Roebuck* was anchored and the men again went ashore in search of water, and here they came into close contact – too close, in fact – with some of the inhabitants of the coast. Dampier was keen to make a peaceful approach to them, partly in the hope that they might be able to guide him to water. He decided to have two armed men accompany him 'purposely to catch one of them'. This led to an undesired confrontation in which one of the 'New Hollanders' was shot, and crewman Alexander Beale was speared through the cheek 'by one of their lances'. Dampier immediately retreated, 'being very sorry for what had happened'.

Consequently, they were no closer to finding water than when they first arrived on the coast, even though the men had dug wells up to 9 feet deep in some places. This meant only one thing for the commander: if they were to survive he must consider where to go to refill the ship's water casks.

It was a decision process that accelerated with the sighting of 'two or three beasts like hungry wolves, lean like so many skeletons, being nothing but skin and bones'. These were probably dingoes, and their appearance left him even more certain there was little, if any, water to be found in the region.

By now, *Roebuck* was only a short distance from King Sound, the huge inlet on the coast of New Holland that Dampier had partly explored when *Cygnet* anchored there some years earlier. Up until this time, his desire had been to reach that sound and explore beyond to the east as far as possible, sailing to places that might lead him to make the grandest discovery of all: the east coast.

Had he achieved this goal and reached the tip of Cape York, he would have almost certainly exposed the secret the Spanish had treasured for so long: the existence of Torres Strait, and the much-discussed passage into the Pacific.

However, as the course east was fraught with navigational hazards, and Dutch charts showed not even the vaguest suggestion that the strait existed, Dampier decided enough was enough. The well-being of his men was his priority, so he would let common sense prevail, and sail to where he knew he could get water:

> And thus having ranged about a considerable time upon
> this coast without finding any good fresh water, or any
> convenient place to clean the ship, as I had hoped for:
> and it being moreover the height of the dry season, and
> my men growing scorbutic for want of refreshments, so
> that I had little encouragement to search further, I
> resolved to leave this coast and accordingly in the
> beginning of September set sail towards Timor.

In the preceding weeks, *Roebuck* had sailed along almost 1000 nautical miles of the north-west coast of New Holland. Dampier had continued writing in his most detailed style regarding everything of interest that he had seen – a treasure trove of information, some of it superbly deduced.

This large and hitherto almost unknown tract of land is situated so very advantageously in the richest climates of the world ... [so] I could not but hope to meet with some fruitful lands, continent or islands, or both, productive of any of the rich fruits, drugs, or spices (perhaps minerals also, etc.) that are in the other parts of the torrid zone, under equal parallels of latitude.

Some two decades later, when his account of this voyage was being absorbed by an adventure-hungry public, Dampier modestly explained in the preface that the things he had discovered 'are most worthy of our diligentest search and inquiry; being the various and wonderful works of God in different parts of the world: and however unfit a person I may be in other respects to have undertaken this task, yet at least I have given a faithful account, and have found some things undiscovered by any before.' He added that these discoveries 'may at least be some assistance and direction to better qualified persons who shall come after me.' They were certainly that for the members of the Royal Society, Captain James Cook and Joseph Banks. They would use Dampier's three remarkable publications for information and research purposes while on the historic *Endeavour* expedition in 1770.

Right then, though, while it was the lack of fresh water rather than research that was his concern, Dampier still pondered the prospect of unravelling the mystery of the missing portion of the Great South Land by cruising across the top of New Guinea. Yes, he told himself, it was a route worth investigating, a passage that might lead *Roebuck*, at some stage, to complete a loop around New Holland.

Once again, he outlined in the preface of his book what influenced his thinking, and his desires:

> I chose to coast along to the northward, and so to the east, and so thought to come round by the south of Terra Australis in my return back, which should be in the summer season there: and this passage back also I now thought I might possibly be able to shorten, should it appear, at my getting to the east coast of New Guinea, that there is a channel there coming out into these seas, as I now suspected, near Rosemary Island: unless the high tides and great indraught thereabout should be occasioned by the mouth of some large river ... But I rather thought it a channel or strait than a river ...

He was similarly mystified by the configuration of the land mass. The large number of islands that he had encountered since sailing north from Shark's Bay caused him to think there might be 'nothing but ranges of pretty large islands against the sea, whatever might be behind them to the eastward, whether sea or land, continent or islands'.

It was on 5 September 1699 – the early days of spring in the southern hemisphere – that Dampier committed to weigh anchor and coast along the shoreline as far north-east as possible, before reaching the point where he had no option but to turn away towards Timor.

Within two days, however, this stretch of ocean became increasingly treacherous. *Roebuck* had sailed out of sight of the low-lying coast, yet the leadsman continually confirmed they were in only 7 fathoms of water. It was an alarming situation, especially considering the velocity and unpredictable nature of the fast-flowing and swirling currents. Dampier later recalled, 'that made me afraid to go near a coast so shallow … for should a ship be near a shoal she might be hurled upon it unavoidably by a strong tide'.

Now, even his faint hopes of reaching King Sound had to be abandoned. All the enticements of this coast were eliminated. The helmsman, holding the vertical whipstaff steering lever in his hands, was directed to change course and 'steer away for the island Timor'. As *Roebuck*'s rudder turned and the wake became a widening arc, so the crew on watch responded by hauling on, or easing the braces and sheets, so the sails were trimmed to best capture the prevailing 'gentle gale' – a light breeze.

Just nine days later, there was cause for jubilation among the crew, and Dampier noted the reason: 'a little before sunset we saw, to our great joy, the tops of the high mountains of Timor, peeping out of the clouds'. This was a relief of sorts, as Dampier was aware of Dutch and Portuguese settlements on the island, but he knew not where. He went looking for water anywhere he thought it might exist, but it did not come easily. *Roebuck* coasted along the island's southern shore towards the east for 60 nautical miles without seeing any sign of fresh water:

> We saw scarce any opening fit for our boats; and the fast land was still barricaded with mangroves; so that here was no hope to get water; nor was it likely that there should be hereabouts any European settlement ...
>
> Weary of running thus fruitlessly along the south side of the island to the eastward I resolved to return the way I came, and compassing the west end of the island, make a search along the north side of it.

It was not until *Roebuck* was guided through a narrow passage at the western end of Timor that the first sign of relief came their way. A Dutch sloop appeared in the distance, coming towards them, and when the two vessels came within hailing distance, Dampier launched one of his boats and sent an officer and men to the sloop.

When the men rowed back to *Roebuck* they brought news that Dampier did not want to hear. The sloop was carrying the governor and about forty soldiers from a Dutch fort not far away and they were surprised that an English ship would be in the region. Worse still, the governor could not be convinced they weren't pirates, so he suggested most strongly that they not go near the fort. The reason was simple: some two years earlier the islanders had been routed by French pirates, so they now detested foreign visitors, so much so that they would have no hesitation in killing Dampier and his crew should they venture onshore, pirates or not.

As alarming as this news was to Dampier, his need for water outweighed the threat. He had no option but to risk a confrontation with the islanders, as well as the governor and his men manning the fort. So he moved *Roebuck* to within two leagues of the garrison and anchored her there – well beyond cannon range. From that anchorage, he could take stock of the situation and implement a plan.

The following morning he sent his clerk to the fort to negotiate with the governor. Initially it was a stand-off: the governor refused to supply the ship with water. But finally, after hours of awkward and sometimes heated discussion, he relented ... on condition that *Roebuck* remained where she was, and that the water casks to be filled were transported by a small boat. Dampier agreed, noting that the governor proved to be a man of his word: 'he sent slaves to bring the casks ashore and fill them; for that none of our men must come ashore'.

That afternoon Dampier decided he should try to appease the governor and possibly even create the opportunity for his men to go ashore. So he sent his boat carrying a senior officer to visit the governor and present him with a token of peace: beer. The offer of the beer was rejected, although the governor did respond in a somewhat positive fashion by sending back an additional ton of water for the ship.

On returning to *Roebuck*, the officer – who was not identified but is believed to be his bosun, John Norwood – told Dampier and crewmates that he had been made feel most unwelcome by the governor, who was 'very rough with him'. Also, the officer reported that more guns had been mounted at the fort and they were aimed out into the bay towards the ship; in other words, there was no doubt that their presence was unwanted and in no way should they even consider venturing to the shore.

Soon after this, without Dampier's knowledge, the same officer consulted with fellow officers, telling them that he believed it was not safe to remain in the port, and they agreed. Dampier soon sensed a rat, realising the officer was manipulating others for his own ends. He was certain the man had concocted the story that *Roebuck* was unwelcome so he could pursue a personal desire to return to England.

Dampier later wrote, 'my officer who occasioned these fears in us by his own forgeries was himself for going no further'. He elaborated, saying this officer was 'as cross and discouraging to my men as possible, that he might hasten our return [to England]; being very negligent and backward in most businesses I had occasion to employ him in … He was also industrious to stir up the seamen to mutiny; telling them, among other things, that any Dutch ship might lawfully take us in these seas'.

Fortunately for Dampier, the remaining officers soon recognised that their shipmate was trying to rouse them into mutiny with no valid reason. They chose to stand by their captain, agreeing they would sail as one until he made the decision to turn for home.

There is no reference to what became of the malcontent officer, but it is apparent that *Roebuck* did not stay within sight of the Dutch fort for much longer. On 29 September, she had cleared Kupang Bay and was being guided along the coast of Timor on a clockwise course, her destination being, hopefully, a Portuguese settlement some 40 leagues away.

Once again Dampier was in awe of the rapid flow-rate and direction of the tidal currents in the area, some tides being so strong that the ship could not make headway. Worse still, these fast-flowing tidal streams almost caused the loss of a number of his key men, who were sent ashore late in the day to search for the still much-needed water. Their boat became marooned among dense and tangled mangroves on a swampy shore, and by the time they managed to free themselves, *Roebuck* had drifted out of sight – carried away by a powerful tide.

Gravely concerned, Dampier lit lanterns on the ship and fired a cannon at regular intervals, all in the hope that the missing sailors would return safely. But at daylight there was still no sign of them. Around 10am there came relief: the boat was seen as a faint speck in the distance. The men were so far away it took more than an hour for them to be recovered.

Once *Roebuck* was again under way she remained on a course towards the north–north–east, until another location seen on land gave new hope for finding fresh water.

Dampier had to investigate, so called for the sails to be hauled up and his ship brought to anchor. With that done, he and many of his men went ashore, where, much to their delight, they found a large freshwater pond 'within 50 paces of the sea'.

This was like liquid gold to them, so much so that within three days they had put 26 tons of additional water into the casks stacked in *Roebuck*'s bilge. Later in the day, there were additional delectable benefits to be enjoyed from what would prove to be a maritime oasis; some men detailed to cast the seine net from one of the small boats caught sufficient fish to feed the entire crew, while others who were 'sent out a-fowling' returned to the ship proudly displaying pigeons, parrots and cockatoos.

With fresh food and ample water now on board, Dampier continued with his exploration and appreciation of the coast, although finding the Portuguese settlement was still his priority. All too often *Roebuck* remained at the mercy of faint breezes and strong, adverse currents, so it wasn't until 12 October when, 'having a pretty brisk seabreeze, we coasted alongshore; and, seeing a great many houses by the sea, I stood in with my ship till I was within 2 miles of them'.

Dampier's pinnace was launched over the side so an officer and a Portuguese seaman – who had joined the ship in Brazil to act as an interpreter in situations such as this – could go ashore and explain to the local governor where the ship was from, and why it was there. Dampier later recorded that the greetings were most cordial, but there was one slight misunderstanding:

About eleven o'clock my mate returned on board and told me he had been … kindly received by the gentleman … who said we were welcome, and should have anything the island afforded; and that he was not himself the governor, but only a deputy. He asked why we did not salute their fort when we anchored; my mate answered that we saw no colours flying, and therefore did not know there was any fort till he came ashore and saw the guns; and if we had known that there was a fort yet that we could not have given any salute till we knew that they would answer it with the like number of guns. The deputy said it was very well; and that he had but little powder; and therefore would gladly buy some of us, if we had any to spare; which my mate told him we had not.

The following day it became even more apparent to Dampier that his English ship was most welcome when the deputy sent aboard

a present of two young buffaloes, six goats, four kids, 140 coconuts, 300 ripe mangoes, and six ripe jacks. This was all very acceptable; and all the time we lay here we had fresh provision, and plenty of fruits; so that those of my men that were sick of the scurvy soon recovered and grew lusty.

Despite the constant, and arduous, demands placed on him as leader of this voyage of discovery, Dampier did not lose his enthusiasm for spending time at his desk in his cabin with goosefeather quill in hand, writing in his usual expressive fashion about anything of interest he had observed. A two-hour meeting onshore with the deputy governor was one such event:

> Our interview was in a small church which was filled with the better sort of people; the poorer sort thronging on the outside, and looking in upon us: for the church had no wall but at the east end; the sides and the west end being open, saving only that it had boards about three or four foot high from the ground. I saw but two white men among them all; one was a padre that came along with the lieutenant; the other was an inhabitant of the town. The rest were all copper-coloured, with black lank hair.

Of particular interest to Dampier during this conversation was the weather: what could he expect at this time of year? Through his interpreter, he was advised that the north-west monsoon could appear any time soon. This news was sufficiently disconcerting for him to write 'that reason desired me to make what haste I could from hence; for that 'twas impossible to ride here when those winds came'.

The weather news meant Dampier's hope for circumnavigating the Great South Land, and thus unearthing the secrets of the unknown east coast, had literally gone with the wind. Common sense and seafaring nous confirmed that, with the monsoon season approaching, it would be too dangerous to venture much further on this voyage.

Dampier was forced to accept that the time was fast approaching when he would have no option but to turn back for home. However, that time was yet to arrive: he would continue on, even though *Roebuck*'s timbers were by now creaking and groaning in an audible protest at the miles the ship had covered, and the punishment she had taken from strong winds and stormy seas. Also influencing his decision to continue on was the knowledge that his men had regained their health, and the water casks were full. There was still time to cruise the coast of New Guinea, and hopefully make discoveries there.

There was, however, a task he must accomplish before he could continue: he had to do what he could to preserve the seaworthiness of his ship. So, after departing the Portuguese settlement on 22 October, he opted to return to Kupang Bay, where he hoped to careen the ship so the seams between the planks could be sealed, and other maintenance carried out. This destination brought an added bonus: his men could catch fish using the seine, and hunt buffaloes onshore.

Unfortunately, after reaching the bay, they realised there was no safe way to careen *Roebuck*; the shore was too muddy and the tides were not suitable. Then, through the fault of his carpenter, it would have been a waste of time careening anyway. Dampier wrote in his journal that 'by that time the ship's sides were caulked, my pitch was almost spent; which was all owing to the carpenter's wilful waste and ignorance, so that I had nothing to lay on upon the ship's bottom'.

Roebuck remained in Kupang Bay for seven weeks, and during that time there was some effort made to clean and protect the hull below the waterline. By moving heavy items to one side of the ship, and possibly by attaching halyards to trees onshore then tensioning, she was heeled so crew could clean off as much shellfish and weed as they could reach, before coating the bottom with the only protection they had in the absence of pitch: a thick, lime-like mixture made from shell grit and water.

Unfortunately for all those on board, there was never a moment when they could completely relax while in the bay, as both Dutch and Portuguese had warned Dampier that they could be attacked by cold-blooded islanders:

[The Kupangayans] have an inveterate malice to their neighbours, insomuch that they kill all they meet, and bring away their heads in triumph. The great men of Kupang stick the heads of those they have killed on poles; and set them on the tops of their houses; and these they esteem above all their other riches. The inferior sort bring the heads of those they kill into houses made for that purpose; of which there was one at the Indian village near the fort Concordia, almost full of heads as I was told. I know not what encouragement they have for their inhumanity.

Finally, with everything in readiness, *Roebuck* sailed from the bay on 12 December 1699 and headed towards the coast of New Guinea.

The imminent arrival of the monsoon season, with its high winds and heavy rain, prompted Dampier to sail as fast as possible so he would have the best possible opportunity to explore the coast of New Guinea and possibly discover regions that were unknown to Europeans.

As had been the case since leaving England, the commander was as much an essayist as he was an expedition leader. His writings relating to his experiences in Timor again highlight the talent that set him apart from all other maritime explorers. His observations during this part of the voyage amount to a remarkable 4000 words, describing almost everything he saw – from the local inhabitants and a most impressive volcano through to the weather, soil, metals, woods, the canula-fistula tree, wild fig trees, fruits, animals, fowls, the ringing bird, fish, oysters so large that 'three or four ... roasted will suffice a man for one meal', and 'cockles as big as a man's head'.

The coast of New Guinea was about 700 nautical miles away to the north-east of Kupang, and Dampier island-hopped for much of the way there. As fate would have it, it was only a few hours after the ship's bell rang out to signal that it was midnight, and the turn of the century, when land was sighted on a hazy horizon ahead. This was Dampier's impression:

On New Year's Day [1700] we first descried the land of
New Guinea, which appeared to be high land; and the
next day we saw several high islands on the coast of
New Guinea, and ran in with the mainland … It is high
even land, very well clothed with tall flourishing trees,
which appeared very green and gave us a very pleasant
prospect … We had fair weather for a long time; only
when near any land we had some tornadoes; but off at
sea commonly clear weather; though if in sight of land
we usually saw many black clouds hovering about it.

The existence of New Guinea had been known since the
Portuguese and Spanish sailed their vessels through the region
in the early sixteenth century. The first known European
sighting was by Portuguese explorer Jorge de Menezes, who
came across the main island some time in 1526 or 1527. He is
credited with having given his discovery the name 'Papua', a
Malay word meaning 'people with frizzy hair'. Less than
twenty years later, Spanish seafarer Yñigo Ortiz de Retez
referred to the same land mass as 'New Guinea' because he
considered the inhabitants to be similar in stature and
appearance to the natives of the Guinea coast in Africa.

Historians would later reveal that the lineage of the
inhabitants of Papua New Guinea dates back 60,000 years, to
when there was a migratory movement towards the Australian
continent. It is suggested that the aggressive demeanour of the
inhabitants of New Guinea was the reason the Spanish and

Portuguese did not consider establishing settlements there. Dampier's *A Voyage to New Holland* gave the world its first insight into these people and their land.

From the outset of this voyage, it was Dampier's intention not to burden his readers with details of latitude and longitude and the daily weather conditions *Roebuck* experienced. But he probably made his first contact with New Guinea somewhere around Triton Bay, to the south of Berau Bay, on the western side of the now Indonesian territory of West Papua.

Roebuck cruised north in fair and favourable weather – 'a fine gale of wind'. Near Berau Bay pillars of smoke were seen coming from a small island, so Dampier decided to head there and hopefully make contact with the natives. Early the next morning, as *Roebuck* closed on the shore, two canoes came very close to the ship, its occupants not making any threatening gestures, but rather encouraging Dampier to follow them to the shore:

> I went after them in my pinnace, carrying with me
> knives, beads, glasses, hatchets, etc. When we came
> near the shore I called to them in the Malayan language:
> I saw but two men at first, the rest lying in ambush
> behind the bushes; but as soon as I threw ashore some
> knives and other toys they came out, flung down their
> weapons, and came into the water by the boat's side,
> making signs of friendship by pouring water on their
> heads with one hand which they dipped into the sea.

The next day in the afternoon several other canoes
came aboard and brought many roots and fruits, which
we purchased.

Dampier also purchased 'fine parrots', and would have bought a slave, 'but they would not barter for anything but calicos, which I had not'.

As there was still no indication of an approaching monsoon, Dampier continued to push his luck, acutely aware that should such a threat appear on the horizon, he would have to run for cover. By 4 February, *Roebuck* had rounded the north-western cape of Papua New Guinea and was set on an offshore south-south-easterly course. On the 16th she had 'crossed the line', this time from south to north. The forever attentive Dampier noted that the compass variation at this point was '6 degrees 26 minutes east'.

He called on the crew to be vigilant around the clock, as 'there were many great logs and trees swimming by us', some large enough to hole the ship should *Roebuck* collide with one. Even so, Dampier saw in this danger a benefit for the ship and his research:

I hoisted out the pinnace and sent her to take up some
of this driftwood. In a little time she came aboard with
a great tree in a tow, which we could hardly hoist in
with all our tackles. We cut up the tree and split it for
firewood. It was much worm-eaten and had in it some

live worms above an inch long, and about the bigness of
a goose-quill, and having their heads crusted over with
a thin shell.

As the weeks went by, the weather became unstable. Dampier
noted that on the 28th *Roebuck* encountered violent tornadoes,
rain, waterspouts and a thunderstorm that delivered more
lightning than seen at any other time on the voyage.

At this stage, Dampier believed he was still pursuing the
coast of mainland New Guinea, even though he could not see
it. *Roebuck* was actually about 30 nautical miles offshore and
traversing a wide and relatively open sea.

Land was again sighted on 25 February. It was an island
about 30 miles long: 'I called it Matthias; it being that saint's
day,' Dampier wrote.

Before long, he became convinced he was back on the coast
of New Guinea, when in fact he was cruising along the eastern
side of a large island, which would eventually be known,
thanks to him, as New Ireland. He and the crew again saw
'many smokes' wisping skywards at a number of spots along
the shore, clear evidence that the area was well inhabited. This
was a signal for him to try to make contact with the natives –
but when it came, that contact was not what he had hoped for.

As *Roebuck* approached the shore she was surrounded by
forty-six proas, the men on board making gestures indicating
that the ship should anchor close to shore. Dampier explained
what followed:

I was not assured of anchorage there, so I thought it not prudence to run in at this time; it being near night and seeing a black tornado rising in the west, which I most feared: besides we had near two hundred men in proas close by us. And the bays on the shore were lined with men from one end to the other, where there could not be less than three or four hundred more. What weapons they had we know not, nor yet their design. Therefore I had, at their first coming near us, got up all our small arms … I resolved to go out again: which, when the natives in their proas perceived, they began to fling stones at us as fast as they could, being provided with engines [slingshots or the like] for that purpose (wherefore I named this place Slingers Bay). But at the firing of one gun they were all amazed, drew off and flung no more stones. They got together as if consulting what to do; for they did not make in towards the shore, but lay still, though some of them were killed or wounded; and many of them had paid for their boldness …

During the month of March 1700, Dampier guided *Roebuck* along the coast of another large island off the coast of New Guinea, now known as New Britain. Dampier is credited with having discovered it, and with being the first European to have gone ashore there. He is also recognised as having discovered what is today charted as Dampier Strait, linking the Solomon Sea to the Bismarck Sea at the western end of New Britain. He wrote:

> As we stood over to the islands we looked out very well
> to the north, but could see no land that way; by which I
> was well assured that we were got through, and that this
> east land does not join to New Guinea; therefore I
> named it Nova Britannia [New Britain].

Dampier was now within 800 nautical miles of discovering the east coast of New Holland: the discovery so many before him had speculated about and sought.

Unfortunately, he would not live to know how incredibly close he came to solving one of the last remaining mysteries on the map of the world. He would die long before Captain James Cook filled in that gap in 1770.

Understandably ignorant of how close he was, and well aware that he should not push his luck with the weather any further, the seafarer in him decided he must turn his ship around and head back to England, much the same way as he had come, via the Cape of Good Hope then north into the Atlantic.

It was destined to be a passage of more than 16,000 nautical miles – but fate would intervene.

CHAPTER SIXTEEN

The Loss of *Roebuck*

With *Roebuck* homeward bound on a course to the north-west, and the coast of New Guinea on the larboard side, Dampier's desire had eluded him. The dream of discovering the east coast of New Holland, and making an indelible contribution to the annals of maritime history, was washing away with the weaving wake that streamed from the ship's stern.

That coastline would remain cloaked in secrecy for another seven decades.

His concerns now lay elsewhere. Apart from the continuing deterioration of his ship and the threat of monsoons, he wrote that there was 'one great reason why I could not prosecute my discoveries further'. His pinnace was leaking so badly it could sink at any time. Without it he and his men would not be able to safely navigate the mysterious east coast when in shallow water, or go ashore and be certain they could get back to the ship. Rebuilding it was a priority, but the crew could not find any safe shore where the pinnace could be hauled onto a beach and repaired.

How he must have rued the excessive delays and shoddy workmanship at the hands of the shipwrights who prepared *Roebuck* at Deptford Dockyard prior to departure! Had they not been so tardy and shown such little attention to detail, he could well have been returning to England with the news that all his supporters, including the king, were hoping to hear. But no: with the start of his venture delayed by weeks, he had been forced to sail to the already known west coast of New Holland and achieve what he could from there. Had he been able to sail, as originally intended, around Cape Horn and directly towards his goal, by this time he might well have been heading home with world-changing news.

Disappointing as this thought must have been, Dampier remained optimistic. He was still exploring – hoping there was more to find in this region.

He did not rest. He continually cross-checked his charts – which were largely based on voyages of Dutch and Portuguese vessels – to see if there was anything he was observing that was not identified there.

Such was the case on 2 April 1700, when he discovered a volcanic 'burning island'. He also registered the presence of huge tidal whirlpools, making 'fearful sounds': a natural phenomenon that brought added pressure to his role as commander:

We found here very strange tides that ran in streams,
making a great sea; and roaring so loud that we could
hear them before they came within a mile of us. The
sea round about them seemed all broken, and tossed the
ship so that she would not answer her helm.

By 26 April *Roebuck* had rounded the western end of Papua
New Guinea and entered the Ceram Sea, her sails trimmed
for a course that would take her towards Timor, more than
500 nautical miles away to the south-west.

The progress was comfortable, and the cares of the crew
few – until a brigantine was seen in the distance, on the
starboard side, heading their way.

Dampier noted:

About eight at night the brigantine … came close along
by us on our weather-side: our guns were all ready
before night, matches lighted, and small arms on the
quarter-deck ready loaded. She standing one way and
we another; we soon got further asunder. But I kept
good watch all the night and in the morning saw her
astern of us, standing as we did …

While Dampier's cautious approach was understandable, in
this case it proved unnecessary. The brigantine was out of
China, carrying a full complement of sailors, along with their
wives and families. The commander assumed those aboard

were on their way to settle at a 'Dutch factory' somewhere in the region. The crews acknowledged each other with waves and welcoming gestures before the vessels continued on their respective courses.

On 18 May, Timor was in sight. Dampier plotted a course towards Babao Bay, where he knew they would be able to replenish their water casks.

He had decided to head for Batavia, where he would be able to repair his decaying ship, and rest his crew prior to the long haul home. He did, however, put this part of the voyage to good use: he decided to search for Tryal Rocks – a much talked about, yet still uncharted, reef that had claimed the lives of more than 100 seafarers seventy-eight years earlier when the EIC vessel *Trial* smashed onto it and was ripped apart. But Dampier's effort was to no avail, partly because *Trial*'s captain John Brookes had deliberately given the incorrect latitude and longitude for the reef, and partly because, at this time, Dampier fell ill:

> … having been sick five or six days without any fresh
> provision or other good nourishment aboard, and seeing
> no likelihood of my recovery, I rather chose to go to
> some port than to beat here any longer; my people being
> very negligent when I was not upon deck myself …

At that point in his account, though, he was pleased to note: 'From hence nothing material happened till we came upon the coast of Java.'

Dampier would write that the layover in Batavia served its purpose in many ways, but he remained concerned about the seaworthiness of his vessel:

> I lay here till the 17th of October following, all which
> time we had very fair weather, some tornadoes
> excepted. In the meantime I supplied the carpenter with
> such stores as were necessary for refitting the ship;
> which proved more leaky after he had caulked her than
> she was before: so that I was obliged to careen her, for
> which purpose I hired vessels to take in our guns,
> ballast, provision and stores …

Roebuck was guided away from the port at 6 a.m., her sails set to harness a perfect land breeze out of the south. Her next destination was the Cape of Good Hope, then the anchorage off Cape Town, a destination more than 5000 nautical miles away.

This proved to be an uneventful passage. *Roebuck* came to anchor there on the second last day of the year, then, on 11 January 1701, she was under sail again: out into the Atlantic at the start of the eagerly anticipated voyage of more than 6500 nautical miles to the entrance of the Thames, and home.

Twenty-three days later *Roebuck* came to anchor off St Helena Island, and after staying there little more than a week, a course was set for Ascension Island, 700 nautical miles away to the north-west.

As with every landfall, the sighting of Ascension Island caused an air of relief and anticipation to spread through the crew. But that atmosphere changed dramatically the following day. Their still-leaky ship was about to give out on them:

> The 22nd between 8 and 9 o'clock we sprung a leak which increased so that the chain-pump could not keep the ship free. Whereupon I set the hand-pump to work also, and by 10 o'clock sucked her: then wore the ship, and stood to the southward to try if that would ease her; and then the chain-pump just kept her free [of water].

The following morning the crew managed to manoeuvre *Roebuck* into a bay, and once there, she was anchored. Dampier and his officers were hoping they might find somewhere suitable to haul her ashore, but the land was most unwelcoming. If the ship were to be saved, the leak had to be traced and plugged there and then.

Dampier ordered that the powder room be cleared of everything stored there, as he believed that part of the ship was where the leak would be found. He then joined the carpenter's mate – 'the only person in the ship that understood anything of carpenter's work' – along with the gunner and the bosun (John Norwood), in search of the source of the leak, but they found nothing. As the water level in the hold continued to rise, a gravely concerned Dampier told the carpenter's mate he would 'always be a friend to him if he could and would stop it'.

While the search for the leak proceeded in haste below deck, where bulkheads and floors were being cut away, the remainder of the crew were manning the pumps – but they were losing the battle. As a despondent Dampier later recorded, 'about 5 o'clock the boatswain came to me and told me the leak was increased, and that it was impossible to keep the ship above water'.

Yes, Dampier was told, the actual source of the leak had been found: a sprung plank. He rushed below to see for himself, and was distressed to find that the men had nothing at hand to jam into the hole, so they could at least slow the ingress of water. He immediately ordered some oakum and 'pieces of beef' to be forced into the breach, but 'to little purpose'.

Every man worked his hardest throughout the day and into the night, trying to devise a way to save *Roebuck*. But she was beyond help:

> About 11 o'clock at night the boatswain came to me and
> told me that the leak still increased; and that the plank
> was so rotten it broke away like dirt; and that now it
> was impossible to save the ship; for they could not come
> at the leak because the water in the room was got above
> it. The rest of the night was spent in pumping and
> bailing. I worked myself to encourage my men, who

were very diligent; but the water still increased, and we
now thought of nothing but saving our lives. Wherefore
I hoisted out the boat that, if the ship should sink, yet
we might be saved: and in the morning we weighed our
anchor and warped in nearer the shore; yet did but little
good.

Throughout the remainder of the night and into the next day,
the challenge was to save every man and whatever food and
equipment possible. *Roebuck* was manoeuvred into less than
4 fathoms of water, close to the shore, then held in place using
a small anchor wedged into the rocks near the tree line.

That done, Dampier, who would be among the very last to
leave the ship, set in motion the procedure that he believed
would be most effective. Without it, they would have almost
certainly all perished:

> I made a raft to carry the men's chests and bedding
> ashore; and before 8 at night most of them were ashore.
> In the morning I ordered the sails to be unbent, to
> make tents; and then myself and officers went ashore. I
> had sent ashore a puncheon and a 36 gallon cask of
> water with one bag of rice for our common use …

When Dampier finally reached the shore, he was most
distressed to realise that some of his men had stolen much of
the rice. But under the circumstances, it was not worth his

while to pursue the matter. More importantly to him, he had suffered a considerable personal loss: many of his books and papers could not be retrieved before *Roebuck*'s deck disappeared below the surface of the bay. Adding to his dismay was the loss of a great number of the specimens of flora and fauna he had collected while on the coast of New Holland. However, he was able to save some charts that showed the course that *Roebuck* had taken off the coast of New Holland and towards New Guinea. For more than a century, these charts would be recognised as the only accurate guide to sailing in this region.

It was late March when *Roebuck* sank, and Dampier and his men made their way onto the shore of Ascension Island, a place that must have felt like the end of the Earth. Measuring just 34 square miles, this uninhabited rocky outcrop was as dry and barren as parts of the west coast of New Holland. Here, though, they were able to find water and, equally important, food:

> [N]ow we were by God's providence, in a condition of subsisting some time, having plenty of very good turtle by our tents, and water for the fetching.

Fortuitously, forward-thinking Portuguese mariners had introduced goats to the island decades earlier to provide food for sailors in a predicament such as theirs. Dampier's men found other food as well, like land crabs, man-of-war-birds and boobies, all of which were delectable. They also discovered a water supply about 8 miles away from their camp.

While *Roebuck*'s hull was now submerged, her masts and yards stood as a haunting backdrop, a kind of mariner's version of the Christian cross. The crew might well have wanted to praise the Lord for their salvation: they knew that had the leak occurred when they were hundreds of miles from land, there would have been little chance that anyone would have survived.

Ascension Island could be considered to be in the middle of nowhere – almost in the middle of the Atlantic, some 2500 nautical miles north-west of Cape Town. But, remote as it was, there was one positive for these sailors in solitude: they were close to the shipping lane for vessels plying a route between Europe and the Cape of Good Hope.

One week after *Roebuck* sank, two ships under billowing sail seemed to be on a course towards the island. Excitement reigned – but it soon proved to be false hope. The ships sailed on, the mariners on board obviously unaware of the plight of fifty fellow sailors on the island they were passing by.

More frustration came about three weeks later, on 2 April, when a fleet of eleven ships cruised past on the windward side of the island, then disappeared over the horizon. *Roebuck*'s crew wondered what it would take to be rescued.

Yet salvation came just one day later:

The day after appeared four sail, which came to anchor in this bay. They were His Majesty's ships the *Anglesey*,

Hastings and *Lizard*; and the *Canterbury* East India ship. I
went on board the *Anglesey* with about thirty-five of my
men; and the rest were disposed of into the other two
men-of-war …

In an unremarkable end to what had been a voyage of great
consequence, Dampier closed his report on his travels thus:

We sailed from Ascension the 8th; and continued
aboard till the 8th of May: at which time the men-of-
war, having missed St Jago, where they designed to
water, bore away for Barbados: but I being desirous to
get to England as soon as possible took my passage in
the ship *Canterbury*, accompanied with my master,
purser, gunner, and three of my superior officers.

*

It was August 1701, more than two and a half years after
Roebuck had sailed away from the coast of England, when
Dampier and his men finally returned to home waters. As
commander, his immediate task was to inform the Admiralty
of the loss of his ship, and in broad terms, of what he had
achieved during the voyage.

When the formal inquiry into the sinking was held about a
month later, Dampier was cleared of all responsibility. But
during the weeks preceding this hearing he realised he had

much more to be concerned about. Some people in high office were quick to deem the voyage a failure because Dampier had returned home without the much-anticipated news of great discoveries – in particular, information and charts detailing the east coast of New Holland.

This was an outcome that frustrated and disappointed Dampier. However, it was nothing compared with what was about to confront him.

Lieutenant George Fisher had, as anticipated, arrived back in England after having been deposited in a jail in Bahia on the outbound voyage. But instead of being charged with insubordination by the Admiralty, he had been able to spend the two years since his homecoming preparing charges of cruelty against Dampier.

A second charge was that Dampier had caused the death of his bosun, John Norwood, whom, it was alleged, the commander had confined to his cabin for four months – probably because because he was 'the officer' inciting others to mutiny when *Roebuck* was at a Dutch outpost in Timor.

It is mooted that Fisher and Norwood's widow, Ursula, conspired to concoct this allegation. The pair would have learned of Norwood's death in Barbados from others in *Roebuck*'s crew when they arrived back in England. At the time, Norwood had been heading home on one of the ships that had rescued *Roebuck*'s crew from Ascension Island. His widow was firm in the belief that her husband's earlier confinement in his cabin for such a long period had precipitated his demise.

The pressure that these allegations brought to bear on Dampier led him to defend himself to some degree in the dedication of his published account of the *Roebuck* voyage, titled *A Voyage to New Holland, etc. in the Year 1699*, which he addressed to 'The Right Honourable Thomas, Earl of Pembroke, Lord President of Her Majesty's Most Honourable Privy Council'. Dampier wrote:

> The world is apt to judge of everything by the success; and whoever has ill fortune will hardly be allowed a good name. This, My Lord, was my unhappiness in my late expedition in the *Roebuck*, which foundered through perfect age near the island of Ascension. I suffered extremely in my reputation by that misfortune; though I comfort myself with the thoughts that my enemies could not charge any neglect upon me.

Fisher had used the time before Dampier's return to prepare a case against him, besmirching his image in the Royal Navy by implying that the commander was not 'one of them' – merely a reformed pirate, if that.

Ten months after Dampier's return – on 8 June 1702 – the court martial commenced aboard HMS *Royal Sovereign,* which was lying at anchor at Spithead, adjacent to Portsmouth on the Solent. The gravity of the charges meant that the Admiral of the Fleet, Sir George Rooke, was appointed to preside over proceedings, assisted by Admiral Sir Cloudesley Shovell. The 'jury' comprised two other admirals and more than twenty captains.

Dampier was acquitted of the charge of causing the death of John Norwood, but was found guilty of the 'very hard and cruel usage' of Lieutenant Fisher. His sentence was harsh: he was ordered to forfeit all pay he had received as commander of *Roebuck* and declared unfit to command any of His Majesty's ships.

*

Such a finding would have ended the seagoing career of many a man, naval or otherwise – but not that of William Dampier. Rather, the establishment in London – in particular the intelligentsia and those with political sway – lauded the achievements of the *Roebuck* voyage, which, through no fault of his own, had been thwarted even before it departed England. Members of the Royal Society, for example, are reported to have been extremely impressed by the uniqueness of many of the plant specimens he presented to them, and by the elaborate detail to be found in his journals about previously unknown flora and fauna.

Dampier's career might have come to an end as far as the Royal Navy was concerned, but his many supporters saw things differently – as would later generations. An 1837 edition of *The United Service Journal and Naval and Military Magazine* called the charge of ill-treatment against Dampier 'an imputation which all circumstances warrant us in denying, and which must have originated from the ignorance or misrepresentation of detracting contemporaries, many of whom were imbued'.

The same story stated that Dampier's 'conduct of the voyage, entitled him to further public employment; but it is not the least singular feature of Captain Dampier's career that all the lists of naval officers of that date, as well as those in manuscript as that published by Admiral Hardy, have uniformly drowned him in the old *Roebuck*!'

Dampier did not go down with the ship. Instead, much to the frustration of those in the Royal Navy who had maligned him and his maritime endeavours, he continued on his ascent to the upper echelons of London society. Edition 3906 of the *Royal Gazette* contained an announcement:

> St James's, April 18th, Captain William Dampier being
> prepared to depart on another voyage to the West
> Indies, had the honour to kiss her Majesty's hand on
> Friday last, being introduced by His Royal Highness the
> Lord High Admiral ...

The announced voyage had nothing to do with the Royal Navy. Instead, it would see Dampier return to a previous form of seafaring employment: he was going back to being a privateer, because England, Austria and the Netherlands were fighting the French and other powers in the War of Spanish

Succession (1701–1714). It was a war that created the opportunity for enterprising businessmen to aid the English cause by funding ships and men to make attacks on enemy vessels and claim what prizes there were to be taken.

Dampier, then aged fifty-two, was well credentialled to lead such a mission: a great seafarer and navigator, with ample experience as a pirate. He was to be part of a two-ship expedition, captaining the 200-ton *St George* while Charles Pickering commanded the considerably smaller galley *Cinque Ports*. The operation was funded by English merchants and supported by the former president of the Royal Society, Sir Robert Southwell. Their plan was to mount raids on treasure-laden Spanish ships (allied with France) off South America.

The two ships were due to sail from Kinsale in Ireland on 11 September 1703, but before *St George* left London and sailed to the Irish port, there was an unwanted surprise for Dampier. An obviously still disgruntled George Fisher had him arrested via a civil claim for '300 shillings or some other great sum', relating once again to the maltreatment he claimed to have endured during the early stages of the *Roebuck* voyage.

Hasty intervention by some of the backers of Dampier's latest enterprise saw bail posted and Dampier free to sail. However, it is possible that in having Dampier arrested Fisher scored a direct hit: no doubt many of his new crew would have been questioning his ability as a leader.

Just as during the early stages of the *Roebuck* expedition, there was a fractious stand-off between the commander and some of the crew as *St George* sailed through often torrid conditions in the Atlantic, bound for the east coast of South America. The word 'mutiny' was even being muttered, but much of the problem was caused by alcohol and delusion.

Off the coast of Brazil, Charles Pickering, the captain of *Cinque Ports*, died. He was replaced by twenty-one year old Thomas Stradling. His quartermaster was a feisty Scotsman, just two years Stradling's senior. His name was Alexander Selkirk, a name which, within a few years, would become famous for all time.

The ships enjoyed little success when it came to plundering enemy ships in the Atlantic, so rounded Cape Horn and went in search of booty off South America's west coast. They encountered a French merchant ship, but their lack of appropriate planning and execution made the attack a humiliating failure.

A similar circumstance arose a few weeks later when a large Spanish ship was overrun. Her cargo of food, wine, wool and linen was considered valuable, but apparently not valuable enough for Dampier, because soon afterwards he inexplicably allowed the ship to continue on her way, her cargo untouched. Some crew speculated Dampier had struck a secret financial deal with the Spanish captain.

By this time *Cinque Ports* faced a pressing problem: her hull was leaking more and more by the day. Stradling advised Dampier he would part company with *St George* and head for the island of Juan Fernández to make repairs. Once there,

Stradling and Selkirk argued heatedly over the seaworthiness of the ship, the latter believing she was close to being beyond repair. There was no resolution to the argument, so, in October 1704, Selkirk demanded he be put ashore on a nearby uninhabited island: a request the young captain had no problem approving. With only a few clothes, some bedding, books, gunpowder and a gun, Selkirk was rowed to the island and farewelled.

However, as *Cinque Ports* began to sail out of the bay, the castaway was having second thoughts. He was seen by those on deck waving frantically, beckoning for the ship to turn back and take him on board. Stradling would have no part of it; he elected to sail on and leave his former quartermaster stranded.

Selkirk was right. *Cinque Ports* was wrecked only a few weeks later, off the coast of Colombia (a Spanish colony). Of her sixty-three man crew, there were only eight survivors, including Stradling. When they struggled ashore they were taken into custody and subsequently imprisoned by the Spanish for an unknown number of years.

Over the ensuing weeks Dampier's ongoing endeavours to plunder enemy ships continued to meet with little success. Some of his crew staged a mutiny of sorts, and twenty men put themselves aboard a small ship they had taken as a prize and sailed off on their own campaign. Dampier did nothing to stop them – in fact, he could well have encouraged the departure of these insubordinates.

His challenge then was to encourage the men who remained with him aboard *St George* to believe there were still prizes to be won. He repeatedly promoted the idea of capturing the ultimate prize, a Manila galleon. These were treasure-laden Spanish merchant ships that sailed the round-trip between Acapulco and Manila once or twice a year. On the outbound passage they would carry huge quantities of Mexican silver; when returning, the cargo comprised valuable fabrics, including silk, as well as precious stones and porcelain.

Just weeks later, on 6 December 1704, a perfect target was sighted. The inevitable battle ensued, but it quickly became apparent that it was a mismatch: *St George*'s 5-pounder cannons were piddling in comparison with the galleon's 24-pounders.

St George had to disengage and run: a move that led to yet another barney between captain and crew. Senior officers claimed that by hoisting the ensign and identifying the ship's nationality so early, Dampier had extinguished any chance they had of making the attack a surprise. Dampier in turn bellowed that had his crew not been so drunk they would have obeyed his orders properly and *St George* would have been the victor.

St George had copped a pummelling from the impact of the 24-pound cannon balls, damage that further weakened her already leaking hull. There was only one solution to this problem: capture another ship as soon as possible, abandon *St George*, and sail their new prize back to England.

Six weeks later, in late January 1705, an appropriate ship was captured off the coast of Mexico. But instead of following their captain onto that vessel, the crew of *St George* conducted another mutiny: three of Dampier's senior men forced him to stay aboard *St George* with more than thirty loyal followers while they, the usurpers, sailed off in the prize.

With his ship's worm-eaten hull planks beginning to resemble honeycomb below the waterline, Dampier knew he and his remaining men had to take another ship quickly if they were ever to see England again. Good fortune came their way off the coast of Peru when they claimed a Spanish brigantine. *St George* was then left to sink while Dampier set a course across the Pacific, probably similar to the track that *Cygnet* had taken all those years earlier; across to Guam, then Mindanao and other islands in that region.

While there are no specific details of this return voyage, it is known they visited Batavia. Dampier and his remaining men finally reached home waters in late 1707 with nothing to show for more than four years on the high seas – much to the disappointment of their backers. However, Dampier could boast of one personal achievement from this voyage: he had become the first man to circumnavigate the world twice.

*

There was no questioning Dampier's ability as a seafarer, navigator, naturalist and author – but generally speaking, as a pirate and privateer, he had missed his mark, even though, after so many years at sea, he had had more opportunity to succeed in that ambit than most.

It was probably because the sea was the only life he knew that he would go in search of riches one last time – at age fifty-six.

Again he needed backers, and refused to give up on his desires. As fellow crewman Edward Cooke wrote in his 1712 account of the subsequent voyage, Dampier did not retreat 'till he had prevail'd with some able persons at Bristol to venture upon an undertaking, which might turn to a prodigious advantage'. Under the agreement, Dampier, whose position would be that of pilot (navigator), not commander, was to receive one-sixteenth of the backers' two-thirds of the profits.

Once again it would be a two-ship venture. The Bristol-based consortium purchased the 30-gun, 320-ton *Duke*, and the 260-ton, 26-gun *Duchess*, which would act as consort. The pair sailed in company from Bristol on 2 August 1708, their first destination being Brazil then, more importantly, the Pacific, via Cape Horn. That landmark was rounded on 15 January 1709, midsummer in the southern hemisphere, but it was a frigidly cold experience for the sailors. As seasoned as these men were to the elements, their clothing was no match for the icy conditions and howling winds in that part of the world. Worse still, it was dangerous for the men who had to go aloft, and who would return to the deck with their hands and feet nearly frozen. Sailing to the north as fast as possible towards warmer weather was the only solution.

Dampier, aboard *Duke*, was now in his element as pilot, being the only man on either ship who had sailed in these waters. His initial destination was a place he knew well, Juan Fernández, whose rugged, saw-like profile came into view sixteen days after the two ships had rounded the Horn.

Duke and *Duchess* were guided into an anchorage with which Dampier was familiar, then their sails were either hauled up or lowered and anchors set. On approach, Dampier and others had been surprised to see smoke rising from among the dense canopy of trees not far from the shore, on what was a supposedly an uninhabited island. The source of the smoke was worthy of investigation, so the master of *Duke*, Woodes Rogers, ordered an armed party to go ashore in one of the small boats. Rogers wrote in his account of the expedition, *A Cruising Voyage Round the World*, that what the men came across was a shock to all:

> Immediately our pinnace returned from the shore, and brought abundance of craw-fish, with a man clothed in goat-skins, who looked wilder than the first owners of them ...

It was Alexander Selkirk, the Scottish sailor who had gone into self-imposed exile on the island after quitting *Cinque Ports*, four years and four months earlier: a man whom Dampier back then had recognised as 'the best man in her'.

This was the first time Selkirk had engaged in conversation since *Cinque Ports* disappeared over the horizon, and initially the joy that came with being rescued made him incoherent. But as he recovered from the initial shock, he began to speak at length, and there was an air of amazement, almost disbelief, among all who heard the incredible story tumble from his sunburned lips.

He explained that he had lit the fire the previous night because he correctly assumed the two ships he saw approaching the island were English. On two occasions ships had anchored off the island and men had been sent ashore, but he had run from them after realising they were Spanish. They had shot at him and pursued him into the forest, where he knew his only chance to avoid capture was to climb high into a tree – the same tree his pursuers later stood under to relieve themselves.

Rogers explained that it took eight months for Selkirk to adapt to the lonely life of a castaway. He built two huts for protection, made clothing from the skins of wild animals, 'and employ'd himself in reading, singing psalms, and praying; so that he said he was a better Christian while in this solitude than ever he was before'. When his gunpowder was spent he had to chase wild goats on foot, killing them with a knife he had made from iron hoops on casks that had washed ashore. Fish, lobsters and wild fruits provided additional food. Other wildlife on the island only caused problems, as Selkirk explained to Rogers:

He was at first much pestered with cats and rats that had
bred in great numbers from some of each species which
had got ashore from ships that put in there to wood and
water. The rats gnawed his feet and clothes while asleep,
which obliged him to cherish the cats with his goat's
flesh; by which many of them became so tame, that
they would lie about him in hundreds, and soon
delivered him from the rats ...

Rogers, like others aboard *Duke* and *Duchess*, was thoroughly
impressed by Selkirk's health, fitness and sanity, despite his
years of isolation:

One may see that solitude and retirement from the
world is not such an insufferable state of life as most
men imagine, especially when people are fairly called or
thrown into it unavoidably, as this man was ...

Yet there was no easy way home for Selkirk: he had no option
but to stay with *Duke* for the remainder of the voyage. When
he finally did reach home his amazing story saw him quickly
become a celebrity – and, as most people believe, the man
whose experiences influenced Daniel Defoe when he wrote
his novel *The Life and Surprising Adventures of Robinson Crusoe*,
published in 1719.

Duke and *Duchess* then continued on their way, first closing
on the coast of Chile then sailing north towards Mexico.

Before long this venture proved far more successful than Dampier's previous foray as a privateer. By the end of 1709, the two ships had claimed a fortune estimated to be worth near 150,000 pounds – some $40 million Australian dollars in today's money. Most of that booty came from the capture of a Spanish treasure ship off the coast of Mexico, that prize he had so fruitlessly sought on his previous privateering voyage.

With this mission complete, the two ships needed to do nothing more than head home on a west-about course. They crossed the Pacific via Guam and Batavia while escorting two prize ships they had also managed to capture along the way. It was a slow passage, since the *Duke* and *Duchess* needed refits as they went. It was not until 14 October 1711 that the anchors of *Duke* and *Duchess* were cast for the final time; they were in the waters of the Thames.

At that moment, William Dampier became the first man to have circumnavigated the world three times.

*

Once more, Dampier's return was engulfed in controversy – claims and counter-claims regarding each man's share of the spoils.

The outcome of these disputes is shrouded in the mystery that engulfs the remainder of Dampier's life. It is believed that he received some level of reward, but there are vague indications that it was not a significant amount – just enough for him to subsist in the company of his cousin, Grace Mercer, in Coleman Street, in the London parish of St Stephen. His wife Judith had died during the *St George* expedition.

He probably passed away in Grace Mercer's home in early March 1715, as his will was confirmed on 23 March that year. This document revealed that the then sixty-three years old Dampier was 2000 pounds in debt: a significant sum in that era.

While his passing was relatively inconspicuous in English society, William Dampier is remembered as one of the greatest seafarers of his era. What might have happened had he discovered the east coast of the Great South Land some seventy years before Captain Cook can only be surmised, but it is safe to assert that such a discovery could have seen the early years of white settlement in Australia follow a course quite different from that we now know. Dampier would have discovered a far more lush and inviting coast than what had been found in the west and north, which in turn would have inspired immense interest; it could well have caused a rush to claim and settle the land. Similarly, had Tasman adopted Visscher's suggestion that they sail west instead of north-west from Fiji, he would have made the discovery almost six decades earlier. One can only hypothesise on where such a happening might have led. Regardless, what the world now knows is that the Dutch opened the door to the Great South Land, but it was the English who entered.

Possibly the most fitting tribute to William Dampier – a barely recognised but remarkable individual – is to be found within the thick stone walls of the medieval St Michael's Church, in his home village of East Coker:

TO THE MEMORY OF

WILLIAM DAMPIER

BUCCANEER EXPLORER AND HYDROGRAPHER

and sometime Captain of the ship *Roebuck*

in the Royal Navy of King William the Third.

Thrice he circumnavigated the Globe

and first of all Englishmen

explored and described the coast of Australia.

An exact observer

of all things in Earth, Sea and Air

he recorded the knowledge won by years of

danger and hardship in Books of Voyages

and a Discourse of Winds, Tides and Currents

which Nelson bade his midshipmen to study

and Humboldt praised for Scientific worth.

Glossary

athwartships Directly across the ship, from side to side

azimuth compass A navigational instrument used to measure the angle of the arc on the horizon between the direction of the sun or other celestial object and magnetic north

ballast Any heavy material (such as gravel, iron, lead, sand or stones) placed in the hold of a ship to provide stability

barricoe A small water barrel or keg

bilge The lower part of the interior of a ship's hull immediately above the keel

braces Ropes or lines attached to the end of a yard which is either eased or hauled in, so that the sail is trimmed to suit the wind direction

burthen Displacement

capstan A large waist-high vertical winch turned by crewmen manning the capstan bars, which lock into the head of the winch. The crew then walk in a circle to work the winch. Used to raise the anchor and other heavy objects

caravel A small, highly manoeuvrable vessel of the fifteenth and sixteenth centuries carrying lateen sails on two, three or four masts

careen To heel a ship over on one side or the other for cleaning, caulking or repairing

carrack A large three- or four-masted sailing vessel featuring elevated structures at the bow and stern

caulking Material making the ship watertight (such as cotton fibres or oakum) forced between the planks to stop leaks

chain pump A water pump where circular discs are attached to an endless chain, which rotates from the deck into the bilge of the ship so water can be lifted to the deck level

chains The area outside the ship where the dead-eyes, rigging and other hardware come together to support the mast

courses A sail set on the lower yard of a square-rigged ship

dead-reckoning A method for estimating a vessel's current position, based on its previously determined position and advanced by estimating speed and course over an elapsed time

doubling To sail around a cape or promontory

factory A trading post

fathom A unit of measurement for depth: one fathom is 1.83 metres or six feet

flood tide Rising tide

freeboard The distance from the waterline to the ship's gunwale measured amidships

ground tackle The equipment used to anchor a vessel

hanger Sword

last/lasten An old Dutch term used to express a ship's carrying capacity

leadline A sounding line with a lead weight at one end, used to record the depth of water under the ship

leadsman The man who, standing in the chains, heaves the lead to take soundings

leeboards Large boards lowered from either side of a vessel to minimise leeway

leeward The direction away from the wind; opposite of 'windward'

lie-a-hull Waiting out a storm by lowering all sails and letting the vessel drift

mainmast The tallest mast on a vessel

mizzenmast On a ship with three masts, this is the mast nearest the stern

painter A rope attached to the bow of a small boat which is used for tying up or towing

pinnace A small ship which, as a multi-purpose design, could operate as a merchant ship, small warship, or a pirate vessel. Alternatively, a small vessel with two fore- and aft-rigged masts, which can be rowed or sailed, and usually carried men between ship and shore

puncheon A large cask of variable capacity, usually between 70 and 120 gallons

quarter: port/starboard The aft parts of a ship on each side of the centreline

ratlines Bands of ropes lashed across the shrouds (the standing rigging on a ship that provides lateral support to the mast) like steps

reciprocal course To return along the course from whence you came

rigging All ropes, wires and chains used to support the masts and yards

shank Part of an anchor

sheerline The upward curve of the deck of a ship towards the bow and stern with the lowest point at or near amidships

sheets Ropes attached to either of the lower corners (clews) of a square sail or the aftermost lower corner of a fore-and-aft sail; also the ropes used to control the boom of the mainsail or mizzen/spanker

sterncastle The structure behind the mizzenmast and above the transom on large sailing ships. It usually houses the captain's cabin

tumblehome The amount by which the two sides of a ship are brought in towards the centre above the maximum beam

whipstaff A bar attached to the tiller to extend the leverage when steering

windlass A horizontal and cylindrical barrel used as a lifting device for a rope or anchor cable

windward Towards the wind

yard A slender wooden spar slung at its centre on the forward side of a mast on a square-rigged ship

Author's note

Millenniums ago there was a belief among the scholars of the empires bordering the Mediterranean Sea that an undiscovered landmass existed way beyond their realm.

This premise was based on their understanding of balance: the weight of the landmass in their part of the world had to be counterbalanced by a similarly large landmass beyond the horizon, regardless of the world being a disc or sphere.

It was declared by some that this land would be inhospitable and uninhabitable due to *'the fury of the sun, which burns the intermediate zone'*. Others were convinced it was simply impossible for humans to exist in a place that was so exceedingly distant from their own world – the cradle of humanity.

While these scholars were only hypothesising, it has been claimed that the earliest contact with the Great South Land by northern hemisphere people might date back to about 232 BCE, when an Egyptian expedition, comprising six ships, departed their shores via the Red Sea with the intention of sailing to the eastern horizon and beyond. Historians identify this as the Maui expedition, Maui being the name of the voyage's navigator.

Whether or not it happened remains a mystery, but there is no denying the Egyptians had the wherewithal to undertake such a voyage: they are credited with having developed sailing vessels around 3500 BCE, and for the following 2000 years Egypt was the world's most powerful maritime nation.

In far more recent times it has been suggested that the Maui expedition might have sailed not all the way, but close to, the coast of Australia; the existence of unique ancient drawings in what are known as the Caves of the Navigators in Irian Jaya seems to support this speculation. It seems possible that the drawings date back to the time of Maui's expedition for two reasons: they are thought to have recorded an eclipse over Australia, and more importantly, they appear to depict the calculation of longitude, albeit in a crude fashion. If this is so then they are quite probably of Egyptian origin because European seafarers did not have the ability to calculate longitude with any degree of accuracy until the eighteenth century. However, the acclaimed Greek mathematician, Eratosthenes, who lived from approximately 276 to 194 BCE, is credited with being the first person to calculate the circumference of earth (incredibly to within four per cent accuracy) and how to establish longitude – and Maui was a disciple of Eratosthenes.

There is one other 'long bow' theory that could link the Egyptians, even the Maui expedition, to the Great South

Land. Darnley Island is one of the easternmost islands in Torres Strait, 100 nautical miles north-east of the tip of Cape York. What makes this place so interesting is that centuries ago bodies of deceased Darnley Islanders were prepared for burial in a manner not dissimilar to that used by the Egyptians between 1090 and 945 BCE. Also, while the Egyptians often ferried mummified corpses along the River Nile to burial places, the Darnley Islanders transported the bodies of their dead to offshore coral reefs. Coincidentally, there is another island 25 nautical miles to the southeast named Mer (sometimes spelled Mir), and the word 'mer' translates to 'pyramid' in Ancient Egyptian, and, when viewed from some aspects, this island takes on the shape of a pyramid.

Speculation aside, it is etched in history that apart from the indigenous inhabitants, Terra Australis Incognita – the unknown Great South Land – remained an unrecorded feature on the face of the earth until the early seventeenth century, and it is because of this fact that I have set the scene for this, my fifth book detailing Australia's maritime history.

In researching the subject I became captivated by one extraordinary fact after another. Most interesting was the realisation that over countless centuries, and for reasons unknown, this huge tract of land – Australia – was never claimed and occupied by any country, not even by the homelands of the earliest documented discoverers. It was only when the English were forced to settle there, not for any strategic reason, but because they needed a distant repository for convicts held in their grossly overcrowded prisons, that settlement of this little known land became important. Equally extraordinary is the fact that, despite the slowness of English expansion across the continent, no other nation took the opportunity to capture any part of it. Because of this, Australia stands today as the largest single nation that is completely surrounded by sea.

Many of the aforementioned 'discoveries' came through misadventure, whereby ships were wrecked and countless lives lost: the west coast of the continent was a maritime graveyard. But when it came to planned exploration, it was the Dutch who led the way, not through any real desire to find and settle the land, but in the process of seeking new markets and sources for their burgeoning spice industry based in the East Indies.

My own discovery was that the finer detail of these planned expeditions and shipwrecks was a fascinating and little known part of Australian history, and it had all the elements for an equally fascinating book.

Consequently, I set myself on a new writing adventure that would take me on a different course to my more recent books. *Great South Land* was not designed to deal with a prominent individual or event extracted from the nation's colourful past; instead, it would document an absorbing century, from when Dutchman Willem Janszoon became the first known European to set foot on Australian soil, through to an amazing individual, Englishman William Dampier. I was surprised by how few people knew about this incredibly talented pirate-cum-explorer. Most identified him as being Dutch, and few, if any, knew he came so close to stealing Captain James Cook's thunder seventy years before the latter claimed the east coast of 'New Holland' in the name of His Majesty, King George III, on 22 August 1770.

I am a writer and a storyteller whose professional background is in the world of journalism, and whose life embraces the sea and sailing. My family heritage dates back to distant relations who were masters of square-rigged ships. My desire is to write to entertain and educate through the retelling our amazing maritime history. It is an endeavour built on some fifty years of writing and broadcasting experience, fifteen books, and near sixty years of sailing.

As has been the case with my four preceding maritime history books – *Bligh*, *Cook*, *Flinders* and *The First Fleet* – considerable information has come from journals and accounts of the day, which can also be enjoyed as free ebooks on Project Gutenberg (gutenberg.net.au). Among the many journals and documents drawn on for this book were: *The* Batavia *journal of François Pelsaert* (1629); Dampier's *A voyage to New Holland etc. in the year 1699*, Volumes 1 and II, and *A continuation of a voyage to New Holland, etc. in the year 1699*; *Voyage of the ship* Leyden *commanded by skipper Klaas Hermansz(oon) from the Netherlands to Java*, a journal kept on board the ship *Leyden* from Texel to Batavia (1623); *Voyage of the ships* Pera *and* Arnhem, *under command of Jan Carstenszoon and Willem Joosten van Colster –*

further discovery of the south-west coast of New Guinea. Discovery of the Gulf of Carpentaria; Carstenszoon's Journal; Abel Janszoon Tasman's Journal; *The voyage of Captain Abel Janszoon Tasman in the year 1642*; *Notices of a second voyage of discovery by Tasman.*

Equally, the free online encyclopedia, Wikipedia.com, provided a mass of information as well as guidance towards the location of finer detail, as did the Western Australian Museum website (http://museum.wa.gov.au). The *Australian Dictionary of Biography*, as Australia's pre-eminent dictionary of national biography, was of considerable value for this project. Google Earth, with its satellite images, gave me the added opportunity to check distances between destinations and points of interest and allowed me to 'visit' and appreciate some destinations. Google Images was also a valuable tool.

The opportunity to complete this historic adventure, *Great South Land*, did not come without considerable assistance; it is here that I salute the 'team'. I must start with the wonderfully professional crew of dedicated book lovers at HarperCollins Publishers, in particular my guiding light, Associate Publisher Helen Littleton, who has been an inspiration right across the period I have been writing maritime history. Special mention must also be made of copy editor Emma Dowden, who did a superb job within a very tight timeframe; HarperCollins editor, Nicola Robinson; the designer of the impressive cover, Hazel Lam; Linda Braidwood, who did a great job researching and securing the images; the always energetic sales team at HCP, and the hardworking typesetter, Graeme Jones. I must also recognise the excellent contribution made by the Emeritus Curator at the State Library of New South Wales, Paul Brunton. Once again Paul did a superb job reading the manuscript and crosschecking the historical detail. (Admittedly Paul and I don't always agree; as ever, history is a contested field. Where I have strayed from Paul's advice, I hope he will forgive me … in such instances I may be thinking like a sailor, not an historian.)

Beyond the publishing house I must thank the booksellers who have been wonderfully supportive of my books for many years.

On a personal note I must thank two special people, Liz Christmas and Christine Power. Liz – my personal assistant – has been a prize possession for me for more than a decade. Her dedication to every project is exemplary, as is her ability to keep me 'on the rails'. For my partner, Christine, this book has been a baptism by fire, and I thank her for her support and understanding.

Finally there are my readers who show inspiring support for my books. To each one of you, and the many, many people who take time to write to me with positive feedback, I say thank you.

I hope everyone enjoys this latest voyage to the Great South Land.

Rob Mundle